Lessons for Social Change in the Global Economy

Lessons for Social Change in the Global Economy

Voices from the Field

Edited by Shae Garwood, Sky Croeser, and Christalla Yakinthou

LEXINGTON BOOKS
Lanham • Boulder • New York • Toronto • Plymouth, UK

Published by Lexington Books
A wholly owned subsidiary of Rowman & Littlefield
4501 Forbes Boulevard, Suite 200, Lanham, Maryland 20706
www.rowman.com

10 Thornbury Road, Plymouth PL6 7PP, United Kingdom

British Library Cataloguing in Publication Information Available

Library of Congress Cataloging-in-Publication Data Available
ISBN 978-0-7391-8775-3 (cloth : alk. paper)—ISBN 978-0-7391-8776-0 (electronic)

∞™ The paper used in this publication meets the minimum requirements of American National Standard for Information Sciences Permanence of Paper for Printed Library Materials, ANSI/NISO Z39.48-1992.

Printed in the United States of America

Contents

Foreword

Mark Barenberg

The global political economy stands at an epochal crossroad. Two related problems are particularly urgent. One is the contest between, on the one hand, the presently ascendant power of corporations and financial institutions in domestic and transnational politics and, on the other, a variety of counter-hegemonic social movements and practical initiatives carrying the banner of social justice. The second is the threat to civilization posed by ever-expanding capital accumulation, its attendant wasteful production and consumption, and the risk of environmental catastrophe on a global scale.

Critical to understanding these two problems is the phenomenon of global chains of production, distribution, consumption, and waste disposal (hereafter "global supply chains"). The global supply chain is a key contemporary institutional form through which corporations and financial institutions wield economic power. And that institution translates economic power into political power, escaping territorial regulatory jurisdiction and weakening sovereign authority. Equally critical are the phenomena of, first, transnational efforts to remake global supply chains and, second, localized communities of production and consumption that either displace or reconstruct links in supply chains. This book makes an important contribution to our knowledge of these problems and phenomena.

The present-day contest between corporate power and what we might broadly call democratic power is an episode in what the sociologist Karl Polanyi termed the "double movement" of modern capitalism. The double movement denotes capitalists' incessant drive to commodify social life in the name of profit maximization and the response by political forces seeking, in the name of social values, to constrain all-out marketization. In recent decades—starting roughly in the years of Reagan and Thatcher—market ideology has been resurgent at a global level. Corporations and hypertrophied financial institutions greatly strengthened their hand in advanced capitalist countries and, often under pressure by advanced countries and corporations, in many countries of the Global South. This was a surprising turnabout after two centuries of increasing state regulation of capitalism under pressure by such democratic social forces as labor movements, women's movements, environmental movements, movements of indigenous people and people of color, and others. Today's global economic constitution—aptly dubbed "neoliberalism"—is much like the laissez-faire domestic regimes of the early nineteenth century.

In the decade before the current Great Recession many countries, most notably in Latin America, turned against the neoliberal hegemony that was manifestly harmful to social and economic development. One might have predicted in 2008 that the aborning economic crisis would amplify democratic revulsion against finance capitalism, which caused the crisis and such great suffering in both rich and poor countries. Instead, global capital seized the still-ongoing crisis as an opportunity to revitalize the neoliberal project and weaken still further the structural foundations of democratic power capable of transforming global supply chains. The policy of austerity is the chosen strategy, even at the expense of medium-term capital accumulation and employment—though not at the expense of short-term compensation of executives and financial elites profiting from each link in global supply chains. Plutocratic governments have weakened labor unions and employee protections, shrunk the public sector, and diminished the provision of collective goods of all sorts, including environmental protection.

Against this historical backdrop, this book's case studies analyze the provisional and contested efforts to bend the arc of global supply chains toward social justice. Some analysts conclude that transnational advocacy networks inevitably fail to transform global capitalism (see chapter 7). They argue that such networks merely serve corporations' public-relations purposes and divert efforts away from democratic sovereign regulation (or dismantling) of capitalism and from collective empowerment in workplaces and communities. Others point to labor-centered and green-centered networks that deeply restructure supply chains in the service of living wages, worker empowerment, and environmental sustainability (see, e.g., chapter 2). Clearly, the jury is still out on whether the rare successes—such as the Alta Gracia factory, the Designated Suppliers Program, and the Bangladesh Accord on Fire and Building Safety—can be scaled up and widely disseminated.

As for local communities of production, distribution, consumption, and waste disposal, this book recounts experiments lodged both in the Global South and in indigenous communities in the Global North—experiments wedding the technical capacity of NGOs with local grassroots struggles for economic survival, equitable social development, and environmental justice. These initiatives range from the linkage between "upcycling" cooperatives in

Buenos Aires and the engineers and social scientists of Waste for Life (WSF); to Chintan's efforts to organize informal sector dismantlers and collectors in the Indian e-waste value chain; and to the Inuit people's use of digital media to participate in dialogue over the environmental impact of extractive industry commodity chains in Canada (see chapters 3, 4, and 8). Ongoing assessment of these initiatives is vital; and the analyses in this book provide important reference points for future evaluation of these experiments and their potential dissemination across the Global South and across indigenous peoples in the Global North and South. In addition, whether these experiments generate new knowledge that is adaptable to localized consumption/disposal circuitry of the enormous production of waste among dominant populations in the Global North, and whether such localization in the North is advantageous to the waste disposal value chains of the South are urgent questions that this volume begins to illuminate.

There is a great deal of irony even in these early success stories. For example, student radicals, labor unions, and NGOs created the Worker Rights Consortium (WRC) as a means to discredit the project of private standard-setting. But in order to delegitimate corporate self-regulation, the WRC designed the gold standard in private labor monitoring and ultimately achieved the first genuine restructuring of supply chains by holding multinational garment retailers and manufacturers financially responsible for their supplier factories' payment of living wages and safety costs (see chapter 2).

The WRC model then inspired private regulatory systems in supply chains outside the garment sector. For example, the Coalition of Immokalee Workers (CIW), a grassroots organization of undocumented migrants working in the Florida fields, succeeded in pressuring fast-food companies to take financial responsibility for raising wages paid by the farms that supply products to those companies (see chapter 5). And in the absence of effective public enforcement of farmworkers' rights, CIW uses a privatized enforcement model adapted from the WRC's.

Critically important, the WRC and CIW have devised enforcement protocols that seek to symmetricize power between Northern activists and Southern worker communities. Their investigative teams are (ideally though not always in practice) composed largely of members of the latter communities, to enable affected worker communities to prioritize their grievances, define applicable legal norms, engage in relevant fact-finding, and order remedies to be undertaken by multinational corporations and their local suppliers. This model advances the values of local empowerment, participation, and equality embraced by other organizations discussed in this volume, such as the Engineering, Social Justice, and Peace project (see chapter 3).

Even more ironically, these experiments in private, labor-centered enforcement have inspired the fortification of labor inspection protocols used by domestic and transnational sovereign entities. Some state and federal labor departments in the United States have adopted the WRC model for their investigation and prosecution of labor rights violations in domestic workplaces and in global chains that supply goods to government departments. Indeed, the WRC and CIW models are the prototypes for proposed methodologies (commissioned by the Obama Administration and incorporated in pending U.S. Senate legislation) for assessing every government's nationwide compliance with international labor rights.

Those proposed methodologies are still under review, as of this writing. Meanwhile, real action has been taken by the U.S. government in the domain of global labor rights: while Bangladeshi labor unions, the International Labor Rights Forum, the WRC, and other organizations achieved the contractual Bangladesh Accord, the Obama Administration used perhaps the most potent existing transnational tool to encourage sovereign enforcement of labor rights by the Bangladeshi government. That tool is the revocation of Bangladesh's favored access to the enormous U.S. consumer market.

This points to a final irony: this volume's analysis of Buenos Aires' regulation of urban waste shows how well-intentioned environmental laws may impede efforts to achieve environmental justice through local empowerment (see chapter 3). But public regulation need not suppress private empowerment; and in some instances private enforcement networks may propel sovereign regulation of supply chains. For example, the foreign economic policy of the United States or other advanced capitalist governments is not monolithic. A state apparatus is a complex, multi-headed organism. While, without doubt, the U.S. government's powerful Treasury Department, State Department, and Trade Representative are key global forces for neoliberalism, the much less powerful Bureau of International Labor Affairs (lodged in the U.S. Department of Labor) occasionally succeeds in forming alliances with White House political staff in order to enforce the little-known labor-rights provisions in U.S. legislation and treaties. And labor unions and community organizations in other countries form alliances with their U.S. counterparts to petition the U.S. president to meet his constitutional obligation to enforce those statutes and treaties. This is the strategy that succeeded in denying special trade privileges to Bangladeshi garment suppliers.

The potential power to transform global supply chains therefore extends not just to grassroots worker and consumer communities and transnational advocacy networks but also to latent components of the very citadels of neoliberalism. To put it differently, hegemonic structures may be fractured, presenting unlikely opportunities for counter-hegemonic action that exploits vulnerabilities and leverage points within the hegemonic structures themselves.

Surely, the self-critical proposition of two authors in this volume is correct: while activists resist injustice, they must also recognize their complicity with unjust institutions (see chapter 3). The converse of this proposition is also true: it is our very implication in the unjust infrastructure of global supply chains that imposes on us a moral obligation to resist and transform it. That is, in light of global economic integration and its dense political scaffolding, we are all—as consumers, investors, and citizens—complicit in the injustices sustained by global supply chains. As consumers, we must choose whether to buy our garments from sweatshops or from factories that pay a living wage; whether to buy from factories in local or distant communities; and whether to dispose of our waste in ways that are environmentally sustainable. As investors, we must choose particular corporations or governments in which to invest our retirement savings and from which to reap profit and interest. As citizens, we inescapably inhabit the political structures that broadly sustain profit-driven global supply chains, and we confront the challenge of participating in and transforming those structures. Hence, as consumers, investors, and citizens, we inevitably face the moral choice between indifference or resistance to the injustices of global supply chains.

Whether the opportunities for counter-hegemonic action will be sufficiently frequent and promising to enable deep transformation of capitalist supply chains, and whether activists will be poised to seize those opportunities, are precisely the questions mooted in this volume. The still unsettled answers to those questions will likely turn as much on the contingencies of history as on academic analysis. But it is of the utmost importance to examine social experiments that can guide researchers and activists in identifying such opportunities and preparing to grasp them when they arise.

Mark Barenberg
Sulzbacher Professor of Law
Columbia University, New York City

Acknowledgments

The idea for this book grew out of a project of the Bluestocking Institute for Global Peace and Justice. As part of that project, we ran a series of workshops in 2010 on social action toward improving the production, consumption, and disposal of everyday items. The interest in these workshops, as well as in a subsequent series addressing globalization in a broader sense, made it clear that there is a growing interest in critical perspectives on social change that make links between local sites and global processes.

Workers and activists around the world are struggling to change the way products are made, goods are disposed of, and information is shared. The authors in this book are redefining people's engagement with the global economy by restructuring workplaces, creating locally controlled media outlets and enterprises, and challenging conventional production models. Their efforts inspired the creation of this book.

Since we began working on this book, we have each had our own experiences living and working in various locations—Cyprus, Lebanon, Greece, Tunisia, Canada, Australia, the United States, and the United Kingdom—researching the ways in which people in different parts of the globe are seeking to create and sustain change in the global economy. We would like to thank all the people along the way who have helped make this book possible. This includes the board members of the Bluestocking Institute for Global Peace and Justice, particularly Kelly Gerard, Michelle Hackett, Kate Riddell, and Liza Beinart. Sky Croeser would like to thank Jason Sharbanee and Claire Litton-Cohn for their ceaseless support and willingness to read drafts, talk through ideas, and provide other support which is often invisible in the final text, but which nevertheless was vital to its production. Christalla Yakinthou would like to thank the University of Birmingham for its support, and understanding that working on something slightly off trajectory does contribute to a worthwhile broader picture. Shae Garwood would like to acknowledge Stephanie Bachman for her friendship and dedication to social justice, Mary and Griff Garwood for their ongoing encouragement, Ethan Blue for his critical engagement and unwavering support, and Amaya and Zadie for giving me hope in the future.

Chapter One

Agents and Methods of Social Change in the Global Economy

Shae Garwood and Sky Croeser

In the face of globalization's massive economic transformations and social dislocation, activists, labor organizers, and advocacy NGOs are seeking change beyond the confines of formal state politics and across national borders. Given the breadth of issues activists face, the ways they define the problem and seek redress vary widely. Some emphasize greater regulation of transnational capital; others seek to reduce environmental waste; still others aim for workers and local communities to have greater control over their labor and local resources.

The challenge of creating social change in the global economy comes, in part, from the complex and convoluted paths that commodities travel. Products are often assembled in one country from raw materials drawn from others, and the final product is shipped and consumed elsewhere still. Consumer goods are then often discarded in landfills or dispatched to recycling centers, where they continue on their journey to other countries. Consider the example of the garment industry: Rivoli (2005) traces the travels of a t-shirt with the cotton produced in Texas, woven and assembled in China, then shipped back to the United States and sold in a shop in Florida. Rivoli further traces clothing that is donated to charities in the United States that fuel second-hand markets in dozens of countries in Sub-Saharan Africa. Such lengthy supply chains and subsequent movement around the globe from points of production, consumption, and disposal are not unique to the garment industry. They are increasingly becoming emblematic of a number of industries, and present specific challenges for those seeking to empower workers and protect natural resources.

Lessons for Social Change in the Global Economy represents an ongoing effort by scholars, practitioners, and activists to understand the global trajectories of commodities, and use that knowledge to address persistent inequality at multiple sites across the planet. This volume provides a unique perspective on efforts toward social change in the global economy, gathering together into one volume concrete examples of the implementation of different strategies for social change. Contributors to this volume are scholars and practitioners from around the world, and draw on strong connections with people working to improve labor conditions and environmental standards of global production systems.

FRAMEWORKS FOR ANALYZING SOCIAL CHANGE

A number of academic fields deal with social change, including development studies, economics, sociology, and gender studies. Each field confronts questions about how people can create social, economic, and political change in slightly different ways. Economics and development studies often emphasize economic growth as the major engine to achieve poverty alleviation and social development. Post-development scholars critique technical fixes and instead analyze the role of power in creating, and constraining, social change (Ferguson 1990). Philosopher and economist Amartya Sen (1999) argues that development should be focused on enhancing agency, capabilities, and freedoms as opposed to the traditional focus of development interventions on economic growth. Activists and NGOs embody different approaches to achieving equitable social change in the global economy, some of which are discussed below, either as ways of analyzing change or applying new practices to alter existing structures.

Social movement scholars analyze the actors and processes involved in social change. Since the 1950s, social movement scholarship has shifted away from the previous emphasis on seeing collective action as largely irrational outbursts and toward an approach that sees movements as attempts to create solutions to problems (or perceived problems) with existing systems. As Giugni (1999, x–xv) has noted, analysis of social movements has tended to neglect their effectiveness in achieving their goals. Despite the tendency to neglect the outcomes of social movement action, different approaches to social movements have offered theories about the factors that shape movements' abilities to affect change. Whereas traditional approaches saw leadership as playing a key role in determining outcomes, resource mobilization theory (also known as the American approach) has focused on the broader political context in which movements work, whereas the European approach has tended to see movements' ability to retain their autonomy and effectively build collective identity as key factors (Hannigan 1985, 436). Increasingly, scholars working within social movement studies are drawing from both approaches in order to build analysis of how movements effect change.

Another framework for analyzing social change comes from politics and international relations. This work seeks to understand how groups of people act as political agents for change within and across political borders. By highlighting the actions of transnational advocacy networks (Keck and Sikkink 1998), nongovernmental organizations (Ahmed and Potter 2006; Garwood 2011), and social movement organizations (Smith 2005) this work uncovers the mechanisms for change within political structures. Those political structures can be actions of states and other layers of government, but also the interaction of private sector actors with economic and social systems. This body of literature examines groups of people as political actors and the ways in which they create change within economic, political, and social systems.

A number of other fields employ practices aimed at assessing the impact of global production systems and developing ways to improve those systems. One such field, drawing from engineering and architecture, emphasizes that negative externalities such as pollution and other waste, or hazardous risks to workers, can be lessened or eliminated through better-designed products and systems. McDonough and Braungart's (2002) work on cradle-to-cradle systems aims to restructure production in order to decrease waste and create more sustainable product lifecycles. Cradle-to-cradle systems focus on technological changes and product design to alleviate environmental hazards and waste in manufacturing systems. Similarly, lifecycle assessment tools are techniques to assess the environmental impact of products and systems. Lifecycle assessments identify energy and material inputs and environmental impacts of a product's lifecycle and how they can be improved (Environmental Protection Agency 2011). Both cradle-to-cradle and lifecycle assessments emphasize the restructuring of business systems to develop more sustainable products.

Other fields focus on improving corporate behavior through better management. There has been a growing emphasis on responsible business management and corporate social responsibility (CSR) in recent years. The literature on CSR highlights self-regulation among corporations. Within this approach, companies are encouraged to take more responsibility for the negative side-effects of their production systems. Traditionally businesses are only legally responsible for the narrow aspects of the direct production of their products. After the point of purchase, there may be limited warranties which allow for a product to be returned if it is faulty, but there is little responsibility taken for the ongoing effects of that product, particularly at the point of disposal. Companies have rarely been forced to reckon with what happens to their products once they are discarded in landfills or recycling centers, or are sold in second-hand markets. Standards of corporate social responsibilities vary widely, yet basically consist of corporations deciding upon, and then meeting, additional ethical or moral standards above and beyond legal minimums. Although many proponents of CSR emphasize its voluntary nature, others call for greater regulation to expand corporations' responsibilities to their stakeholders.

POINTS OF INFLUENCE IN THE GLOBAL ECONOMY

There are many different ways that people can intervene in social, political, and economic systems. Leverage points are places in systems where a small change can trigger broader behavioral change (Meadows 2008; Forrester 1990). Meadows (2008) distinguishes between points of leverage and a silver bullet or quick fix. She explains that strategic points of intervention in a system are often counterintuitive. These points include, among others, identifying and changing the flow of information in systems, altering the rules in a system, and transforming paradigms (Meadows 2008). The type of intervention required is dependent on the type of the system, actors involved, and access points for activists.

People seeking change in global production systems have targeted different points in the system. For example, labor movements often focus on the point of production to organize workers to demand better working conditions, fair pay, and/or safe working conditions. Workers are best placed to know their needs and collectively bargain for better conditions and protections. However, in many cases workers are limited in what they can achieve because of lengthy supply chains. Global supply chains present challenges for traditional unions. Unions are structurally reliant on bargaining between two parties. Yet, that two-sided model does not always apply in global supply chains since many decisions that impact workers are actually made by large-scale retailers even though they do not own the factory or directly employ the workers.

Environmental movements utilize a range of approaches due to the multi-dimensional (and multi-spatial) nature of threats to the environment. Because the environmental impact of a product is not tied to the point of production, environmental movements have been successful at accessing various points of leverage. Some actions focus on more environmentally sustainable production systems while others aim to establish new regulations or ensure the implementation of existing environmental laws. Other activists have targeted companies to take responsibility for their product at the end of its lifecycle. For example, activists are pressuring companies that produce electronics to be responsible for the disposal of their products when they are no longer used. The idea behind these campaigns is that companies will have more incentive to design products that last longer and provide less environmental waste at the end of their usefulness if the companies are financially responsible for their disposal. Activists have met with varying degrees of success with each of these points of influence.

Consumer movements are linked with environmental and labor movements, but differ in the position of consumers in the global economy and the points of influence available to them. Just as companies cannot exist without workers to produce commodities, neither can they survive without consumers. People are using their roles as consumers to pressure companies to improve social and environmental standards. With increasingly complex supply chains, people are often distant politically and geographically from the point of production. Global supply chains also mean that consumers and producers do not share many political institutions that can be used to regulate the behavior of manufacturers and retailers. In these cases, what is available to consumers is to pressure retailers. In the clothing industry activists focus on reforming the mainstream clothing market, because making small changes to the $583 billion industry (WTO 2008) can create significant changes in millions of peoples' lives. Consumer campaigns use a variety of tools including boycotts, buycotts (promoting products that adhere to higher labor and environmental standards), certification and labeling of products, and greater regulation of transnational corporations. One example of this is the Clean Clothes Campaign, which pressures European companies to improve conditions in garment factories worldwide. The Campaign puts pressure on companies through demonstrations, media campaigns, and demanding that those companies join initiatives to make their supply chains more transparent and accountable to codes of conduct. Each of these strategies seeks to galvanize consumer politics to create change.

SEEKING ALTERNATIVE GOVERNANCE SYSTEMS

Industries are governed by domestic and international laws, treaties and trade agreements, and codes of conduct. Some governance systems rely on voluntary participation while others require greater transparency and reporting to governments. Voluntary, multi-stakeholder initiatives (MSIs) that involve companies, non-government organizations (NGOs), and sometimes governments, are growing as a result of activist pressure to monitor industry compliance with codes of conduct. Esbenshade (2004) distinguishes between private monitoring by corporations and independent monitoring by NGOs. MSIs can improve labor standards and lessen environmental damage within production systems. However, when in place of government regulation, MSIs are limited in what they can achieve, particularly when they essentially privatize regulation and close off more democratic forms of regulation (O'Rourke 2006; Lipschutz 2005). Nevertheless, MSIs represent an alternative form of governance (from state regulation), and given the political economy of global supply chains, MSIs may be what is feasible within these constraints at this time.

Multi-stakeholder initiatives use a number of tools to reform industry practices, including labeling and certification regimes. In some industries there are multiple labeling systems in use, promoted by different MSIs and in different countries. For example, requirements to allow products to be labeled organic vary from country to country. Certification and labeling can ensure that certain health and safety standards are met and can provide consumers with information they need to make informed decisions. However, some labeling may be more about "greenwashing" than actually reflecting healthier and more sustainable processes. Regardless of the form of governance, changing an industry often requires behavioral changes beyond existing minimal regulations.

VOICES, PERSPECTIVE, AND SOCIAL CHANGE

We use the term voice in the book to value the perspectives of the authors and the different subject positions of activists and organizations in seeking social change. Many of the chapters have multiple authors and therefore have a collaborative or collective voice. The use of the term voice is not intended to valorize one true "authentic" voice, but rather to highlight different perspectives and engagement at different points in the global economy as a counter-balance to dominant "voices" of states and corporations. In *Why Voice Matters: Culture and Politics After Neoliberalism*, Couldry discusses voice as process and as a value:

> Voice as a process—giving an account of oneself and what affects one's life—is an irreducible part of what it means to be human; effective voice (the effective opportunity to have one's voice heard and taken into account) is a human good. "Voice" might therefore appear unquestionable as a value. But across various domains—economic, political, cultural—we are governed in ways that deny the value of voice and insist instead on the primacy of market functioning (Couldry 2010, vi).

While writing from different geographic locations and geopolitical subject positions, the authors in this book are all engaged in counter-hegemonic struggles against the primacy of market functioning over the well-being of workers and the environment.

The term "the field" in the subtitle is meant to convey the realm of engaged advocacy. Many of the authors are NGO practitioners, labor organizers, and activist-scholars, overlapping categories in which the authors simultaneously operate on multiple fronts. "The field" is used here in a political sense to designate a sphere of advocacy and activism, often in conversation with scholarly debates on how to create change in global production systems and the waste created from such systems.

STRUCTURE OF THE BOOK

The chapters in *Lessons for Social Change in the Global Economy* demonstrate the use of different points of leverage in the global production system for creating change. They analyze efforts from labor, environmental, and consumer movements as well as technical assessments and improvements to product lifecycles and alternative governance structures. The strength of this volume is in the balance between breadth and specificity. It provides an overview of the themes of social change, which contextualizes and draws common threads from the chapters grounded in specific geographic locations and political spaces of change.

The chapters analyze environmental and social problems and the varying degrees of success activists have had in regulating industries, containing environmental hazards, and/or harnessing aspects of an industry for positive social and economic change. The chapters draw upon different ways of creating change, which include corporate social responsibility schemes, fair trade regimes, and community radio. The chapters vary in terms of the emphasis, providing perspectives on campaigns of reform for specific industries, community-based action focused on a particular product, or wider social change. By providing an insight into the potential and limitations of actions taken at different sites, the book encourages a critical perspective on efforts for social change, grounded in an understanding of how conditions around the world can affect these activities. This introduction along with the conclusion and supporting material connect the studies with broader discussions around the strategies examined, helping to provide a theoretical framework for a critical understanding of the case studies.

In the chapter 2, Sarah Adler-Milstein, Jessica Champagne, and Theresa Haas show how consumer and labor movements have come together to work towards improving labor conditions in the garment industry in three case studies. They argue that these actions—collective efforts among workers, universities, students, consumers, and advocates—point the way to broader change in the industry. The first case study examines the Alta Gracia factory in the Dominican Republic, which produces t-shirts and sweatshirts for hundreds of universities across the United States, pays a living wage, accepted unionization without resistance, and allows independent and transparent verification of its commitments. Initial research is demonstrating the impact that a living wage has on workers' health, their children's health, and the economic well-being of the community. A second case examines direct agreements between global brands and workers' representatives, which create enforceable obligations that go beyond the non-binding corporate pledges that define CSR programs. Adler-Milstein, Champagne, and Haas profile agreements in Honduras as well as an unprecedented legally enforceable contract between brands and retailers, international union federations, and unions in Bangladesh following the collapse of Rana Plaza in April 2013, which killed 1,129 workers. A third case highlights how the Designated Suppliers Program for universities, now under consideration at universities throughout the United States and Canada, will force apparel brands that do business with universities to align their pricing and sourcing practices with their labor rights obligations, a reform that is essential if respect for worker rights in global supply chains is to be more than an empty corporate promise. The chapter analyzes the ways in which these campaigns are restructuring relationships between workers and global brands and creating enforceable obligations to improve labor standards in the industry. The authors reflect on their work in seeking these changes and the potential for change in other industries using these models.

While Adler-Milstein, Champagne, and Haas focus on improving labor practices at the point of production, in chapter 3 Caroline Baillie and Eric Feinblatt turn to labor practices at the point of destruction or re-use. Applying a post-development framework, Baillie and Feinblatt conduct a critique of Waste for Life, an organization that aims to provide an urban recycling service in Buenos Aires. Baillie and Feinblatt argue that the model for social change used by Waste for Life presents a socially just alternative to traditional public/private profit-making approaches to recycling, and may provide lessons for other efforts to reform the waste industry. Waste for Life has shown that different groups work within the recycling system in different ways. Some important principles and practices include assemblies and equal pay, *sin patrón*—working without a boss—and people before profit. The chapter demonstrates how Waste for Life works to reinforce these features with the ultimate purpose of contributing to the larger discussions and experimentations in alternative modes of social and productive life, including social, environmental, and economic relationships to commodities and commodity disposal.

Unlike the workers in Buenos Aires engaged in a cooperative, workers in the electronics industry in Asia are faced with little decision-making power in a highly hierarchical global supply chain. In chapter 4, Bharati Chaturvedi discusses ways to improve conditions in the electronics industry at the point of destruction and recycling. Chaturvedi examines the work of Chintan, a non-profit organization based in India that works in partnership with workers in the informal sector (the part of the economy that is outside of government regulation or taxation) of the recycling industry in India. Chintan aims to help workers "convert waste into social wealth." Chaturvedi analyzes the impact of legislative changes in the disposal of electronic waste, and the ways in which Chintan is helping workers in the informal sector to partner with manufacturers and consumers, in order to create "green jobs" in the context of the new regulatory environment. To do this, Chintan is creating new strategies and partnerships with generators, the government, and with recyclers. The chapter argues that amid legislative changes intended to reduce hazards in electronic waste disposal, workers in the informal sector are subject to increased regulation, which places this vulnerable population at risk of losing their livelihood. The chapter presents a model for social change based on harnessing environmental legislation to benefit poor and disenfranchised populations, and the significant challenges and setbacks in doing so.

While Chaturvedi focuses on governance through state regulation, Michael Heasman and Ralph Early assess a range of alternative governance systems in chapter 5. They investigate activities designed to help reassure consumers about a company's ethical and environmental credentials. They do this through a broader conceptual framework of social justice and fairness in food supply chains. Heasman and Early argue that a notion of fairness is a useful analytical lens to help consumers to "re-connect" to their food through their purchasing and consumption practices and create greater structural changes to our food systems. Heasman and Early argue that the broader concept of fairness and equity can be a powerful analytical tool with which to hold corporations accountable for activities across their supply chains. This includes the consequences of food industry actions as they operate in globalized markets and through complex business networks. The reconceptualization of fairness and equity reveals the range of factors affecting the lifecycle of commodified foods and that impact consumers in surprising ways. These might include food insecurity, labor practices, and human rights, in addition to considering notions of "fair" trade and the deepening environmental crisis facing the future of food production.

As Heasman and Early point out, numerous corporations have responded to social movements and challenges with testaments to corporate social responsibility. They proclaim that they are globally minded citizens with the interests of consumers at heart. Yet as Marisol Sandoval and Kristina Areskog Bjurling reveal, workers' rights in the electronics industry continue to be violated. They provide evidence of labor rights violations in the electronics industry in China, Vietnam, the Philippines, and India based on numerous reports by members of the makeITFair Campaign. These reports cover a range of critical areas including wages, working hours, workplace safety, discrimination and harassment at work, and rights to unionize and to collective bargaining. Sandoval and Bjurling argue for abandoning simplistic versions of CSR that improve corporate image without adequately addressing workers' rights and conditions. In their place, Sandoval and Bjurling advocate for a nuanced approach to CSR, which establishes more direct links between workers and brands in order to develop clear relationships of accountability and improve conditions for workers in the sector. The chapter concludes with lessons from their campaigns to secure workers' rights in the supply chain of the global IT industry and the relevance for other industries.

In the next chapter, Sanjiv Pandita and Fahmi Panimbang extend Sandoval and Bjurling's critique of CSR and present an impassioned call to reject existing efforts to reform global supply chains. They argue that the global supply chain system cannot be reformed because of its reliance on corporations being able to externalize risk to workers in developing countries. Pandita and Panimbang contend that efforts that promote the adoption of "top down" labor codes and standards are limited in their efficacy and actually undermine the sovereignty of nation states and the potential for grassroots action. The chapter challenges prevailing ideas about supply chain reform and presents a compelling argument from activists working in the field.

Chapter 6 by Claire Litton-Cohn and Sky Croeser presents another voice on social change, extending the discussion beyond product supply chains to another type of production and consumption. Litton-Cohn and Croeser reveal how digital media is an increasingly important "product" in the global economy, both in terms of its economic impacts and in terms of its importance in creating social and political change. They demonstrate how IsumaTV, which hosts and builds networks around First Nations media, represents efforts to bring about social change in the global economy. These efforts depend in part on gaining increased visibility for marginalized voices, and especially for indigenous peoples around the world. IsumaTV provides a model for using new media to do this effectively.

Lastly, the concluding chapter summarizes the findings from the other chapters, highlighting some of the similarities and differences across different interventions and the implications for those interested in addressing problems in the global economy. It draws out lessons for social change from the chapters and contributes to further understandings of how people can change systems to respect workers' rights and increase environmental and social sustainability.

Lessons for Social Change in the Global Economy reveals links between activists across the globe in efforts from production to consumption and waste. It seeks to reintegrate seemingly disparate sites of experience in struggle. The volume is unique; bringing together academics and activists directly engaged in advocacy work for social justice to offer case studies and share analysis based on their locally grounded experience. As such, it collects a range of perspectives that reveal the multiple crises of globalization, as well as the successes and setbacks that activists have confronted in the quest for social change in the global economy.

REFERENCES

Ahmed, Shamima and David M. Potter. 2006. *NGOs in International Politics*. Bloomfield, CT: Kumarian Press, Inc.

Couldry, Nick. 2010. *Why Voice Matters: Culture and Politics After Neoliberalism*. Sage.

Environmental Protection Agency. 2011. *Life Cycle Assessment*. Accessed Sept 24, 2011. http://www.epa.gov/nrmrl/lcaccess/

Esbenshade, Jill. 2004. *Monitoring Sweatshops: Workers, Consumers, and the Global Garment Industry*. Philadelphia: Temple University Press.

Ferguson, James. 1990. *The Anti-Politics Machine: "Development," Depoliticization and Bureaucratic Power in Lesotho*. Cambridge, UK: Cambridge University Press.

Forrester, Jay Wright. 1990. *Principles of Systems*. Cambridge, MA: Pegasus Communications.

Garwood, Shae. 2011. *Advocacy Across Borders: NGOs, Anti-sweatshop Activism and the Global Garment Industry*. Bloomfield, CT: Kumarian Press, Inc.

Giugni, Marco. 1999. *How Social Movements Matter*, edited by Marco Giugni, Doug McAdam, and Charles Tilly, xiii-xxxiii. Minneapolis and London: University of Minnesota Press.

Hannigan, John A. 1985. "Alain Touraine, Manuel Castells and Social Movement Theory a Critical Appraisal." *The Sociological Quarterly* 26(4), 435-54.

Keck, Margaret and Kathryn Sikkink. 1998. *Activists Beyond Borders*. Ithaca: Cornell University Press.

Lipschutz, Ronnie D. 2005. "Global Civil Society and Global Governmentality: Or, the Search for Politics and the State Amidst the Capillaries of Social Power." In *Power in Global Governance* edited by M. Barnett and R. Duvall. Cambridge: Cambridge University Press, 229-48.

McDonough, William and Michael Braungart. 2002. *Cradle to Cradle: Remaking the Way we Make Things*. New York: North Point Press.

Meadows, Donella. (ed by D. Wright). 2008. *Thinking in Systems: A Primer*. London: Earthscan.

O'Rourke, Dara. 2006. "Multi-stakeholder Regulation: Privatizing or Socializing Global Labor Standards?" *World Development* 34, 5, 899-918.

Rivoli, Pietra. 2005. *The Travels of a T-shirt in the Global Economy*. Hoboken, NJ: John Wiley & Sons, Inc.

Sen, Amartya. 1999. *Development as Freedom*, New York. Alfred A. Knopf.

Smith, Jackie. 2005. "Globalization and Social Movement Organizations." In *Social Movements and Organization Theory* edited by G. Davis, D. McAdam, W. R. Scott and M. Zald, 226-48. Cambridge, UK: Cambridge University Press.

WTO. 2008. International trade statistics tables ii65 and ii70, World Trade Organization. Available from: http://www.wto.org.

Chapter Two

The Right to Organize, Living Wage, and Real Change for Garment Workers

Sarah Adler-Milstein, Jessica Champagne, and Theresa Haas

In almost every campus bookstore in the United States, Yenny Perez's face smiles out from the tags of Alta Gracia brand T-shirts. Yenny is an unlikely celebrity spokeswoman; she is a thirty-five-year-old single mother of five who has been working in apparel factories since she was fourteen years old. She is also a courageous union leader who is now a quality inspector at the Alta Gracia factory, the first ever living wage, unionized factory in the global apparel industry.

The Alta Gracia factory is located in and named after Yenny's hometown of Villa Altagracia in the Dominican Republic. Yenny's own words appear on the hangtags on Alta Gracia garments at University stores, where she explains that Alta Gracia products:

> . . . are made in a unique factory where workers have united to form a union. Our factory has a living wage which allows us to have a better life where we know we can provide a good education, healthcare and food for our families. Every t-shirt helps support the hope of a better life, not just for each one of our children, but for our whole community.

Alta Gracia is the only apparel factory in the Global South which pays workers a genuine living wage (more than three times the prevailing wage), welcomed unionization without resistance, and has been shown by truly independent monitoring to be in full and consistent compliance with domestic and international labor standards.

From Yenny's beaming smile on the Alta Gracia tag, it is hard to believe that five years earlier, she was the spokeswoman for a very different message—that workers in the global garment industry faced myriad abuses, including forced overtime, dangerous health and safety conditions, and brutal harassment, while struggling to survive on poverty wages. In 2001, Yenny and her coworkers at the BJ&B hat factory, which produced for Reebok, Nike, and other major brands, had formed a union to fight against dangerous, inhumane working conditions. For years, workers and their US allies, including the union UNITE, had unsuccessfully fought for improved conditions at BJ&B; this time, they succeeded despite continued resistance by management. After a year-long struggle, including international support from United Students Against Sweatshops (USAS), the union was recognized and negotiated a contract that eliminated the worst abuses at BJ&B and began bringing workers up to a decent standard of living—starting with a 10 percent raise. BJ&B was hailed as an example of the progress that could be achieved through a combination of tenacious worker organizing and effective international solidarity.

However, it ultimately fell victim to the "race to the bottom" (Collins 2003), the cut-throat competition between apparel factories to produce at the lowest possible cost in order to secure orders from apparel brands who scour the globe for the lowest possible labor price. International brands steadily decreased their orders to BJ&B, and the factory's owners shifted their production to lower-wage facilities. Finally, in 2007, the plant closed. Along with her co-workers and with support from allies, Yenny fought successfully for severance payments above the legal minimum, but they could not keep the factory open. Union leaders, including Yenny, were blacklisted for their activism. With limited employment options available in Villa Altagracia, they and their families slid into even deeper poverty along with many of their former co-workers.

This story has repeated itself in El Salvador, Indonesia, Thailand, Honduras, and in fact, in most countries where apparel is produced. What makes Yenny's story different is that the workers' years of struggle inspired the creation of the Alta Gracia factory in 2010. Yenny's experience provides important insights regarding the value of independent monitoring, worker organizing, and international activism for winning concrete gains in workers' rights as well as about shortcomings of the strategies to address the supply chain practices of major brands. This chapter reviews strategies that have been undertaken in the past by both worker advocates and the apparel brands themselves to address labor rights issues at the factory level, and evaluates what has been effective and what has simply been corporate spin. The chapter then describes three promising new initiatives designed to confront this reality which represent the best hopes for change in the garment industry and other manufacturing sectors.

In the mid-1990s the anti-sweatshop movement first raised awareness among US consumers that the factories that produced their clothing had unsafe working conditions and poverty wages. The anti-sweatshop movement grew particularly strong on university campuses, where students used lucrative licensing agreements between universities and major apparel brands to leverage support for enforcement of labor standards. Universities and student activists were effective in using this power to compel disclosure of which specific factories were producing for universities, implement labor codes of conduct, and establish the Worker Rights Consortium as an independent monitor to report on and enforce these codes of conduct. The BJ&B factory where Yenny worked is an example of both how these tools were used to achieve concrete victories at the factory level, and their limitations in an industry where maximizing profits remains brands' top priority (Ross 2006).

Under fire from activists and under a media spotlight, apparel brands developed their own strategies to respond to the public awareness of widespread abuses in their supplier factories. In the late 1990s the leading brands in the apparel industry trumpeted new corporate social responsibility (CSR) programs and pledged to raise standards in the factories that produced apparel for export. However, the evidence from a decade of implementation of voluntary CSR programs in the garment industry indicates that they have done little to change workers' lives. While global brands showcase their CSR commitments, they continue to place downward pressure on prices and switch rapidly between suppliers to find the products at the lowest price. The focus on fast, cheap production brings poverty wages, deadly health and safety violations, and constant repression of workers' efforts to organize and speak out against these conditions (Locke et al. 2006).

What would it take to create real change? Despite the ineffectiveness of CSR programs, workers, universities, students, consumers, and advocates are winning meaningful victories that point the way to broader change in the industry. The three promising new avenues for change reviewed in this chapter are as follows. First, as described above, in the Dominican Republic, Alta Gracia serves as a model for apparel production where the factory pays a living wage, accepts unionization, and allows independent and transparent verification of its commitments. Initial research is demonstrating the positive impact that a living wage has on workers' health, their children's health, and the economic well-being of the community (Kline and Soule 2011). Second, in Honduras and in Bangladesh, direct agreements between the global brands and retailers and worker representatives create enforceable obligations that go beyond the non-binding corporate pledges that define CSR programs (Greenhouse 2009, 2010). Third, the Designated Suppliers Program (DSP), now under consideration at universities throughout the United States and Canada, will force apparel brands that do business with universities to align their pricing and sourcing practices with their labor rights obligations, a reform that is essential if respect for worker rights in global supply chains is to be more than an empty corporate promise (Kline 2012).

CODES OF CONDUCT AND MONITORING

The contemporary US anti-sweatshop movement is relatively new, birthed in the mid-1990s as a series of sweatshop scandals led to a growing public awareness of labor conditions in the global apparel industry. Exposés about young female workers in Mexico and abusive conditions at Gap factories in El Salvador, among others, sparked student activism on college campuses where much of this clothing was sold.[1]

As an increasingly global economy brought the brutal realities of garment sweatshops into the public eye, students across the country recognized the important leverage they could exert over brands producing their collegiate logo apparel. Through a process called licensing, universities grant major sportswear brands including Nike, adidas/Reebok, Gear for Sports, and others, the right to produce and sell apparel bearing their university name and logo, in exchange for a portion of the sales revenue. Students realized that through these valuable licensing agreements, universities could hold brands accountable for conditions in their supply chains. If brands were unwilling to meet these labor requirements, they risked losing their share of the valuable collegiate market and access to young consumers, whose brand loyalty was still up for grabs.

Uniting themselves into a national organization called United Students Against Sweatshops (USAS), anti-sweatshop activists at campuses around the country demanded that universities take concrete and enforceable action to ensure that their logo apparel was being produced under fair and humane working conditions.

Through a series of protests, sit-ins, and other campaign tactics in the late 1990s, students and labor rights activists demanded that universities require licensees (brands that have obtained licenses to produce collegiate apparel) to disclose the names and locations of their supplier factories, which had long been considered a trade secret by companies seeking to prevent their competitors from gaining access to, they claimed, proprietary information. But thanks to pressure brought to bear on universities through student activism, factory data for the collegiate market was ultimately made public, exposing the first of many corporate deceptions—that each apparel brand did not have its own private list of suppliers; instead, licensees shared factories, each of which could be producing for dozens of different brands at any given time. Brands that are arch-rivals in the marketplace, such as adidas, Nike, and Under Armour are often producing t-shirts or even more technical products such as shoes at the same factories; in one recent example, Nike and adidas were both key buyers for the Pinehurst factory in Honduras, where workers recently organized a union in 2011–2012 despite initial employer resistance.[2]

Students also demanded, with widespread success, that universities adopt labor codes of conduct, including requirements in areas such as wages and hours, freedom of association, women's rights, and occupational health and safety. University licensees would then be responsible for ensuring that all of their supplier factories complied with these codes.

Realizing that codes of conduct would be meaningless without a mechanism for enforcement, in April 2000 students joined with labor and human rights groups to create the Worker Rights Consortium (WRC), which was tasked with uncovering and documenting labor rights abuses in university supply chains and providing support for workers seeking to organize and improve conditions. To carry out its investigative mission, the WRC hired staff in countries where a significant amount of collegiate apparel was produced, and began to develop an extensive network of labor unions and NGOs in the Global South. Using a complaint-based system in concert with this network, the WRC could identify factories in which serious labor abuses were occurring and where real gains could be achieved by and for workers. When the WRC found that codes of conduct had been violated, students could use this information to press universities to ensure that licensees corrected the abuses.[3]

The organization's model was first put to the test when on January 18, 2001, four workers from the Kukdong facility in Atlixco, Mexico submitted a complaint to the WRC alleging serious labor rights abuses. The complaint stated that that the factory engaged in the use of child labor, physical and verbal harassment, failed to provide legally mandated maternity leave, locked workers inside the factory during lunch breaks, served rancid food in the cafeteria, and had illegally fired workers for participating in a work stoppage a week earlier. The complaint also alleged that Kukdong, a supplier of collegiate apparel to Nike, had called in the local police to disband the stoppage through physical force, injuring several workers in the process. Within a week, the WRC assembled an investigative team which, through worker interviews, review of relevant documentation, consultation with Mexican legal experts and local human rights organizations, and interviews with senior factory management, found overwhelming evidence to substantiate the workers' claims, and issued a public report of its findings (WRC 2001).

The WRC notified universities of its findings in the case. With students around the country encouraging their schools to take action, the universities pushed Nike and Reebok to compel Kukdong to remedy the violations. This led to the reinstatement of the illegally fired workers, improvements in the cafeteria food, two wage increases, and recognition of the factory's independent, democratically elected union.[4] This represented a substantial victory in a country whose manufacturing sector was dominated by a corrupt, management-friendly organization that claimed to represent workers' interests, but which existed primarily to prevent the sort of genuine worker organizing that had taken place at Kukdong.[5]

The success achieved at Kukdong proved that students, in solidarity with workers, could force major apparel brands to take responsibility for conditions at their supplier factories, and win real gains for workers. As it had at Kukdong, the WRC continued to use its on-the-ground network to identify and document violations at collegiate suppliers, and students pressed their universities to hold brands accountable for remedying these abuses. At factories like BJ&B in the Dominican Republic, PT Dada (WRC 2002) and PT Kolon Langgeng in Indonesia (WRC 2003), CODEVI in Haiti (WRC 2006), and Primo in El Salvador (WRC 2004), workers began to achieve genuine victories, and substantial improvements were made. It seemed that students had found a way to hold brands accountable for conditions in their subcontracted factories in a way that garnered unprecedented improvements in the global supply chain.

But even as workers in individual factories won tremendous victories against billion-dollar corporations, the WRC continued to uncover abusive conditions at nearly every factory it investigated, and plants that had been the site of major labor rights breakthroughs often began to report losses in orders as brands refused to support the higher costs that come with improved conditions, as in the case of BJ&B. It was clear that no matter how vigorously the WRC investigated or how hard the students campaigned, the fundamentally flawed structure of the global apparel industry was preventing sweeping progress from being achieved and maintained.

SUPPLY CHAIN PRACTICES OF GLOBAL APPAREL BRANDS

Collegiate apparel production, like the rest of the industry, is spread among thousands of individual facilities. In most factories, university logo apparel accounts for only a very small percentage of the factory's overall business, giving an individual licensee limited leverage to compel the necessary changes to improve labor rights compliance. As a result, factories remain primarily accountable to non-university buyers, which typically have less incentive to press factories to achieve labor rights compliance, thus dragging conditions in these collegiate factories down to the low industry norm. This atomization of production makes it virtually impossible to effectively monitor the collegiate supply chain. Because of the time and resources required, no monitoring organization, including the WRC, can effectively keep tabs on what is happening in thousands of individual factories.

Despite the voluntary labor standards adopted by virtually all major apparel brands, and the codes of conduct imposed by universities, corporations remain accountable to one standard above all else: profit. In order to maximize profit, corporations put enormous price pressure on their suppliers to keep costs as low as possible. Brands pit factories against each other to push prices down; suppliers understand that if they cannot meet a brands' price demand, another factory somewhere else will. As a result, factory owners look for every possible way to cut costs, which inevitably comes from labor, the most flexible cost in a factory. Although brands pay lip service to their public commitment to labor rights compliance, the economic message they send to factories is quite different: keep prices down, or risk losing business. Inevitably, workers suffer as a result.

Even in situations where factories have made genuine progress on labor rights, through intervention by the WRC, students, and universities, they still face enormous pressure to minimize production costs. Instead of rewarding a supplier that has improved conditions by providing larger order volumes, longer-term contracts, and higher prices, brands respond by reducing orders at the facility, unwilling to accept the inevitable increase in costs that come with producing under decent labor conditions.[6] As a result, factories that move toward code compliance, as universities ask them to do, actually render themselves less competitive in the marketplace.

In seeking out the lowest price, apparel brands jump constantly between suppliers, often shifting orders every few months, creating economic instability for factories and a lack of job security for workers. These short-term relationships make it difficult to exert substantial pressure on a factory to correct labor violations. Once such abuses are uncovered, a licensee may already have left the facility, taking with it the valuable leverage necessary for improvement. Nor are factories generally eager to implement costly changes in labor practices at the behest of a customer who may well not be around a few months down the road.

These factors—price pressure, atomization of production, order volatility, and failure to reward compliance—have created an environment for factories in which labor rights compliance is incompatible with economic success. As a result, despite more than a decade of efforts by universities and other stakeholders to improve conditions, workers continue to face grueling hours of forced overtime, to be threatened or fired for organizing unions, and to earn wages that are lower in real terms than they were a decade ago. Meanwhile, factories that have made genuine improvements have either closed or reverted back to previous sweatshop conditions.

Industry practices have led to undermining real wages for garment workers. A recent study released by the WRC and the Center for American Progress indicates that real wages for garment workers have generally decreased in the last ten years; for workers in the top ten apparel-exporting countries to the United States, real wages have actually declined since 2001. Even in the few countries where real wages increased, the majority of countries still made limited progress toward a living wage. Even if wages continued to grow at the same rate in those countries where real wages increased, it would still take workers decades to achieve a living wage. In 2011, prevailing wages among workers from the top four apparel exporting countries to the United States were only 14 to 36 percent of a living wage (WRC, Center for American Progress, and Just Jobs Network 2013).

Unsurprisingly, voluntary corporate social responsibility (CSR) initiatives, developed in response to the sweatshop exposes of the late 1990s, have been substantially less effective than the system of binding obligations imposed by universities; these industry-controlled programs have, with minimal exceptions, yielded no meaningful improvements for workers. Though brands and retailer CSR programs are sometimes staffed by well-meaning individuals who genuinely want to create change, CSR staff do not control the pricing and sourcing decisions made by their employers and therefore cannot ameliorate the cost cutting demands that virtually guarantee that these programs will fail to generate labor rights improvements at the factory level. Thus, while the industry pays lip service to the need for meaningful improvement, the reality is that very little has changed for garment workers since the inception of corporate codes of conduct and monitoring.

THE FIRE AND BUILDING SAFETY CRISIS IN BANGLADESH

Nowhere else is the failure of CSR more obvious than in Bangladesh, the second largest producer of apparel in the world (Yardley 2012), where 80 percent of the country's export income comes from the garment sector (BBC News 2012). Garment workers there earn approximately 18 cents an hour, less than their counterparts in any other significant apparel-exporting country in the world. Bangladesh's ultra low wages are part of a concerted strategy by the industry there to establish itself as the world's cheapest source of labor in direct response to the relentless price pressure exerted by the global garment industry. This strategy has had a devastating impact on workers.

On April 24, 2013, Bangladesh became the site of the deadliest accident in the history of the global apparel industry when the Rana Plaza building collapsed, killing 1,129 workers and injuring more than 2,000. The day before the collapse, workers at the eight-story building noticed large cracks in the walls and the engineer that was called in to inspect the structure warned that it was dangerously unsafe and should be shut down immediately. The next morning, although most of the businesses in the building, including a shopping center and bank, remained closed, workers at the five garment factories were ordered to report to work and threatened with the loss of up to a month's pay if they refused. Less than two hours later, the building collapsed, trapping more than 3,000 workers inside. The rescue effort continued for more than two weeks and on May 10, the final survivor, a 19–year-old garment worker named Reshma was pulled from the rubble. She had survived under the debris for 17 days.

In the immediate aftermath of the collapse, the brands producing at the factory including Wal-Mart, Children's Place, JC Penney, and United Colors of Benetton denied any connection to the tragedy in the press. However, when faced with increasing evidence that made their connection to the factory impossible to deny, the brands claimed that they had done everything they could to police their factories and expressed shock and despair that such a disaster could have befallen them.

Yet to anyone with knowledge of the history of the garment industry in Bangladesh, the Rana Plaza collapse was inevitable. Eight years earlier, in April 2005, the Spectrum sweater factory collapsed under eerily similar circumstances: workers noticed cracks in the walls and expressed concerns to managers, who ignored the warnings and forced workers back to work. Sixty-four workers were killed when the factory collapsed the next morning. In response, brands and retailers, factory owners, and the Bangladesh government vowed to move swiftly to clean up the industry. However, nothing changed.

The tragedy at Rana Plaza was only the latest in a series of deadly fire and building safety disasters that have taken the lives of more than 1,800 Bangladesh garment workers since 2005. Exactly five months before Rana Plaza, 112 workers were killed in a fire at the Tazreen Fashions Limited factory, a major supplier to Wal-Mart, as well as Disney, Sears/Kmart, and ENYCE, Sean Combs' clothing line. In December 2010, a deadly fire at That's It Sportswear (a supplier to several major brands and retailers including Gap and Phillips Van Heusen) left thirty dead and dozens more injured, as many workers jumped to their deaths after locked exits prevented their escape. Less than a year prior, twenty-one workers at Garib and Garib, an H&M sweater facility, were killed, most succumbing to smoke inhalation after guards padlocked the factory's exits. And the list goes on.

These tragedies are part of the reality of the Bangladesh apparel sector. which is defined by utter disregard for the most basic safety precautions. The result is an industry so grossly unsafe that most of the factories, if located in the United States or any country that actually enforces its building code, would be identified as a grave threat to human life and shut down. In order to keep up with new orders, factory owners have established production facilities in shoddily constructed multi-level buildings which lack proper fire exits and safe electrical wiring. These factories become death traps as shoddy electrical wiring is overloaded by hundreds of machines running twenty-four hours a day combined with piles of flammable clothing blocking aisles and exit paths. When fires inevitably ignite, workers attempting to escape find the exits locked, purportedly to prevent theft.

Brands and retailers know that these conditions exist, but did nothing to prevent these disasters from happening. However they tell their customers a story that is opposite of the reality: they are deeply committed to protecting the rights and safety of workers who make their clothes and have put in place robust and highly effective systems to ensure safe and responsible practices by their suppliers. These claims could not be further from the truth. Virtually every single factory where major disasters have occurred in the past decade has been audited repeatedly by industry audit schemes, none of which did anything to prevent the massive death tolls. In the wake of the Tazreen fire and the Rana Plaza collapse, the brands and retailers have publicly admitted that their monitoring systems, which they have long asserted were top-notch, do not even look at basic fire and building safety issues.

Experience shows us that workers in Bangladesh cannot rely on the goodwill of the brands and retailers to make their factories safe. For this reason, it is critical that workers have a meaningful way to sound the alarm about building and fire safety hazards. If, on the morning of April 24, workers at Rana Plaza had had the option to refuse to enter an unsafe workplace, thousands of children, parents, husbands, wives, sisters, and brothers would not have lost their loved ones that day. Toward this end, labor rights NGOs play a critical role in educating workers about their rights and advocating on their behalf. From the perspective of industry, and its allies in the Bangladesh government, however, this advocacy threatens the nation's low-cost production strategy and it has drawn increasingly harsh repression in response. In August 2010, Babul Akhter and Kalpona Akter, the two principal leaders of the Bangladesh Center for Worker Solidarity (BCWS), one of the country's most prominent labor rights advocacy organizations, were arrested and charged with numerous crimes, some of which carry a possible sentence of life imprisonment (Bajaj and Manik 2010). Although they were released on bail a month later, the charges against them remain, and the organization's license to operate has been rescinded. Thus far, no legitimate evidence has been presented in support of these charges, and it appears that the criminal cases were brought as a means of scapegoating peaceful labor rights advocates for the unrest among workers that results from the poverty wages in the country's apparel sector and the government's failure to enforce its labor laws. In April of 2012, one of BCWS' most effective organizers, Aminul Islam, was found murdered, his body bearing visible signs of torture (Manik and Bajaj 2012). To date, the perpetrators of this crime remain unpunished.

Despite Bangladesh's near total failure to achieve compliance with basic labor standards, and despite the government's violent repression of lawful labor rights advocacy, the volume of orders from international brands continues to grow. If brands were serious about labor rights compliance, they would base their sourcing decisions on a country making labor rights a priority and a country like Bangladesh that makes a mockery of its labor rights obligations would be punished in the marketplace; instead, the opposite has happened. Bangladesh's strategy of minimizing production costs by running roughshod over the rights of workers has paid off handsomely, making it an increasingly attractive source of apparel for brands and retailers whose real priority is low prices, not high labor standards. As Bangladesh's share of global apparel production continues to rise, Bangladeshi garment workers continue to work for poverty wages and risk their lives every time they enter their workplaces.

Unfortunately, Bangladesh is only one example of this strategy. In places like Cambodia and the Philippines, manufacturers have actively lobbied against increases to the minimum wage, citing the very real danger that orders will diminish as brands refuse to support higher costs (ABS-CBNnews.com 2012). It is clear that codes of conduct and increased monitoring are not sufficient to address the economic pressures perpetuated by brands and retailers.

NEW DIRECTIONS

Achieving real change in factories around the world will require approaches that fundamentally alter the way brands do business. Widespread noncompliance with labor standards, and the closure of the rare factory that does improve its labor practices, are inevitable unless brands provide factories that live up to high labor standards with long-term production commitments at prices that make it possible for factories to maintain those standards and still turn a profit.

Workers, universities, students, consumers, and advocates are winning meaningful victories that point the way to this broader change. Three initiatives currently in progress are examples of genuine reform. First, the Alta Gracia Project in the Dominican Republic provides an example of how a commitment by an international buyer can bring sustained improvements, including living wages and full respect for workers' rights to organize. Second, a union in Honduras has broken new ground by signing two agreements with multinational brands that cover multiple factories and contain specific, legally enforceable obligations. The Accord on Fire and Building Safety in Bangladesh builds on this model with more than 60 brands committed to a binding agreement to prevent future disasters. And third, the Designated Supplier Program (DSP) will ensure that collegiate apparel producers change the way they operate their supply chains.

Alta Gracia

The Alta Gracia factory serves as a model for apparel production with a living wage and full respect for workers' rights including freedom of association with a democratic union and independent monitoring to ensure compliance. Alta Gracia products are now in hundreds of college bookstores as a result of more than ten years of campus activism focused on the need to source sweat-free products. The initial results indicate that not only is it possible to achieve exemplary labor standards in the apparel industry, but that it is possible to do so and remain economically viable (Kline and Soule 2011).

A study conducted by Georgetown professors John Kline and Edward Soule found that workers identified the living wage paid by Alta Gracia as emblematic of the model as a whole and describe the transformational effects that the Alta Gracia model has on workers' lives. One worker stated that living wage meant:

> . . . being taken into account; you are actually valued at work. People are able to get a higher education, better intellectual development, and better nutrition; without this, we can't have goals. Before, we were excluded from the whole system. (Kline and Soule 2011, 12)

Another worker said of Alta Gracia:

> . . . It allows one to accomplish dreams. In [a previous factory], the road was always dark. We always had to be borrowing money and taking out loans. You don't get to see the results of working. A [living wage] allows you to be identified as a human being. (Kline and Soule 2011, 12)

Alta Gracia provides a powerful example of the profound impact on workers' lives that can be achieved if the apparel industry fundamentally changes its practices.

What has allowed the Alta Gracia model to be radically more successful than other factories in implementing exemplary labor standards? For one, Alta Gracia has aligned its supply chain practices with its labor rights commitment by incentivizing compliance at the factory level and providing the necessary funds for labor rights compliance. A key element in Alta Gracia's success is the fact that the parent company, Knights Apparel, owns and operates the Alta Gracia factory directly and buys 100 percent of its products. This gives Knights Apparel full leverage and control to ensure that labor rights standard are met by the factory. In addition, Knights provides the factory with the funds necessary to pay a living wage and invest in necessary infrastructure for labor rights compliance (everything from a living wage and contributions to pension and health insurance systems to ergonomic chairs, adequate ventilation, and safe industrial-grade electrical wiring.) Lacking stable long-term orders at a fair price, other apparel factories cannot afford to make such improvements. Because Alta Gracia is sold specifically as a sweat-free product it incentivizes both the brand and the factory to put in the necessary resources to achieve labor rights compliance.

The living wage paid by Alta Gracia is unprecedented in the apparel industry. Such a wage will only be tenable for other individual supplier factories if they receive a fair price from their buyers. The current living wage at Alta Gracia is 21,499 Dominican pesos per month, about US $540; this is more than three times the free trade zone minimum wage for the Dominican Republic (6,320 Dominican pesos a month, about US $160). Alta Gracia's living wage was calculated by the WRC to include a decent standard of living for an average family, covering housing, nutrition, clothing, education, childcare, transportation, medical care, and a cushion for emergencies and savings, and is adjusted each year for inflation.[7]

Kline and Soule's study found that the living wage allows workers to make strides toward their life goals such as: education for themselves or their children, home ownership or improvements (such as indoor plumbing or sturdier construction to protect against hurricanes), better diet, and the financial wherewithal to afford necessary medical procedures they previously could not afford. In addition, Kline and Soule's study found that the living wage also positively affected the local economy through the "multiplier effect" of workers having more available income to support and invest in new businesses and community infrastructure. Their study found that the local economy was stimulated by the increased need for:

> . . . construction materials for home improvements as well as appliance purchases such as refrigerators, stoves, washing machines and motor scooters. Paying back money borrowed from family and friends increases their potential spending power. Banks gain new customers with sufficient financial stability to qualify for first-time loans. Childcare centers improve their quality with more children attending from the families of Alta Gracia workers. Small restaurants open outside the FTZ's gates to provide lunchtime options. (Kline and Soule 2011, 14)

While some critics of living wages raise concerns of unrest or inequality among workers, the evidence from Alta Gracia is that a living wage generates a high level of community support because of the indirect positive effects to the local economy.

Alta Gracia is also unique in that Knights, who buys 100 percent of the products, provides both funds and incentives for high levels of labor rights compliance across the board. Alta Gracia's occupational health and safety (OHS) program is an excellent example. While the vast majority of apparel factories cut corners on OHS infrastructure in order to compete, Alta Gracia proactively invested in OHS by working with Maquiladora Health and Safety Support Network (MHSSN), a respected and independent network of volunteer OHS professionals. Alta Gracia made improvements recommended in MHSSN's initial consultation and responded promptly to feedback from additional factory inspections. The MHSSN coordinator, Garrett Brown, writes that at Alta Gracia, "In a refreshing change from many garment operations . . . issues have been rapidly addressed by plant management, assisted by both their international customer, Knights Apparel, and by the union" (Brown 2010).

While the sourcing practices at Alta Gracia created the incentives and provided the resources necessary to reach labor rights compliance, the Alta Gracia union and the WRC play crucial roles in ensuring day-to-day compliance. Both the WRC and Fedotrazonas were involved in establishing and ensuring labor rights standards from the setup and hiring process to the current date.

Prior to opening the factory, Knights Apparel and Fedotrazonas reached an unprecedented agreement which allowed the union federation full access to the factory and a role in the orientation and worker rights training provided to all new employees. As a result, the union of Alta Gracia workers (SITRALPRO) officially formed in June of 2010—just months after the factory opened—with no resistance from management. The union has been extremely effective in addressing workplace issues and has resolved potential labor rights violations with management with little need for outside intervention. For example, when the government health insurance program assigned workers to a plan with no local coverage, the union quickly worked with management to solve the problem collaboratively; at other factories such a problem could last for months or years. A collaborative approach by management, based on open dialogue, has opened the door to both management and the union cooperating for the benefit of the workers and the enterprise. The union has taken the lead on promotion of the Alta Gracia products, acting as the spokespeople for Alta Gracia on campuses through video conferences, worker tours on US college campuses and various delegations and factory visits by US student groups.

In the first public monitoring report on labor conditions at Alta Gracia, the WRC noted that Alta Gracia's positive and open attitude to union formation was "a first, in our experience, in any export apparel factory in the Global South that supplies a US brand or retailer" (WRC 2010). Kline and Soule found that the positive relationship formed between the management and the union has concrete benefits to the workforce. They note that all stakeholders noted that:

> . . . the overall state of management-labor relations was by far the best of any factory in their experience. Workplace conditions drew consistent approval

> with several workers commenting on how training alerted them to safety risks they had disregarded in other jobs. (Kline and Soule 2011, 11)

The WRC also has an extensive monitoring program which makes Alta Gracia likely the most rigorously monitored factory in the apparel industry. The WRC has complete and unfettered access to the factory and all relevant documents. It conducts unannounced factory visits on a regular basis and does monthly payroll review to ensure compliance with the living wage standard. In addition, the WRC also regularly conducts off-site interviews with workers to identify any potential issues and resolve them quickly. As a result the WRC has been effective in identifying potential violations and ensuring remediation. For example, the WRC was able to ensure back pay for post-natal benefits that the workers had not used and worked with the affected workers, union, and factory management to ensure a practical long-term solution for the use of these benefits in the future.

Alta Gracia's full transparency with an independent labor rights monitor is in stark contrast to the norm for the apparel industry where brands themselves conduct monitoring or hire organizations to carry out monitoring on their behalf. As the recent deadly factory fires and collapses in Bangladesh discussed earlier in this chapter demonstrate, the inherent conflict of interest that occurs when monitoring is paid for by the brands themselves renders such monitoring ineffective. The WRC receives no funds from Knights or any other brand to carry out the monitoring program and thus can ensure rigorous and impartial monitoring.

The combination of incentives and resources to implement model labor practices and a union and an independent monitor to enforce these standards has enabled Alta Gracia to be radically more effective in achieving high labor standards. MHSSN's coordinator, who has worked in factories across the globe, commented:

> Global supply chains in electronics, toys, apparel, sports shoes and equipment, remain riddled with sweatshops—some of which hide behind the façade of corporate codes of conduct and "third party" monitoring schemes. . . . In the case of the Alta Gracia brand's plant, however, "no sweat" actually means "no sweat." (Brown 2010, np)

The long-term economic viability of Alta Gracia will have implications for the apparel industry as a whole. Occidental College Professor Peter Dreier wrote that if Alta Gracia can continue to provide apparel made under humane conditions at a competitive price it

> . . . will challenge the basic race-to-the-bottom economics of the apparel industry and prove that conscientious consumers can have an impact on humanizing the forces of global capitalism. (Dreier 2011)

The first years of Alta Gracia sales in college bookstores seems to indicate that this is the case. Kline and Soule write that:

> Alta Gracia garments offer consumers a compelling proposition: equal or better quality as compared to the most recognizable brands at an equivalent or slightly lower price. On top of that, point of purchase signage highlights the human dimension of the Alta Gracia brand. It is not surprising that the merchandise has sold at the same pace as established brands and commensurate with the floor space allocated to it. (Kline and Soule 2011, 5)

The Designated Suppliers Program and multi-factory agreements with brands, discussed below, are informed by the Alta Gracia model. Alta Gracia demonstrates that it is possible to dramatically improve labor standards through providing factories with a fair price, stable orders and real incentives and resources for reaching labor rights compliance.

Enforceable Agreements between Brands and Unions

Groundbreaking Agreements in Honduras

While Alta Gracia remains unmatched in its commitment to workers' economic well-being, two hard-won victories by unions in Honduras have shown that direct agreements between unions and multinational brands can bring change for thousands of workers. In October 2008, Jerzees de Honduras, a collegiate apparel supplier, closed while in the process of negotiating its first ever collective bargaining agreement. The company had already worked through much of the anti-union playbook, including repeatedly firing workers who took part in organizing and threatening to blacklist pro-union workers so they would not be able to find other work.

Norma Estela Mejia Castellanos was a leader in forming the union at Jerzees de Honduras. Recalling the day that factory management announced the closure, she recalled in an interview with the WRC,

> They [the factory management] called the union's leadership committee into the conference room to have a meeting with the head of personnel. We were happy at first because we thought that this was related to the mediation process. But instead she told us that Jerzees de Honduras was closing. We began to look at each other and breathe deeply and I began to cry, I could not contain myself. My coworkers began to cry too. When we left the room, we entered the main area of the plant and we saw that a whole group of workers was crying and hugging each other, because they had been told about the closure. The pregnant women were rubbing their stomachs and asking themselves how they would survive with their children, it would be so hard. And when it was time to leave, the leaders of the union, we decided to leave together because we were afraid of what might happen, the way people were looking at us. They

> were saying "It's your fault that we will go hungry, that we will have no jobs." And I just thought, "Please God give us strength and courage."

A WRC investigation revealed that the closure was motivated, at least in part, by anti-union animus, and recommended that the factory be reopened. The company's owner, Russell Athletic (owned by Fruit of the Loom), refused to do so. The union and its allies around the world, notably including USAS, launched a campaign that lasted for over a year. As a result of student pressure, more than 90 universities terminated their licensing contracts with Russell. Students publicly lambasted Russell at the NBA finals, at Sports Authority stores across the country, and at the shareholder meeting of Russell's parent company, Berkshire Hathaway (Greenhouse 2009).

As a result, in November 2009, Russell signed a legally enforceable agreement directly with the union representing the Jerzees de Honduras workers. The company committed not only to reopen the factory, respect the union, and provide back pay, but also to respect workers' freedom of association at eight Russell factories in Honduras. The idea that Honduras's largest private employer would not only reopen a factory after closing it down to eliminate a union, but also make specific freedom of association commitments throughout its Honduran operations represented a major breakthrough for Honduran workers and for garment workers around the world.

On May 19, 2011, the union at the reopened factory, now known as Jerzees Nuevo Dia, negotiated a collective bargaining agreement that brought not only significant wage increases, but also a commitment to increased hiring and investment in the factory (WRC 2011). Fruit of the Loom's international top management was directly involved in the negotiations.

Norma, who was on the union's bargaining team, describes the negotiations as a "beautiful experience." "Before, no line operator would have been able to sit down with an employer to demand her rights and ask for benefits, but now we can do that thanks to our union organization," she told the WRC. In addition, she reports, the new contract "has changed my life because now I have time to rest, time to be with my children. Now, I have enough money to pay for all of my basic food supplies and sometimes I have enough for a treat." Norma has been able to pay off debt, pay for much-needed medication for her mother, pay for her son's graduation fees, and donate to her church.

The partnership between the factory union SitrajerzeesND, an affiliate of the Confederacion General de Trabajadores (CGT), and Russell has set a new standard for labor-management relations in Honduras. In an environment marked by rampant disregard for labor law, this agreement has created a context where SitrajerzeesND has been able to consistently engage directly with Russell to resolve disagreements and negotiate improvements. Freedom of association trainings performed jointly by managers and the CGT have also begun at other Russell plants in Honduras, and Russell and the CGT have repeatedly demonstrated their ability to resolve plant-level issues through the dispute resolution mechanism established by the agreement.

Building on their experience with Russell, the CGT waged another international campaign and, the following year, signed another international agreement. Two Nike suppliers, Hugger de Honduras and Vision Tex, closed in January 2009 without paying legally required terminal benefits to some 1,500 workers and without paying required sums into a national health care system on behalf of the workers. Nike initially stated that it was not required and was not willing to ensure that the workers receive all the funds they had been illegally denied, since the obligations were accrued by a subcontracted facility, rather than by Nike itself. Students and universities refused to accept this argument; as one professor told *The New York Times*, "if apparel companies can't take responsibility for the factories where they have contracts, they can't claim to be adhering to a code of conduct" (Greenhouse 2010).

In July 2010, after significant advocacy in the United States including engagement by students and universities, Nike committed to provide $1.54 million to a worker relief fund, to arrange for the workers to receive health care for one year, and to ask its suppliers to offer priority hiring to former Hugger and Vision Tex workers (Greenhouse 2010).[8] In signing this agreement, Nike took financial responsibility for correcting a violation committed by a supplier factory and set an example by addressing a significant case of one of the most common forms of wage theft in the industry. While the Nike agreement does not prospectively address ongoing factory conditions, it set an important precedent and provides another example of the potential of agreements directly between labor unions and international brands.

Unprecedented Commitments in Bangladesh

As the death toll from fire and building disasters in the Bangladesh garment industry continues to rise, labor rights advocates have pushed to move away from voluntary self-regulation by the industry to binding agreements between workers and the brands for which they produce. This has led to the development of the Accord on Fire and Building Safety, a legally enforceable contract between brands and retailers, international union federations, and local Bangladeshi unions. The Accord will require that factories in Bangladesh undergo not just inspections by independent experts, but that these facilities are subject to an industry-wide program of renovations and retrofitting to make these buildings fundamentally safe. In the likely scenario that factories cannot pay for these fixes, the buyers will be required to provide the necessary financial support, not only for the physical upgrades, but also in the form of higher prices and long-term commitments to factories that undergo renovations. If any factory refuses to undergo renovations and operate safely, the signatory companies must cease doing business with that plant. By imposing higher costs and constraining sourcing decisions, the Accord blunts the relentless push for lower prices and faster delivery that define the industry sourcing strategy.

The Accord also includes a central role for workers and unions, giving workers the ability to fight for their own protection. Factories are required to provide access for union representatives to the plants, allow for the establishment of joint worker-management occupational health and safety committees and respect workers' rights to refuse dangerous work.

Thus far, nearly 60 companies have signed the Accord, including H&M, the single largest buyer from Bangladesh; Inditex, the largest fashion retailer in the world; PVH Corp, which owns Calvin Klein and Tommy Hilfiger; ENYCE, the clothing line owned by Sean Combs; and Abercrombie and Fitch. Yet many others in the industry are reluctant to do so. In particular, Gap and Wal-Mart have exhibited strong opposition, specifically because the agreement is such a large departure from the voluntary systems they have put in place.

The Accord has been a tremendous breakthrough because it is the first binding agreement in the contemporary apparel industry committing brands to pay to improve working conditions and to align their sourcing decisions with their labor rights obligations; it sets a model for labor rights reforms going forward on which future efforts can be based.

Key Principles

Five key elements were crucial to the Russell agreement and the Bangladesh Accord, and are necessary elements for any future agreements. Taken together, these five elements will ensure that workers have the opportunity to organize and improve their situation without either direct retaliation by factory management or the threat of brand flight and factory closure.

First, any commitment must be binding in a court of law. While most multinational firms are accustomed to self-enforced codes of conduct, for these commitments to be meaningful they must be legally enforceable contracts including a dispute resolution mechanism, such as arbitration. Both the Russell agreement and the Bangladesh Accord, for example, provide recourse to arbitration as a last-resort dispute mechanism, as well as creating an Oversight/Steering Committee as an intermediate mechanism. Workers can only be assured that labor rights commitments will be taken seriously if brands use the same legally enforceable agreement with workers as they do with their other business partners.

Second, specific commitments on freedom of association are crucial. Associational rights are foundational to improving factories' compliance with other standards. If workers cannot join their voices to speak out against abuses, and engage directly and meaningfully with the decision-makers to address these abuses, long-term change is impossible. These commitments may include providing a clear statement to workers regarding freedom of association, allowing union organizers access to the facility, and a commitment to end any existing anti-union practices.

Third, multinational brands must commit to pay prices that enable supplier factories to comply with their obligations. Too often, brands pay lip service to the importance of suppliers' compliance, while at the same time insisting on flat or even decreasing prices, making it impossible for factory owners to make significant improvements in workers' wages or conditions. Under the Bangladesh Accord, brands and retailers are obligated to provide financial assistance, either directly or indirectly, to factories so that they can afford to undergo the necessary renovations and repairs to make their workplaces safe.

Fourth, brands must commit to produce in a given facility over a period of years so that the factory and the workers have some guarantee that the investment required for change will not be undercut by an immediate loss in orders. A long-term purchasing commitment ensures that the factory will have time to make real progress.

Fifth and final, a living wage is key to making real change in workers' daily lives and must be part of any scheme where factories or products are designated as socially responsible. To date, brands have been reluctant to make serious commitments to increase or even stabilize workers' real incomes. As a result, as noted above, real wages in key garment producing countries have dropped over the past decade (WRC 2013). Specific, time-bound commitments to a clearly defined living wage are essential.

Designated Suppliers Program

These same principles form the basis of the Designated Suppliers Program (DSP), which was proposed by USAS, and endorsed by the WRC, in 2005. Under the DSP, universities can require that their licensees source university logo apparel from supplier factories that have been determined, through independent verification, to comply with workers' rights standards including those above. The licensees, in turn, commit to fair pricing and to produce in specific designated factories for long enough to lend some stability.

Nearly fifty universities have expressed agreement in principle with the DSP. Many were waiting to implement based on concern regarding the program's legal status. However, in December 2011, the Department of Justice released a favorable Business Review Letter, stating that the DSP is consistent with US antitrust law.

The DSP creates a framework for universities to align their values more completely with their licensing practices and have a much more significant impact on the real conditions in factories around the world. By requiring that licensees choose factories that are achieving a high level of compliance, and make commitments to pay those factories enough to continue that compliance, the DSP will make it possible to sustain the type of factory-level victories that have been swept away in the past by shifting orders. With the DSP, the workers at the next BJ&B, PT Kolon Langgeng, or Gina Form Bra (WRC 2006) will keep their jobs and the high standards they have achieved by selling to collegiate licensees that are committed to finding factories that meet DSP standards.

CONCLUSION

A decade ago, students and universities were at the forefront of demanding transparency and responsibility in apparel supply chains. While they have achieved some reforms, the full promise of these initiatives has yet to be realized. The deck is stacked against the universities, students, workers, and consumers seeking to ensure that workers' rights are respected. Multinational apparel brands can still shop around the globe for the lowest prices. They can repeatedly place orders in factories that are documented serial rights violators, and pull orders from factories that are making progress toward compliance, without facing any negative consequences. They enjoy the profits made possible by denying workers legally earned compensation and failing to provide basic health and safety equipment.

Reviewing the victories and setbacks of the anti-sweatshop movement to date, it is clear that to achieve more factory-level victories, and defend victories already won, workers and advocates must win a new level of commitment from the apparel brands that control the global supply chain. Over the past fifteen years, thanks to public pressure, brands have moved from a complete denial of their responsibility for conditions in their supply chains to acknowledging that they have the power and the capacity to raise standards. Now, it's time to push them to the next level through the DSP and direct agreements between brands and worker representatives—transnational, legally binding documents that require a commitment that brands pay high enough rates and make long enough commitments to enable sustainable change at supplier factories.

As this work proceeds in the garment industry, it can also inform the struggle for workers' rights in other industries' supply chains. In 2012, news coverage of the intense pressure, illegal overtime, and occupational injuries faced by workers producing iPods and other Apple technology, and Apple's inadequate response, sparked anger and dismay among consumers.[9] In response, Apple is following the apparel companies' early model of hiring "independent" monitors that report to the brand itself, hiding behind these self-funded monitoring reports, and pledging gradual improvements that never seem to come (Shapiro and Nova 2012).

As international pressure grows on Apple and other international electronics brands, the experience of workers in the garment industry is instructive. We have seen over and over that unilateral pledges by international brands in CSR documents or press releases are worthless if they are not backed by signed agreements and organized workers. Unless basic labor rights compliance trumps price in international brands' sourcing decisions, low prices will continue to undermine high standards in all of their production.

Alta Gracia and Jerzees Nuevo Dia show that it is possible to sustainably operate a different kind of factory, with decent wages and respect for workers' rights—if there is a commitment from international buyers. The DSP and the direct union-brand agreements in Honduras and Bangladesh offer a framework that can allow more such factories to flourish. Where commitments to workers' freedom of association and living wage are guaranteed by binding agreements and a commitment to pay sustainable prices, workers can see a true realization of the promises that the international garment industry has made for so long. Without those commitments, workers will be left with CSR policies worth less than the paper they are written on, lower and lower real wages, and deadly fires.

NOTES

1. For a more in-depth description of the early years of the student anti-sweatshop movement, see Featherstone (2002).
2. The WRC now maintains a public database of factory locations disclosed by university licensees, which can be searched by country, licensee name, factory name and location, or university. This database is available at http://www.workersrights.org.
3. In addition to the cases described below, all WRC final reports can be found at http://www.workersrights.org/Freports/.
4. See Thompson (2001). This article and other coverage of the Kukdong case is available at http://www.workersrights.org/Freports/Kukdong.asp.
5. See, for example, American Center for International Labor Solidarity (2003).
6. Examples include Gina Form Bra in Thailand, which closed in 2006. Another example is the Indonesian shoe factories PT Tong Yang and PT Dong Joe, which were the sites of an early Reebok social audit and ongoing engagement but subsequently closed. Oxfam Australia alleged that the closures were due to fluctuations in orders from Reebok after the firm was purchased by adidas. More information is available about Gina Form Bra and PT Kizone on the Worker Rights Consortium website.
7. More information about Alta Gracia is available on the Worker Rights Consortium website.
8. Additional information on this agreement and its implementation is available on the Worker Rights Consortium website.
9. See, for example, Duhigg and Barboza (2012).

REFERENCES

ABS_CBNnews.com. 2012. "Foreign businessmen say wage hike will turn off investors." May 21. http://www.abs-cbnnews.com/business/05/21/12/foreign-businessmen-warns-against-wage-hike.

American Center for International Labor Solidarity. 2003. *Justice for All: The Struggle for Workers' Rights in Mexico.*

Bajaj, Vikas and Julfikar Ali Manik. 2010. "Bangladesh Arrests 21 After Rallies." *New York Times*, August 16.

BBC News. 2012. Bangladesh Garment Factories Reopen After Protests, June 21. http://www.bbc.co.uk/news/world-asia-18530579.

Brown, Garrett. 2010. "'No Sweat' In the Dominican Republic." *Industrial Safety and Hygiene News*, October 1. Accessed August 31, 2012. http://www.ishn.com/articles/90036–no-sweat-in-the-dominican-republic.

Collins, Jane L. 2003. *Threads: Gender, Labor, and Power in the Global Apparel Industry.* Chicago: University of Chicago Press.

Dreier, Peter. 2011. "Is the Perfect Factory Possible?" *The Nation.* October 19.

Duhigg, Charles and David Barboza. 2012. "In China, Human Costs Are Built Into an iPad." *New York Times*, January 25.

Featherstone, Liza and United Students Against Sweatshops. 2002. "Students Against Sweatshops." London: Verso.

Greenhouse, Steven. 2009. "Labor Fight Ends in Win for Students." *New York Times*, November 17.

Greenhouse, Steven. 2010. "Pressured, Nike to Help Workers in Honduras." *New York Times*, July 26.

Kline, John. 2012. "How Colleges Can Improve the Lives of Sweatshop Workers." *The Chronicle of Higher Education*, October 29.

Kline, John and Edward Soule. 2011. "Alta Gracia: Work with a Salario Digno." Research Progress Report, Reflective Engagement Initiative, Georgetown University. http://www12.georgetown.edu/sfs/docs/Research_Progress_Report_11–29b_with_cover.pdf.

Locke, Richard M., Feui Qin, and Alberto Brause. 2006. "Does Monitoring Improve Labor Standards?: Lessons from Nike," MIT Sloan Research Paper No.4612–06, http://papers.ssrn.com/sol3/papers.cfm?abstract_id=916771.

Manik, Julfikar Ali and Vikas Bajaj. 2012. "Killing of Bangladeshi Labor Organizer Signals an Escalation in Violence." *New York Times*, April 9.

Ross, Robert J.S. 2006. "A Tale of Two Factories: Successful Resistance to Sweatshops and the Limits of Firefighting." *Labor Studies Journal* 30, 4: 65–85.

Shapiro, Isaac, and Scott Nova. 2012. "Polishing Apple: Fair Labor Association Gives Foxconn and Apple Undue Credit for Labor Rights Progress." Economic Policy Institute Briefing Paper #352. http://www.epi.org/publication/bp352–polishing-apple-fla-foxconn-labor-rights/.

Thompson, Ginger. 2001. "Mexican Labor Protest Gets Results." *New York Times*, October 8.

WRC, Center for American Progress and Just Jobs Network. 2013. "Global Wage Trends for Apparel Workers, 2001–2011." Working paper. Worker Rights Consortium: Washington DC.

WRC. 2001. *Investigation re Complaint against Kukdong (Mexico): Preliminary Findings and Recommendations.* Worker Rights Consortium. http://www.workersrights.org/Freports/Report_Kukdong_1.pdf.

WRC. 2002. *WRC Assessment re PT Dada (Indonesia), Remediation Progress Report.* Worker Rights Consortium. http://www.workersrights.org/Freports/PTDada_Remediation_Report_09–30–02.pdf.

WRC. 2003. *Assessment re PT Kolon Langgeng (Indonesia), Findings and Recommendations.* Worker Rights Consortium. http://www.workersrights.org/Freports/PTKolonLanggeng_10–08–03.pdf.

WRC. 2004. *Statement on Agreement with Lands' End.* Worker Rights Consortium. http://www.workersrights.org/Freports/LandsEndWRCStatementOnAgreement.pdf.

WRC. 2006. *Case Summary re Gina Form Bra*. Worker Rights Consortium. http://www.workersrights.org/Freports/.

WRC. 2006. *Factory Assessment Update*. Worker Rights Consortium. http://www.workersrights.org/Freports/Update_Feb2006.asp#GrupoM.

WRC. 2010. *Worker Rights Consortium Verification Report Re Labor Rights Compliance at Altagracia Project Factory (Dominican Republic): Findings*. http://www.workersrights.org/freports/WRC%20Verification%20Report%20re%20Altagracia%20Factory%2012–23–10.pdf.

WRC. 2011. *Second Progress Report re Implementation of Russell Athletic/Fruit of the Loom Remediation Agreements for Operations in Honduras: Findings and Status Report*. http://www.workersrights.org/linkeddocs/WRC%20update%20on%20Jerzees-Russell%208–16–11.pdf.

Yardley, Jim. 2012. "Export Powerhouse Feels Pangs of Labor Strife." *New York Times*. August 23. http://www.nytimes.com/2012/08/24/world/asia/as-bangladesh-becomes-export-powerhouse-labor-strife-erupts.html?_r=1.

Chapter Three

Waste for Life

Poverty-Reducing Technologies for Repurposing Waste at the Margins

Caroline Baillie and Eric Feinblatt

Waste for Life (WFL) is a loosely joined network of engineers, architects, academics, and designers who work alongside waste-picking cooperatives to co-develop poverty-reducing strategies and technologies to repurpose scavenged waste. Specifically, they work with the cooperatives to introduce income-generating schemes by creating manufactured goods from waste that has little or no resale value. The most common waste lifecycle they adopt is to turn plastic and fiber into "reinforced plastic" or "composites." The waste fiber is a natural fiber, which is regionally specific e.g., waste agricultural fibers from flax stem (Canada), corn stalk (Lesotho), rice husk (China), or wood chip, tissue, and paper (Buenos Aires). The plastic is toughened and strengthened in this upcycling process into a Natural Fiber Composite (NFC), but the final product can also be completely recycled and reprocessed at its end-of-use life.

This chapter explores questions the WFL team raise in pursuit of their social goals, which focus on the ability of waste scavenger cooperatives to provide urban recycling services to local populations while remaining self-sufficient under increasing economic and governmental pressures. The ultimate purpose of WFL's interventions is to contribute to the larger discussions and experimentations in alternative modes of social and productive life, including investigations into the social, environmental, and economic circuitries of commodities and commodity disposal. WFL is very much at the beginning of its relationships with the cooperatives that are in a position to work with us. We do not yet know the long-term impact of what we are doing, but as part of that knowing process this chapter explores and self-critiques WFL as a socially just alternative to traditional public/private profit-making approaches to recycling.

Waste for Life has framed it goals within the norms of social *and* environmental justice. There are many ways waste can be reprocessed to accrue environmental benefits, but the main objective of WFL is to enhance justice. We work with marginalized community groups to support the development of new income streams by "upcycling" (enhancing the properties of) waste into Natural Fiber Composites (Baillie 2005). Industry calls these NFCs "green composites," though in industrial settings these are rarely waste-based. Such composites can have environmental advantages—particularly in transport applications—where utilization of these lighter/stronger materials contributes to fuel savings. However, these savings are counterbalanced by a dependency upon virgin plastic manufacturing and toxic, non-recyclable resins, which do not compute into an environmental cost/benefit analysis. Materials engineering, like any other industry, is not immune to "greenwashing," labeling a product "green" without evidence that its production and usage result in a net reductive environmental impact. Claims of "sustainability," also attached to "green composites," rarely take into consideration the third pillar of what it means to be sustainable; while environmental and economic impacts are calculated, social impacts, which are core to any deep notions of sustainability, are more often than not ignored.

WFL was formed in part to begin to redress this balance—to use engineering knowledge about recycling and production of composites to support and enhance marginalized communities by giving them access to the technology and scientific knowledge from which, because of their economic, social, and political status, they would otherwise be excluded. This chapter tells part of the story of WFL, Buenos Aires—an attempt to disturb the usual lifecycle of waste-for-profit (for those in power)—and repurpose it as waste-for-life (for the powerless). WFL was founded by the authors in 2007, arising out of the technical research of Baillie. It became a registered not-for-profit organization in the United States in 2011. An international volunteer network of researchers, academics, practitioners, and students in engineering, architecture, urban design, sociology, geography, and business studies supports our work on the ground.

WASTE FOR LIFE, BUENOS AIRES

During the crisis of 2001, Argentina and, particularly, Buenos Aires, experienced a precipitous decline in economic activity accompanied by spiraling unemployment. Overnight, 60 percent of the population lost their jobs and 100,000 people became "waste pickers" or *"cartoneros,"* scavenging the streets of Buenos Aires City for recyclable materials to sell (Parizeau 2006; Gutierrez et al. 2005). In 2012, there are an estimated 6,000 to 25,000 cooperative, family, or individual *cartoneros* (officially referred to as *Recuperadores Urbanos* or Urban Recoverers) who collect, separate, sort, and sell waste as their sole economic activity (Schamber et al. 2007). These unpaid informal workers live in outlying shantytowns but move through the city with their carts at all times of the day, and in 2007 (date of last report) were collecting and recycling 90 percent of whatever Buenos Aires throws away (CEAMSE 2007). The informal recovery of materials from waste is an important survival strategy for marginalized groups in the Global South. Medina (2005, 2) contends that "waste picker cooperatives can increase the income of their members, improve their working and living conditions and promote grassroots development." Medina estimates that 15,000,000 people worldwide survive from other people's waste.

The recycling waste that is collected is sold to agents or middlemen, though some more organized cooperatives separate, sort, and sell the materials directly to industry. In some cases cooperatives have the machinery to reprocess the waste and even to produce products, but this is rare. Income generated by the cooperatives in Buenos Aires ranges from $100 to $300 per month per person, and though this figure is generally higher than what individual *cartoneros* gain working on their own, it is barely sufficient to feed a family. As Medina points out "low incomes can be explained by the low prices paid by middlemen" (2005, 9) who, themselves, are also squeezed by market fluctuations in the value of trash.[1]

Zero Garbage (*Basura Cero*) went into effect in Buenos Aires in late 2005 as part of a comprehensive law dealing with urban waste (Ley No. 1.854, 2005). It stipulates that the total amount of garbage in landfills is to be reduced 50 percent by 2012 and 75 percent by 2017 from 2004 levels, and one of its ancillary benefits is that recyclable materials will no longer end up in landfills. For environmentalists this appears to be a desirable outcome, however, its consequences for most *cartoneros*—whose livelihood depends upon collecting recyclables—is potentially negative. It will be impossible for the government to professionalize the work of the thousands of informal workers and absorb them into a "legitimate" workforce in order to fulfill Zero Garbage. This is causing strife among the different *cartonero* groups and with Greenpeace, which was instrumental in drafting the legislation and has always been a strong and dependable ally of the *cartoneros*. As pointed out by Medina, "scavengers respond to market forces not to environmental considerations. If there is a demand for a particular material and the price is right, they will collect it" (Medina 1997, 25). Scavenging is rarely a choice. It is an economic imperative. The *cartoneros* we met in Buenos Aires do not descend from generations of garbage scavengers but, more often than not, are previously employed skilled or semi-skilled laborers who had lost their jobs.

They are not motivated by ecological purpose, and single-focused environmental solutions to waste problems are inevitably counter to their interests.

Buenos Aires does not yet have a visible and/or official systematic recycling program, though it generates about 4,500 tons of garbage everyday—11 percent of which is disposed of by the *cartoneros*. The municipal government has partnered with private trucking companies to build six sorting centers or *Centros Verdes* scattered around the city, two of which are currently up and running. Each center will be managed by a different cooperative and receive waste hauled to it by one or more of the trucking companies. They can also receive recyclables brought to them by *cartoneros* in trucks (only). The sorted waste is sold somewhere up the recycling food chain and all of the proceeds benefit the cooperative. But it is unlikely that six centers will be able to support more than 300–400 *cartoneros* by giving them the opportunity to turn their informal work into formal work. (Cooperative numbers fluctuate between 10 and 50 members, though these numbers could swell if there were sufficient work available. Unfortunately, the flow of recyclables to the *Centros Verdes*—which is largely orchestrated by government—has been erratic at best.)

Although sorting waste for recyclables is currently shared between *cartoneros* and government, garbage collection in Buenos Aires is almost entirely privatized. The city government contracts different trucking companies, each of which is assigned to specific city districts. Each company is responsible for cleaning the streets of waste and hauling that waste to transit points or directly to the CEAMSE (*Coordinación Ecológica Area Metropolitana Sociedad del Estado*) landfill. There is a single government-owned company that hauls waste from a transit point in Buenos Aires' poorest district in the southwest of the city. CEAMSE is a municipal and regional government amalgam with private affiliations, which manages the landfill that receives the waste of the 13,000,000 people of the greater metropolitan area of Buenos Aires in 1,000 trucks per day. CEAMSE has only one landfill that is currently operational, *Norte III*. Others have either collapsed or are being turned into "eco-parks."

The question of who owns the waste is constantly being asked in Buenos Aires. The private hauling companies, which own the trucks that collect the waste, believe they own the garbage, but they have little environmental incentives to do something else with it since they are paid to deliver all waste to the landfill. The *cartoneros* who pick their way through the bags left on pavements late at night know they don't own the waste, but they are legally allowed to take the recyclables as long as they have registered with the local authorities. CEAMSE has no interest in who claims waste ownership as long as all of it is hauled to their landfill where they are remunerated by the tonnage they receive and dispose of.

All of the above issues have a strong impact on the feasibility and social impact of any new waste management scheme. Hence before starting to work in Buenos Aires, the Waste for Life team spent six months in situ in Buenos Aires as prelude to a three-year feasibility and social impact assessment, along with a detailed stakeholder analysis (Baillie et al. 2010).

RECYCLING AND REPROCESSING WASTE INTO NATURAL FIBER COMPOSITES

Rather than focus only on material re-use, WFL works with composite materials—for which "the whole is greater than the sum of the parts"—because reinforced plastics are stronger than the constituent plastic and tougher and more flexible than the constituent fiber. It is also possible to gain an environmental advantage by "upcycling" waste plastic using reinforcing waste fiber. Lifecycle assessment (LCA) is a tool used to evaluate environmental impacts associated with a particular product throughout its entire lifecycle (from extraction of raw materials to the end of life; from cradle to grave) (Murphy 2003). LCA can be used to compare two or more products to find out which of them is preferable from an environmental point of view. For a fair comparison, products should meet the same service requirements. Also, since different products have different impacts at different stages in their lifetimes, comparing them at only one stage can give misleading results. Their whole lifecycles should be considered. Researchers in the field of NFCs claim that these products can help reduce environmental impact, however, environmental impacts of a product are case specific. For instance, one study that analyzed impacts of hemp fiber plastic door panels against glass fiber plastic panels for housing using LCA demonstrated that both panels had almost similar impacts on the environment (Murphy 2003). According to Baillie (2003), LCA reports from EU CRAFT projects showed that NFCs had more impacts on the environment than glass fiber plastic composites except for automotive applications where NFCs performed better due to fuel savings owing to their lighter weight. NFCs, though ostensibly a "greener" approach to manufacturing, must be evaluated case-by-case to determine their long-term environmental impact. This is exactly what has been done in automotive applications, but it is by no means necessarily transferable to other applications.

A review of studies on NFCs in automotive applications has concluded that NFCs are more eco-friendly than glass fiber composites in automotive applications because (1) natural fiber production has lower impacts than glass fiber production; they depend mainly on solar energy to grow and they absorb CO2 during growth, (2) natural fibers take more volume per unit weight of a composite, therefore NFCs require less polymer matrix (which has more impacts on the environment) than glass fiber composites, (3) owing to their light weight, NFCs improve automotive fuel economy, thereby reducing emissions during use, and (4) it is possible to recover and use energy by incinerating natural fiber but not glass fiber (Joshi et al. 2004).

In order for NFCs to have a lower impact on the environment for other products as well, it is critical to consider the "matrix" or plastic material, which is reinforced, as well as the reinforcing fiber. The first step is to ensure that this is a plastic, which is itself recyclable. This means that even though there will be small amounts of chopped up natural fiber present in the recycled material, it is in fact possible to melt and re-use. A further benefit is, of course, that the material has already had one or more lives, and is itself waste. Waste for Life clearly works in this domain.

In Buenos Aires, for example, which is an urban setting, the most appropriate reinforcing fiber is from paper, and the matrix is from recyclable (technically known as "thermoplastic") plastic products. Conventional waste paper recycling directed toward new paper production may require sorting to avoid unclean waste, pulping, de-inking, and bleaching, depending on the intended products. These processes can be costly and demanding in time, water, and energy (Berglund and Söderholm 2003). Expensive processes such as de-inking may produce toxic waste ink sludge containing both ink and various paper fillers. Other uses of waste paper include production of activated carbon but these require specialized equipment and large energy expenditure. By making composites from waste paper and plastic we can eliminate de-inking and pulping and create "upcycled" products that are stronger than the plastic alone, yet with a reduced environmental impact in comparison to paper recycling processes.

Alongside a positive environmental impact, due to the widespread availability of waste materials, and the low threshold/high impact technology WFL has developed, products made from waste-based materials offer great potential for poverty reduction and positive social and economic impacts, especially for communities that depend primarily on waste collection as their sole economic activity. In Buenos Aires the *cartoneros* collect waste paper and plastic that they could potentially use to make natural fiber composite material products, which could be far more valuable to them than the waste alone. Some forms of plastic, such as bags and bottle tops, have very little market value, and so are generally ignored by the *cartoneros*. If collected, they yield little value (4–8 US cents per kg). One of the larger sources of plastic and paper waste which WFL uses is food packaging waste which has no other pathway to a new life. It is important to note that WFL is very aware that cannibalizing sales of plastic waste that has resale value in the recyclable market is counter-productive, and we only work with waste that has little or no resale value in its raw state.

WFL has put years of research into looking at composite manufacturing as a means to develop usable and "upcycled" materials from recycled plastics and natural fiber waste as materials (Thamae and Baillie 2007, 2008, 2009; Thamae et al. 2008, 2009a,b). The challenge, however, which WFL needed to address when working outside of the lab, in a real context, was to develop low-cost manufacturing processes and technology to create the composites. The ability to manufacture composites from food packaging and other waste at reduced cost, and by local teams, became WFL's goal. The design of a low cost hotpress was completed by Queens University Professor, and WFL member, Darko Matovic, and industrial prototypes were made to test and improve its functioning (Baillie et al. 2011). The first production hotpress was manufactured locally in a suburb of Buenos Aires by a "recovered" factory. These recovered enterprises emerged after the 2001 economic crisis as a means for local workers to continue to work and support themselves and their families. They formed cooperatives and took over or "recuperated" the factories they worked in, which had often been abandoned by the owners at the time of the economic crash. In many cases the groups gained the legal right to work in the factory and expropriate the means of production, even though they were not the original legal owners. One of these factories, a metallurgic factory that produces automotive parts, agreed to manufacture the hotpresses on demand at a reasonable price. Workers cooperative "19 de Diciembre" thereby became a local source for the machinery and generated an additional niche income stream for themselves.

WFL also explored possible avenues for non-affiliated funding, which resulted in a combination of volunteer support, public donations for processing equipment, and a micro-loan system that make the entire process sustainable. At the time of writing, one cooperative has successfully started to produce goods (commercial and domestic trash cans, wallets, and CD covers), and is receiving commissions from the local municipality. It is beginning to pay back its loan. More details may be found in Baillie et al. 2011.

It is too early to evaluate the environmental impact of the individual products themselves. We know they are manufactured with waste that was destined for landfill, and every product is accompanied with tagging that suggests it be returned to the cooperative for re-processing at its end of life or use. However, because the products have been in the marketplace only briefly, we have no data available for tracking. The trajectory of individual lifecycle depends largely upon the habits of the eventual consumer who can determine whether or not the products find easy pathways back to the cooperative. For this reason WFL is concentrating on operating within a "constrained" economic environment. The cooperatives we work with have close ties with their surrounding communities and often go door-to-door to collect recyclables. We are now targeting these neighbors—up to 5,000 individual households for every cooperative—as potential customers for the products the cooperatives manufacture from the households' own recyclable waste. This is part of a larger effort to integrate the waste recyclers into the local communities whose waste they recycle and, by implication, to make the consumption/disposal circuitry more tangible and visible. We expect that one of the results of such integration/implication would be increased cognizance and responsibility vis-à-vis waste, and that the notion of returning a product to the cooperative for reprocessing would replace throwing it away as normalized behavior.

A CRITICAL LENS TO VIEW WASTE FOR LIFE

Waste for Life works from a social justice perspective. To this end we are cognizant of Young's (2000) "five faces of oppression"—exploitation (benefiting at the expense of others), marginalization (being pushed away from participation in social life), powerlessness (being unable to make one's voice heard due to lack of status or respect), cultural imperialism (the dominant culture becomes the way of interpreting social life), and violence (the risk and reality of being targeted with acts of violence). We apply to our work the commitments of the Engineering, Social Justice and Peace network (ESJP), founded by Baillie in 2004, which were developed to actively address these faces of oppression. ESJP is a network of engineers, academics, activists, social scientists, and practitioners who work toward a socially just engineering practice and question the assumptions of dominant practice. They state their commitments in relation to social justice (which may be found on the website http://esjp.org) as follows:

- Actively working to reduce injustice and enhance equity,
- Working for peace and non-violence,
- Supporting local networks,
- Considering power and participation,
- Maintaining self-critique and critical voices.

We also draw on post-development literature to frame our work. The "development agenda," as post-development scholar Ferguson (1990) points out, has become a machine that implements technical solutions to problems that are far from technical in nature. He questions "developers" socially constructing a third world in such a way that the technical solutions the North has to offer seem to be the solution to move toward "progress." He does not completely reject the idea of people from the North working together with those from the South, but he gives certain criteria for this—groups should understand the politics surrounding the particular issues, and these groups should be "counter-hegemonic," representing a movement toward local empowerment. Over the past decade, the kind of critical research that has influenced us has generally moved away from holistic theorization toward more empirically informed and inductive approaches; what Leys (1996) refers to as "development studies," rather than "development theory." In development practice, there has been a parallel move toward "participation" and "empowerment." However, this position often represents a top-down strategy for institutional reform, in the sense that it is an effort by state agencies and collaborating nongovernmental organizations to make institutions more efficient and to include identified target groups as "owners" in the development process. This conceptualization of participation and empowerment is often based on the erroneous assumption that power is equally shared and that government structures are intrinsically just—that power resides with individual members of a community and can increase with the successful pursuit of individual and collective goals. The implication is that the empowerment of the powerless could be achieved within the existing social order without any significant negative effects upon the power of the powerful (Craig and Mayo 1995/2004). A post-development critique would question this assumption and this is what WFL attempts to do.

CRITICAL REFLECTION—SOCIAL JUSTICE

In this section we adopt the social justice commitments of ESJP to critique the work of Waste for Life.

Actively Working to Reduce Injustice and Enhance Equity

> We are committed to resisting injustice in its many forms through promotion of diversity and inclusivity, and by working towards fair, equitable, and sustainable treatment of people and their environments. We are committed to equity and sharing where they support justice goals. We are committed to participatory decision-making. We are committed to collaboration within the group–to assisting one another personally, intellectually, and professionally—recognizing interconnectedness and shared resources. We are committed to practice reciprocity between the group and other groups with similar goals.

Because the aim of WFL is to enhance the capacity of *cartoneros* to remain economically autonomous, we strive to enhance equity, especially equity of access to economic security and the benefits this will provide. However, it is unclear to us if we are reducing injustice. The *cartoneros* will remain at the bottom of the social ladder, vulnerable to changes in local community and government attitudes vis-à-vis their scavenger/informal worker status. The conditions under which the *cartoneros* work are fragile, often entirely disrupted due to illness, fire, equipment failure, market fluctuations, and family obligations. Only if the funding from WFL eventually supports a sustainable income through manufacturing will any social benefit become apparent. It remains a remote question as to whether this contributes to a more just society.

Working for Peace and Non-Violence

> We are committed to working for peace and nonviolence—within ourselves, our group, the engineering profession, and the wider world. We understand peace and social justice to be mutually constituted, each requiring the other to be meaningful. We are unsettled by the close relationship between engineering and militarism, both historically and in the present, and are committed to engineering that alleviates suffering caused by violence of all sorts.

Cartoneros in Buenos Aires are not violent nor are they at war. However, waste management is often suspected of being entangled with crime syndicates. Waste is neither physically nor metaphorically clean—there is simply too much money at stake for the latter. The *cartoneros*, in their limited capacity to collect waste and make a living, appear to have some sort of agreement with the major players. We have heard that streets are "shared." There is evidence, though, that when a cooperative becomes too successful or infringes upon other "waste stakeholder" territory—truckers, for instance—they invite more violence into their lives. As an example of this, we know of one cooperative that operates outside of Buenos Aires City and regularly collects waste from residents of a suburban gated community. Representatives of the local trucking union recently visited the coop and let its president know in no uncertain terms that they were infringing on the truckers' territory. If they wanted the garbage they would have to hire the truckers to deliver it to their door. Power positioning such as this is not uncommon, and WFL is fully aware of the high stakes of garbage collection, and we make every effort to anticipate and mitigate potential frictions.

Supporting Local Networks

> We oppose globalized economic policies that lead to the breaking of local networks of labor, production, and food provision.

Waste for Life directly supports local markets and local participation, both of which are central to our mission. The machines that we have designed are built locally in recovered factories, which themselves are organized around principles of solidarity and social justice. Nonetheless, the open or not-so-open "market" looms heavily on any manufacturing enterprise. The cooperatives can produce their goods in an equitable environment, but they need to sell those goods to someone. What we had not initially fathomed was how conflicted we would feel when it came to assisting the co-ops to find a market—and we must as they have little experience at commodity selling. We spent time doing actual market research of selected products in markets and in local stores, and actually found ourselves thinking about the "competition"—other wallets, for example, made by other artisans or cooperatives. We were unwittingly becoming part of a market system in ways we never wanted to.

Other opportunities then arrived—large manufacturers offering huge money to co-ops to recycle their plastic food containers. Who were we to say, "no thanks, we don't believe in working with these people"? It took many days of examining our thoughts, feelings, and actions before the team was convinced that this was the exact point at which charity and social justice collided. We could help make the co-ops a quick profit going down that route by helping industry publicize its opportunistic embrace of all things "green." If real structural changes were ever going to be made, then we had to understand our positioning better and take a longer view of our project. Working with large manufacturers intent on creating more goods at whatever cost, at enhancing consumption and, thus, pleasing shareholders with "green coating" strategies was not a game plan we were willing to buy into. These companies were not even attempting to tackle the knotty, problem-ridden consumption/disposal circuit; they were merely interested in making consumption more palatable to increasingly suspicious audiences. Waste for Life has intended all along to straddle the line between artisanal and mass production. We hoped that enough products could be made to develop a sufficient business to give extra income to the cooperative members without contributing to an economic system—however local it may be—that needs to expand, outsource, sell out, and compete with major local economic powers. This is an ideological position that we have not had to defend, not because it isn't being challenged by cooperative members, but because the capacity simply does not exist at the moment to compete in a broader consumer marketplace and, thus, it is not yet an issue. This is true for two reasons: the limitations of the process technology, which is inherently slow and puts an automatic governor on how many products can be produced per hour, and issues of design aesthetics, standardization/repeatability, and quality control which, though necessary and inherent attributes of large scale merchandising manufacturing, have not been internalized in scavenging labor. We do not shy away from routinizing these skills, but it is a slow process. In the meantime, we have identified a local and, perhaps, more fertile marketplace that has social and environmental norms embedded within and alongside consumer norms. This marketplace consists of the neighborhood families from whom the *cartoneros* already collect waste and with whom they already have established relations. Cooperative members have surveyed these neighbors' domestic needs and are in the process of manufacturing products that can serve them. A commercial relationship between co-op members and their neighbors only serves to legitimatize the *cartoneros'* work, and make more visible the habits and patterns of consumption and disposal.

At the time of writing, and under pressure of remaining close to our own commitments and the ideals of cooperativism, we have veered off in another direction—originally through serendipity and, now, by design. In late 2011, the cooperative we work with in the Buenos Aires suburb of Morón received a commission from the local municipality, which has eagerly supported its scavenging work. In a surprise move, having learned of the WFL project within the co-op, they asked us to manufacture 50 trash bins for a park that was being rehabilitated and transformed into a public eco-space. This official recognition of the co-op as a manufacturing source, not merely a scavenging source, capable of providing a service to the community at large has allowed us to rethink what the "market" means for WFL. Commissions from the municipality continue, and the co-op is formally surveying the 4,500 households from whom they collect the rubbish that they then separate, sort, and sell to determine their consumption and disposal routines. Their idea is to manufacture and sell compact recycling bins to these families, which will make it easier for them to separate the rubbish at its source, and eliminate one stage of tedious work for the cooperative members. So the marketplace is essentially built-in—there is no need to stray from the neighborhood or compete with others—and aside from the potential financial advantage, there is the additional community benefit of knitting the families and co-op members more tightly together within the mutual circuitries of consumption and disposal.

Power and Participation

> We are committed to reflexivity—to resisting injustice even as we recognize our complicity with it. As members of different engineering communities, we recognize the structural forces impinging on the profession that perpetuate and reinforce problematic forms of power and privilege. Our participation in these structures necessarily affects how we view social justice and peace. We therefore seek to work critically and inter-disciplinarily to interrogate these structural forces and our relationships to them.

One of the clearest commitments that Waste for Life has is in its non-affiliation with any form of government or corporate entity, especially in the early stages of needs assessment. In some countries working with government funding appears to be neutral, but this is certainly not the case in Buenos Aires, which is still in the midst of distancing itself from a ruthless, dictatorial past. The cooperatives we work with are mainly interested in gaining and maintaining autonomy and independence. Waste for Life intends to support this by generating sustainability through the loan system and an alternative funding stream for set-up costs. However, there is still no clear answer to the dilemma of all development projects. Who are we to think that we can help build capacity or empower other groups? What right have we to give any of our stolen power to those without?

Critical Voices

> We are committed to maintaining independent and critical voices. We oppose extractive approaches to research in which the knowledge of one community becomes the property of another. We celebrate the diversity that exists beyond our shared commitments, and we respect variation among us in priorities and strategies employed to propagate social justice and peace.

The independent and critical voice is clear in what we do in Waste for Life. However it is important that we continually reflect upon the knowledge of the *cartoneros*, ensuring that any information we gather will be used to support them in their enterprise to manufacture goods from waste. We have noticed a huge difference in the way in which we are received by the cooperatives as engineers, intent on co-creating solutions to poverty reduction, and their attitude toward social scientists intent on creating a PhD for themselves. The set-up stages took so long, and we were often embarrassed to return yet again to a cooperative for additional information and mutual updates, which all seemed like an endless process going nowhere. But after three years we realized that the groups were patient enough and that our dogged pursuit of the project meant we were serious in their eyes. But even then we were hesitant. Every time we would visit the cooperatives we would ask if we were just infringing on their time and once again raising hopes without any actual benefit, because we still had no viable working scheme. However, we were determined to work with the groups in a participatory way, so we felt that at all stages we must ask cooperative members what products, what markets, and what processes would be most useful?

CRITICAL REFLECTION—A POST-DEVELOPMENT CRITIQUE

In this section we attempt to apply the above-stated post-development frameworks and address some of the following questions, which are considered in more detail in Baillie and Feinblatt (2010): Can Waste for Life help cooperatives remain independent and economically self-sufficient? Can this "help" be non-oppressive and non-patronizing? Is it possible for waste management practices to be co-developed and applied in a counter-hegemonic way to support cooperatives through initiatives such as WFL?

There are many well-founded criticisms for doing this type of work from a post-development perspective, but through continual self-reflection and critique, WFL attempts to understand what it might mean to share technical knowledge with the *cartonero* cooperatives while remaining cognizant of asymmetries of privilege and status. During a period of six months in 2007 and another visit in 2008, the team conducted their social assessment and feasibility study on the ground and began to answer these questions.

In Buenos Aires we were introduced to the notion of "socializing knowledge," which works on a very local level. One of our first encounters with a cooperative was encouraging—we were told, "you share the knowledge with us and we will share it with others." They had the "scientific" knowledge about what could and could not be recycled locally and what processing methods were realistic and manageable. We had the knowledge of how to make the composites. The challenge was to work in this shared, non-exploitative, counter-hegemonic way with other cooperatives in Buenos Aires.

We made it clear to the cooperatives that we did not represent our universities in any formal way, but we were there simply to support their efforts if we could. We came to Buenos Aires with few things pre-planned, except to remain as steadfastly unaligned as possible, which proved to be a prescient decision of ours given the country's long history of divisiveness. We reached out to anyone and everyone who could help us understand the complex maze of garbage and the role of the cooperatives within that maze. We recorded many of our experiences and encounters in the blog and on video and are in the process of making a documentary about WFL in Argentina. Though our main purpose was to act and not record, we diligently created contemporaneous text, audio, and visual documents and commentaries on our work. We wanted to find out if the technology was useful, what products they thought could be made and sold in local markets, if the hotpress machine could be made by local recovered enterprises with local resources, if the money they would make would be worth the effort, if they could borrow the money to make the press from the local micro credit organization we discovered, The Working World (*La Base*), if this was a good idea and, most importantly, if it would support them in their struggles to stay autonomous and survive economically. Or, would the cooperatives be better off without our involvement?

Our work with the cooperatives demonstrated that different groups work within (and outside of) the system in different ways. Some critiqued privatization, saying that the government should take over garbage collection and employ the *cartoneros*—that they were in fact "shirking their responsibility" by leaving it to the *cartoneros* to clear up the city's waste. Others supported the "*sin patron*" notion of independence—that *cartoneros* were quite happy working for themselves, and any way of assisting them to do that would be welcomed as long as they could remain unencumbered by allegiances. Some welcomed government subsidies and others refused them. But it became quickly clear to us that few cooperative members had any political critique or motivation for what they were involved with or the way they were working. They wanted to eat, to feed their families and, in all cases, they wanted to share and help others do the same—not out of a sense of duty but out of solidarity first and a historical belief, born from experience, that "no government will help us so we have to help each other."

We certainly saw examples of people who were very vocal in rejecting cooperativism because they felt it infringed upon their independence, and others who embraced it because the mutual dependency/responsibility enabled them to survive, but we witnessed only rare instances of ideological commitment to cooperativism and, less often, a political analysis. When these did occur, it was a cooperative spokesperson, leader, or president who articulated them, and we were never certain how deeply or strongly within the organizations that commitment or analysis reverberated. It did not serve our purposes to map the *cartoneros'* experiences to the mostly academic debates buzzing around clientelism, automonism, or socialism.

Our work with the cooperatives showed us that different groups work within the system in different ways. All fight for the right to work, to own their own time, and to not labor for others but to share the proceeds equitably of the work they contribute. Some important features of this include:

- Assemblies and Equal Pay—many co-ops have weekly membership assemblies or workshops in which major decisions are made and issues of "being a cooperative" (which are neither evident nor easy) are collectively worked through.
- *Sin Patrón*—despite the fact that all the co-ops we worked with had a designated leader, this person, for the most part, did not have any power over wages, conditions of work, or any other important considerations. Decisions are made together in a non-hierarchical, participatory decision-making process, and in most cases pay is equally distributed. Although we heard this phrase ("without a boss" or "without an overseer") most often from independent *cartoneros* who used it to differentiate, positively, their lives from those subject to the collective decision-makings of a cooperative, *sin patrón* gained currency as an idea during the recovered factory/self-management movement that began with the 2001 crisis and is grounded in the ideas of cooperativism.
- People Before Profit—one of the clearer forms of resistance we encountered was how people were brought into the co-ops. In most cases, if they needed to be included in group or family cooperatives, they were included. We were in fact told that the priority for employment would be "need" as opposed to merit or qualifications.

Ultimately the answers to our three questions were not clear but the questions became better defined as we continued working in Buenos Aires. We believe we are able to help the cooperatives become more independent and at the time of writing have proof-of-concept that the system works to enhance self-sufficiency and pride in work. We have remained at arms length and in many cases do not think the cooperatives know of our existence, hence it is easier to remain "non-patronizing." We have been particularly careful (and have endeavored to insist on this with volunteers) not to try to reap glory by photographing ourselves with the cooperatives for newspaper articles and other media—hence creating a false and unsustainable sense of fame and success for the co-ops.

FINAL THOUGHTS

This chapter may seem a little out of place in a book about lifecycles of products. We have not spent much time talking about the packaging waste, products made from them, nor where they end up. However we address directly the question of change in potential lifecycles—particularly change in the way that materials are collected, reprocessed, and redistributed, taking an explicitly post-development and social justice perspective. We have given some details about the way in which Waste for Life works, a not-for-profit network, which supports marginalized cooperatives through co-creation of waste composite products. We have demonstrated the way we continually self-critique through lenses which we feel are important, in order to address past injustices and maintain sustainable, social, and environmental justice for the future. Recycling products to begin a new life is not enough. We need to consider the consequences of the processes, and determine *who* benefits and *who* pays—socially, environmentally, and economically (Franklin 1999)—not only for initial production but also for recycling and re-purposing. WFL does not claim to have *the* answer or even *an* answer. It is clear from this chapter that despite our continual reflections and iterative adjustments toward our end goal, we still feel we will always be in flux, moving toward our ever more challenging, previously unrecognized goals. We simply present our work here as an alternative model to the dominant ways of thinking that we have become accustomed to, even within the environmental movement.

NOTE

1. For example, see Richtel and Galbraith (2008).

REFERENCES

Baillie, Caroline. (Ed.) 2005. *Green Composites: Polymer Composites and the Environment.* Boca Raton: CRC Press.

Baillie Caroline. 2003. "Why Green Composites?" In *Green Composites: Polymer Composites and the Environment,* edited by C. Baillie. Cambridge: Woodhead Publishing Limited.

Baillie, Caroline. 2012. "Waste for Life: Socially Just Materials Research." In *Engineering and Social Justice in the University and Beyond,* edited by C. Baillie, A. Pawley, and D. Riley. West Lafayette, Indiana: Purdue University Press.

Baillie, Caroline and Eric Feinblatt. 2010. "Recycling Technologies and Cooperativism: Waste-for-Life in the New Cooperativism." *Affinities: A Journal of Radical Theory, Culture, and Action,* 4(1).

Baillie, Caroline, Eric Feinblatt, T. Thamae, and E. Berrington. 2010. *Needs and Feasibilty: A Guide for Engineers in Community Projects, the Case of Waste for Life.* San Rafael, California: Morgan and Claypool.

Baillie, Caroline, Darko Matovic, Timothy Thamae, and Shamil Vaja. 2011. "Waste-based Composites: Poverty Reducing Solutions to Environmental Problems." *Resources, Conservation and Recycling* 55: 973–978.

Berglund, C. and P. Söderholm. 2003. "An Econometric Analysis of Global Waste Paper Recovery and utilization." *Environmental and resource economics* 26: 429–456.

CEAMSE. 2007. *Estudio de calidad de los residuos solidos urbanos.* CEAMSE Report, January 2007, Buenos Aires, Argentina.

Craig, Gary and Marjorie Mayo. 1995/2004. *Community Empowerment: A Reader in Participation and Development.* London, UK: Zed Books.

Ferguson, James. 1990. *The Anti-politics Machine: "Development," Depoliticization and Bureaucratic Power in Lesotho.* Cambridge, UK: Cambridge University Press.

Franklin, Ursula M. 1999. *The Real World of Technology.* Toronto, Canada: House of Anansi Press.

Gramsci, Antonio. 1971. *Selections from the Prison Notebooks of Antonio Gramsci* edited by Q. Hoare and G. N. Smith. New York, NY: International Publishers.

Gutiérrez, Ageitos, Pablo Javier, Jessica Koehs, Pablo Javier Schamber, and Franciso Martin Suárez. *Informe sobre trabajo infantil en la recuperación y reciclaje de residuos.* UNICEF Buenos Aires, Argentina.

Joshi, S. V., L. T. Drzal, A. K. Mohanty, and S. Arora. 2004. "Are Natural Fiber Composites Environmentally Superior to Glass Fiber Reinforced Composites?" *Composites Part A: Applied Science and Manufacturing*, 35(3): 371–376.

Ley N. 1.854 de la Ciudad Autónoma de Buenos Aires.

Leys, C. 1996. *The Rise and Fall of Development Theory.* Oxford, UK: James Currey.

Medina, Martin. 1997. "Informal Recycling and Collection of Solid Wastes in Developing Countries." *Issues and Opportunities*, UNU/IAS Working Paper 24.

Medina, Martin. 2005. "Waste Picker Cooperatives in Developing Countries." Presented at the Wiego/Cornell/SEWA Conference on Membership-Based Organisations of the Poor, Ahmed, India.

Murphy, Richard. 2003. "Life Cycle Assessment." In *Green Composites: Polymer Composites and the Environment* , edited by C. Baillie. Cambridge: Woodhead Publishing Limited.

Parizeau, Kate. 2006. "Theorizing Environmental Justice: Environment as a Social Determinant of Health." *Munk Centre for International Studies Briefings: Comparative Program on Health and Society Lupina Foundation Working Paper Series 2005–2006*, 101–128. Toronto: University of Toronto.

Richtel, Matt and Kate Galbraith. 2008. "Trash has Crashed." *New York Times*, December 8, New York.

Schamber, P. J., F. M. Suárez, and E. Valdés. (Eds.). 2007. *Recicloscopio, Miradas sobre recuperadores urbanos de residuous de America Latina.* Buenos Aires, Argentina: Prometeo Libros.

Thamae, Timothy and Caroline Baillie. 2007. "Influence of Fibre Extraction Method, Alkali and Silane Treatment on the Interface of Agave Americana Waste HDPE Composites as Possible Roof Ceilings in Lesotho." *Composite Interfaces* 14, (7–9): 821–836.

Thamae, Timothy and Caroline Baillie. 2008. "A Life Cycle Assessment of Wood Based Composites: A Case Study." In *Wood-polymer Composites*, edited by Oksman K. and Sain, M. Cambridge: Woodhead Publishing Limited.

Thamae, Timothy and Caroline Baillie. 2009. *Natural Fibre Composites: Turning Waste into Useful Materials*. Saarbrücken, Germany: VDM Publishing House Ltd.

Thamae, T., R. Marian, C. Wu, L. Chong, and C. Baillie. 2008. "Developing and Characterizing New Materials Based on Waste Plastic and Agro-fibre." *Journal of Materials Science* 43, (12): 4057–68.

Thamae, T., Aghedo, S., Baillie, C. and D. Matovic. 2009a. "Tensile Properties of Hemp and Agave Fibres." In *Handbook of Tensile Properties of Textile and Technical Fibres*, edited by Bunsell and Schwartz, Cambridge: Woodhead Publishing.

Thamae, T., S. Vaja, Y. Shangguan, C. Finoro, N. Stefano, and C. Baillie. 2009b. "Mechanical and Moisture Absorption of Corn and Wheat Flour Composites for Developing Countries." In *Green Composites: Properties, Design and Life Cycle*, edited by F. Willems and P. Moens, Hauppauge, NY: Nova Publishers.

Young, Iris Marion. 2000. "Five Faces of Oppression." In *Readings for Diversity and Social Justice*, edited by M. Adams, X. Zuniga, C. R. Castenada, M. L. Peters, H. W. Hackman, and W. J. Blumenfeld, 35–49. New York, NY: Routledge.

Chapter Four

From Toxic to Green

Turning Mountains of E-Waste into Green Jobs

Bharati Chaturvedi[1]

Electronics has emerged as the fastest growing segment of Indian industry both in terms of production and exports. Between 1993 and 2000 in India, the growth of personal computers was 604 percent, compared to the world average of 181 percent. Many of these computers are now ready to be discarded as electronic-waste or will become available for recycling very soon. E-waste is one of the largest growing waste streams in India. Electronic and electric waste (or e-waste), such as old computers, printers, and televisions, is emerging as a serious environmental problem in India. Most electronic waste in India is picked by and sold to the informal sector, where precious elements, such as copper, gold, etc. are extracted under highly hazardous conditions. Typically, such units are raided and sealed. But Chintan, a non-profit organization that works in partnership with the informal sector, converting waste into social wealth, believes that despite its toxicity, e-waste can provide green jobs if collection systems are inclusive of the informal sector and a framework of Extended Producer Responsibility (EPR) can be strategically deployed to fill in key gaps required for safe e-waste handling. This poses a dual challenge of eliminating pollution while ensuring green jobs for existing e-waste recyclers.

To do this, Chintan is creating new strategies and partnerships, deviating from given thinking on these issues. The chapter will explore the evolution of such partnerships. It will detail why India should turn to its traditional informal sector to solve a new age problem.

OF CANNIBALISTIC CONSUMPTION

It's a warm afternoon on the border of Delhi. Two young men slouch on a shop floor, with just basic tools in their hands and around them. Like magicians, they take apart a desktop computer in seconds. First, they use a screwdriver, freeing large chunks of the machine from the case. Then, they get to each chunk, taking it apart too. All manners of computer entrails spill out—chips, boards, screws, stuff that's green, orange and steely silver. Wires poke out—thin and fat. Some components will be removed from each other using a blow torch. In a matter of minutes piles of computer residue lie neatly around them. Their shop floor is no bigger than a king-size bed. It isn't unique either. In this part of Delhi, as in many other parts of North India, shop after shop dismantles computers, phones, and other electronic goods. They are scrap malls, selling over 80 percent of what they dismantle as components that someone will reuse (Chaturvedi et al. 2007). *Some parts will be fed into metal extraction units, known for their toxicity. All across India, nearly 95 percent of electronic waste will be dismantled like this, by sheer human skill and enterprise* (Chaturvedi et al. 2007). *But none of these businesses are listed on the yellow pages. They are informal, the stuff that is not accounted for, not registered and often, not included in plans.*

How do we find ways to make dismantlers like these a part of a formal, recognized way to handle such stuff? This is a particularly serious issue for India, where, there are indications that the disposal of e-waste is increasing rapidly. The data is diverse, and sometimes, incongruous. According to the Indian Ministry of Environment and Forests, between 2004 and 2012 e-waste has increased seven times by weight. According to another study, by 2011 India was forecasted to have generated 470,000 MT of e-waste annually, up from 330,000 MT in 2007 (Chaturvedi et al. 2007). In the absence of monitoring or data registries, this is not easy to triangulate or verify. The UNU Institute for Sustainability and Peace points out that by 2020, e-waste from discarded refrigerators will double or triple.[2] A popular argument is that an increase in "high tech trash" (Grossman 2006)[3] is one of the by-products of the disposable income of a growing middle class. This is true. There is also another trend impacting e-waste generation. This is the access to cell phones among Indians.

According to a news report (Vaidyanathan 2012), there are more than 898 million mobile subscribers in India, of which 292 million live in rural areas. From an e-waste perspective, this means 900 million cell phones that will be trashed in the coming eight years. Along with these will be chargers, headphones and other accessories.[4]

In short, India's e-waste is increasing at a fast pace. There is reason to consider the best options for recycling as the volumes increase. As the story of the everyday working lives of those involved in recycling e-waste shows, there is also reason to consider other, less exploitative ways of handling the detritus of our consumption.

Sunder Singh Kabari is in his 30s, he has spent nearly 17 years riding a cycle around India's most privileged addresses. From about 6:30 in the morning, until at least one in the afternoon, he cycles around the inner lanes, calling out to residents to sell him their high value scrap. Kabari, he says, referring to both his own profession and to scrap itself. Across India, nobody sells low value plastics and paper: it's discarded in the trash. But old refrigerators, washing machines, and printers, all these are sold to itinerant buyers like Sunder Singh. Sometimes, I see him with a single computer, its chords and wires intact, on his cycle carrier. He pedals to an informal transfer station where he will store the computer and continue looking out for more waste to buy. By three, too exhausted to cycle and feeling famished, he sells what he has invested for a small profit. By this time, Sunder Singh would have had to find his way through a maze of hostility: police inspecting his bag of goods to see if he has any especially valuable goods that might have been stolen, the local security guard asking for free drinks, and civic authorities threatening to seize his cycle because he is vagrant and unauthorized. His profits are important, but they are much less important than wriggling out of this daily mess. The computer has a predictable path. It will enter a chain. It is likely to be sold to a small dealer, who will sell it ahead to another dealer specializing in old electronics. This dealer will test it. If the computer still works, it goes to a refurbisher, someone who will repair it, replace some parts, and sell it ahead. That's if it is relatively new. If it is old, the dealer will sell it to a dismantler, someone who will take the computer apart and sell off each section. About 80 percent of all e-waste is actually reused (Chaturvedi et al. 2007). *The plastics will be recycled, the screws will be sold in a second hand market, and the mother-boards will end up as sheets of copper.*

Sunder Singh's routine tells us that not only are dismantlers important actors for e-waste handling, but those who collect e-waste and channelize e-waste are key actors too. He holds a solution to the dilemma of how to safely recycle electronic waste and create decent, green jobs.

Currently, the e-waste chain in the informal sector starts with collection by itinerant buyers and others, aggregators, or people who purchase and store the waste, feeding it to various chains. One such chain is the dismantlers, who sell off usable parts for reuse, plastics for recycling, and motherboards and other parts for metal recovery. Almost all parts of this chain are informal. Big e-waste collection companies, entering the market in the last few years, don't know, and possibly, don't much care, about this bevy of actors who handle their brands after the consumer trashes them. The challenge is to help informal sector actors formalize and collect e-waste, feeding it into the formal value chain, where it is safely handled. Such a perspective accepts that those extracting copper will not be able to do so anymore, because it is a highly toxic process. On the other hand, the bulk of those working in e-waste, namely the collectors, aggregators, and dismantlers, would be able to upgrade and formalize their work. In the long term, better technologies that are commercially viable at a smaller scale have to be explored and piloted even for metal extraction.

The solution sounds simple, but as Chintan's experience of implementing it shows, it has a long history of incremental steps, some failing and others succeeding.

WORKING THE TERRAIN

Before 2008, there was little impetus to find a win-win solution for e-waste in India. Some environmental organizations did routine exposés about the horrors of e-waste recycling. Their key objective was to stop the imports of toxic e-waste into India, which they saw as ecocide and unjust (MEDIndia 2007).[5] In the many exposés that took place, there were dramatic visual indicators about the dangers of the existing forms of recycling. There was no discussion about the people whose livelihoods were based on such toxic work. Nonetheless, there was a small degree of public consciousness raised about the issue, although it seemed to vilify the informal sector. Rather than frame the sector as one that was bearing the brunt of such consumption, its role remained ignored.

Apart from such environmental groups, other actors were also engaging with the issue. Among these was Deutsche Gesellschaft fur Internationale Zusammenarbeit (GIZ), the German bilateral agency for technical cooperation, along with the Manufacturers' Association for Information Technology (MAIT), who jointly undertook a detailed study of the e-waste sector.

Not surprisingly, a part of GIZ's mandate was to find a way for existing informal sector actors to be included in the e-waste management. Chintan, on the other hand, had been following the issue of e-waste, but not actively working on it until 2005. At this point, the earliest discussions at Chintan were related to evaluating the e-waste value chain. However, it was only in late 2007 that this began to become a reality as Chintan began to work with GIZ. This first partnership served as a cornerstone for the kind of work Chintan would do in the coming years. The Chintan-GIZ partnership was related to formalizing the informal sector.

There were several compelling reasons to work with the informal sector. The livelihood imperative was clear. If, as the GIZ-MAIT study (MEDIndia 2007) suggested, approximately 25,000 persons from the informal sector worked in the e-waste business, it was clearly an important livelihood. Not strengthening it would mean creating vulnerability, leading, with policy shifts, to livelihood loss. Including them in e-waste handling would mean creating green jobs and reducing poverty levels. There was also the argument around efficiency. Data from a recent study showed that the informal sector was much more efficient than the formal sector in waste recovery in general (see table 4.1).

Chintan argued that collection should be improved to direct e-waste to safe recycling units. Table 4.1 shows that except in cities where the informal sector is absent, the informal sector generally handles more waste than the formal sector globally. Hence, even if formal sector collection systems were

Table 4.1. Global city-wide waste recovery (in tonnes and percent)

City	Tonnes recovered, all sectors	% materials prevented or recovered	% recovered by formal sector	% recovered by informal sector	Total % recycled as materials	Total % to agricultural value chain
Adelaide	2,611,214	54%	54%	0%	28%	26%
Bamako	392,893	85%	0%	85%	25%	31%
Bengaluru	524,688	25%	10%	15%	15%	10%
Belo Horizonte	145,134	7%	0.1%	6.9%	6.9%	0.1%
Canete	1,412	12%	1%	11%	12%	0%
Curepipe	NA	NA	NA	NA	NA	NA
Delhi	**841,070**	**33%**	**7%**	**27%**	**27%**	**7%**
Dhaka	210,240	18%	0%	18%	16%	2%
Ghorahi	365	11%	2%	9%	11%	NA
Kunming	600,000	38%	38%	NA	38%	0.05%
Lusaka	17,446	6%	4%	2%	6%	NA
Managua	78,840	19%	3%	15%	17%	2%
Moshi	11,169	18%	0%	18%	NA	18%
Nairobi	210,240	24%	NA	NA	20%	4%
Quezon City	287,972	39%	8%	31%	37%	2%
Rotterdam	90,897	30%	30%	0%	28%	1%
San Francisco	366,762	72%	72%	0%	46%	26%
Sousse	4,168	6%	0%	6%	2%	4%
Tompkins County	36,495	61%	61%	0%	61%	NA
Varna	37,414	27%	2%	26%	27%	NA
Average		30%	16%	15%	23%	9%
Median		25%	4%	11%	22%	4%

Source: UNHABITAT (2010).

instituted, the informal sector could play a critical role in upgrading and improving such systems. Third, the reach of the informal sector is unparalleled. Workers in the informal sector are able to collect an old mobile phone even from a home that has nothing else to sell. Such reach is essential when the objective is to plug leakages into toxic recycling. The collection services that the informal sector could provide should be viewed as an environmental service when harnessed to channel materials into cleaner recycling.

Finally, there is the value addition the sector brings in. Even in the case of e-waste, the sector is able to contribute in many ways that are currently unaccounted for. It segregates the various kinds of e-waste into neat categories. Furthermore, various components are tested for functionality, and many are repaired and re-sold into the second hand market. Others are refurbished, which requires some replacement of parts, and sold as intact, usable objects to local markets. This, too, is an environmental service. The GIZ-MAIT study pointed out that 80 percent of the components were reused.

Chintan's understanding around formalizing the informal e-waste handlers was based on three key ideas. To create green jobs was obvious. The second idea was to establish a formal space and identity as legitimate actors in the space ahead of the development of legislation and industry standards for handling e-waste. Experience in the solid waste sector clearly indicated that the development of formal legislation is typically followed by the entry of private companies who seek contracts to handle the legislated type of waste. Players who are not organized are likely to be left out. In 2000, after several iterations, the Solid Waste (Management and Handling) Rules, 2000 were created. Within a few years, a large number of companies began to enter the market, bidding for collection and transportation contracts, followed by waste processing contracts. These companies displaced wastepickers and traders at different points of the waste lifecycle and reversing such contracts proved hard, and sometimes not possible. Chintan's perceived need for urgently organizing the informal sector in e-waste came from its previous experience with the solid waste sector. It was clear that regulation around e-waste was required and in the offing. But this time around, Chintan was hoping to pre-empt a similar situation by organizing and claiming a space beforehand. It also felt the need for inclusive recycling, even if the goods being recycled were classified as hazardous. The point was to explore and demonstrate how actors from the informal sector need not be removed from value chains in the case of even toxic materials, while reducing toxicity across the chain.

Despite having already worked with the informal sector in the municipal solid waste stream, Chintan decided not to begin with strengthening them as an e-waste collection mechanism, but to seek out new partners directly working in electronic waste. In part, this was based on our understanding that dismantlers were the most vulnerable, and could lose their livelihoods most easily, if they were not organized. In Delhi, specific areas exist where electronic waste is traded, dismantled, and the metals extracted. Chintan began organizing in two such sites, Seelampur and Shastri Park, both in East Delhi. For many reasons this was, as expected, an entirely different experience to organizing waste pickers and traders.

Most dismantlers are literate and therefore able to absorb much more written information about the issue. This makes it quicker to discuss new ideas. However, they are also relatively wealthy, and the stakes for organizing are lower. Unlike even small waste traders, they do not face public hostility or even constant closure by the municipality. They are also spatially differently organized. Many of them operate from their own living rooms, located on the ground level of their two-storied homes. They are not spread out across the city either—they appear to be ghettoized to specific areas, unlike informal actors in the solid waste space. Areas like Mustafabad, in East Delhi, appears as a mini-industrial complex, protected by the sheer number of people working here. This leads to a certain isolation from everyday negotiations with government officials, from police to municipal actors, who otherwise demand pay-offs and threaten eviction. Such isolation meant that there was no immediate need for organizing. "I am working now, and I am not unhappy with the way I work. No one really troubles me," a dismantler once announced. "Why should I take the trouble to start organizing myself? My business? How will it change anything?"

For these reasons, Chintan decided to work with dismantlers, the section of the chain that buys e-waste, primarily computers, and takes them apart component by component. The challenge was to transfer Chintan's experience in the solid waste sector to e-waste, considered hazardous. In the context of Delhi, the challenge was also to demonstrate an alternative to the widespread government strategy of sealing polluting formal or informal units, instead of working to upgrade them to provide green jobs to workers, who bear the harshest impact.

At this point, Chintan conducted a survey as a means of becoming familiar with the social and political landscape of the area and speaking with people, as well as understanding the dismantlers' point of view on a range of issues. When the organizing began, through door-to-door conversations, the key issues were related to the need for a clearly defined body that could demand inclusion for its work. The nature of inclusion was primarily land and legal recognition. For most dismantlers, legal recognition seemed to be a vague proposition. But the need for formal land was a concern that they shared. "Look at our work. We have to run the entire business from our own spaces. I work downstairs and then I go upstairs to have lunch and rest. If I get more money, I could own a small shop, but it will be so small, I am not sure it will be helpful," said Mohammed Irfan, explaining his situation. His colleague, Mohammed Safeeq, made a community wish: "We would be much better off if the government agreed to give us some space nearby where we could work and expand the business . . . everyone here can pay for something if it is useful. But if we unite and ask for it, and don't get it, will they come and close us down here?"

During the process of discussion, many e-waste dismantlers and traders were interested in upgrading their work. It was not possible for such persons to be part of Safai Sena, an organization of wastepickers, itinerant buyers, and small dealers of solid waste, because they saw themselves as socially more accomplished than wastepickers. In Delhi, where the wastepickers are migrants from other states, living in slums and handling the lowest quality of dry waste, they are stigmatized. The dismantlers did not wish to embrace this social marginalization as part of their own reality.

As in the case of the waste recyclers, Chintan was inclined toward establishing an association because it was relatively easy to run and administer, served as a useful first level organization for a business and the e-waste dismantlers already had the expertise to run it. In this, Chintan and GIZ worked to set up such an association for nearly two years. In 2009, the first of these was set up—4R, Responsible Reduction, Reuse and Recycling. The association comprised a range of e-waste traders and dismantlers. It also comprised a lawyer, whose role was to ensure that the association functioned well and met all legal requirements. Key leadership was provided by a dismantler and trader who specialized in computers, both from within India and those imported from other countries. Those specializing in computers, in printers, and in refurbishing were also included. At this point, in 2012, it is still the only association to have been formed within the e-waste dismantling space. Companies, as opposed to associations, have been a more common form of organization among e-waste dismantlers.

Chintan and the e-waste handlers jointly created a list of objectives of this association. In addition to this, Chintan also provided training to key 4R members on various key issues of concern, including the procedures for creating an association and how associations work. However, members of 4R were not satisfied with this input. They wanted Chintan not to be an external facilitator, but an internal part contributing equally. In other words, their understanding of Chintan's stake in e-waste was different from that of Chintan's. In the end, Chintan, represented by two people, became a partner of 4R and contributed to its functioning and toward its fees and expenses.

The key plans that 4R outlined were:

- To set up a dismantling unit.
- To establish 4R as a legitimate player in the e-waste sector.
- To set up a code of conduct for 4R members in the future, in order to enable them to benefit from 4R membership but without jeopardizing the

credibility of the sector. For example, members could not sell e-waste for gold extraction, and peer monitoring would determine this.

At the same time, Chintan was working in another partnership, with the Silicon Valley Toxics Coalition, or SVTC, a diverse non-profit organization based in the United States engaged in research, advocacy, and grassroots organizing to promote human health and environmental justice in response to the rapid growth of the high-tech industry. Until that point in 2007, SVTC was concerned about the mass dumping of e-waste from the United States into India. Their key concern was that such dumping did not result in sustainable consumption. The SVTC-Chintan partnership was based on advocacy, but the common concerns were unidentified until SVTC visited India to see the on-the-ground reality for themselves. During a visit in August 2008, a key issue that emerged for SVTC was related to the informal sector. In particular, both SVTC and Chintan believed that by allowing workers in the sector to work in hazardous, informal conditions, the producers of the electronics were exploiting them and free-riding on their work. To drive the point home a film, *Citizens at Risk*, was produced. The film clearly shows the dilemmas of the informal sector, the toxicity of the work, and the precarious nature of recycling. In particular, through its arresting visuals, the film showed how children were participants in electronic recycling. This was the first, and continues to be, the only, film that examines corporate free-riding on the informal sector in e-waste. The partnership with SVTC helped Chintan sharpen its focus on the informal sector, and increase the areas of overlap between the two organizations. Chintan also learned about trends in e-waste handling in the United States and jointly analyzed their relevance in India through discussions, as a means of understanding how e-waste could be handled in the Indian context.

At the end of the first phase of work, ending in early 2009, Chintan had been able to identify partners in the formal and informal sector, help create one organization of the informal sector in e-waste and clarify its own voice for further advocacy. From 2009 onward, Chintan took these two streams ahead within a rapidly changing context.

Deepening the Work

From about 2009 onward, with nearly three years of practical experience, Chintan decided to push for deepening its work. The key pillars of this were helping 4R set up a dismantling plant, building capacity within Safai Sena to become part of the collection mechanism, advocating for inclusive rules on e-waste, and seeking new partners to help implement this phase.

Enter Safai Sena

Chintan had also facilitated the establishment of Safai Sena, an association of wastepickers, doorstep waste collectors, itinerant and other small buyers, small junk dealers, and other types of recyclers, based in various cities in North India. The association was established in 2001 but registered only in 2009. One of its aims is that the work of waste recyclers should be recognized and that they should have safe and secure work conditions. The association comprises of around 11,000 recyclers working in solid waste management.

In the second phase of its work, Chintan began building the capacity of Safai Sena to also provide collection services. In fact, Safai Sena was already collecting e-waste, because itinerant buyers typically purchase computers and old electronic items from households who wish to dispose of these. Several Safai Sena members also sold small quantities of e-waste in the Sunday Market, a weekly bazaar for second hand goods. An approximation showed at least 40 percent of the bazaar comprised of e-waste and refurbished e-waste sellers. Safai Sena was already a well-organized entity, working in partnership with Chintan. It also had the experience of handling solid waste. The key task was to help build the capacity of itinerant buyers, in the first instance, to collect e-waste in a formalized manner. Chintan directly, and with GIZ, conducted training for a combination of itinerant buyers and leaders from Safai Sena.

By May 2011, the Ministry of Environment and Forests had already declared the new E-Waste (Management and Handling) Rules, 2011. These were to come into force on May 1, 2012. Among the provisions of the rules were that any company or association wishing to collect waste would have to seek authorization from the State Pollution Control Board or the State Pollution Control Committee, based on their area of operation.

There were several provisions in the laws, or at least, interpretations, which make it hard for a new player in the scene to comply. The most difficult to handle was the Delhi government's unwillingness that a collection center, required by every collector, could only be set up in an industrial area. Unfortunately, industrial areas in Delhi have recently succumbed to the processes of gentrification and the accompanying high real estate values. Instead of the manufacturing units that once dominated Delhi's 31 notified industrial areas, there are offices, automobile showrooms, export factories, and other new kinds of services that have rented most of the space in such areas. In fact, in the case of plastics, approximately 80 percent of the total reprocessing units are in the informal sector.[6] They simply cannot get registered without showing collection centers in an industrial area, and industrial areas command exorbitant rentals.

When Safai Sena first informally approached the Delhi Pollution Control Committee (DPCC) to inform it of its intention to apply for authorization, it did so with the help of Chintan. However, the DPCC was not confident that Safai Sena, with a small bank balance and no demonstrated experience of working in the area, would be able to comply with the regulations. The discussions around e-waste were also frenzied, and any such consent to operate functioned as a closely-watched pilot. It was clear that Chintan was more likely to get the authorization in Delhi. After several rounds of filling in and correcting forms, and answering various queries of the DPCC, Chintan obtained a Consent to Establish from Delhi Pollution Control Committee for an e-waste collection center. It is the first non-profit to have been authorized to collect e-waste in Delhi. At the time of writing this, there is no public announcement of any other non-profit receiving such authorization.

The Morphing of 4R

To accomplish the previously decided objectives of the association, 4R decided to set up a dismantling unit. They were able to work with a consulting firm, Sycom Projects Consultants Private Limited, to produce a business plan. Sycom's costs were met by GIZ to help 4R. The plan was co-created by 4R, Chintan, and Sycom after several discussions on dismantling.

Unfortunately, an unhappy asymmetry of information resulted in a setback for 4R. Based on the understanding that a vibrant recycling belt on one of Delhi's borders was an authorized industrial area, 4R set up a dismantling unit and applied for various permits. The area it had selected was not an authorized area, but only a proposed authorized area. The investment was futile. Not just this, but during the discussions that followed, it became clear that 4R would be unable to undertake its core competence, dismantling, in the jurisdiction of Delhi. There was consensus that dismantling was toxic and should not be permitted, regardless of what the e-waste legal regime permitted. 4R would have to turn to collection, a downgrading of its fine skills.

This failed project created a great deal of acrimony within 4R, and some members decided to register themselves as a company under the Companies Act 1956. Their new company was named Green E-waste Recyclers Pvt. Ltd. They believed that they stood a better chance of being accepted by the DPCC as a company. Since the actors in 4R were not poor, in contrast with Safai Sena's wastepickers, they also had adequate capital.

However, not all 4R members were part of this new company. Nevertheless, all 4R members began to seek formalization opportunities, aware of the vulnerability of staying informal. The new company has applied for authorization to the State Pollution Control Committee as a collector and the status is pending. Another company formed by members of 4R is working without authorization. The uncertain authorization process serves as a barrier to entry into the informal sector.

Chintan has set up guidelines on collection for recycling and is working with both Safai Sena and with another company set up by e-waste traders that is still in the process of filling in its application form for authorization. Chintan believes that if protocols are created and monitored, it can seek to offer partnerships to a range of informal sector players to formalize and work legally under the umbrella of its authorization.

Advocating for Inclusive Policy

While Chintan was working with the informal sector to set up systems on the ground, it was also advocating for improved policies in e-waste management. From November 2009, when it made its first presentation to the Ministry of Environment and Forests (MOEF), to December 2010, when it offered its final comments on the Rules, Chintan's focus was on creating a level playing field for organized informal sector actors as an essential means of improving e-waste handling and reducing pollution. In order to help create the rules, Chintan identified key actors within the Ministry of Environment and Forests. These were both at the level of political leadership and at the senior executive and technical levels. As various iterations of the policy were shared, it became clear that refurbishers would benefit the most if their non-polluting work, already good for the environment, were not included in the rules because this both created barriers in their operations and was likely to lead to greater corruption. The new legal system has a provision for local kabaris to handle e-waste. The law clearly defines a collection center as a "Centre established, individually or jointly or a registered society or a designated agency or a company or a association to collect e-waste."[7] This means any local kabari either individually or collectively can establish an e-waste collection center after formalizing through an association or company, and obtaining consent from the concerned authorities.

OF NEW PARTNERS AND PARTNERSHIPS

Chintan's work—within the e-waste landscape and otherwise—has always been hinged on synergistic partnerships. The unfurling scenario and fresh challenges demand not only strengthening old partnerships but also creating new ones. These include finding authorized companies to sell the e-waste to, linking up with e-waste producers to help implement Extended Producer Responsibility and the general public, key sources of e-waste. But these partnerships require both Safai Sena and Chintan to upgrade their capacity and systems. At the point of writing this chapter, Chintan is putting into place a system that will allow it to monitor the e-waste collected, identify key areas for improvement within itself and Safai Sena, and scale up Safai Sena's ability to handle consumer feedback. Not only is this an essential process for service delivery, but it is also an essential means to seek financing for its grassroots collection operations.

Within a few weeks of the new rules coming into force, Chintan has already begun negotiating a Memorandum of Understanding with a major mobile phone manufacturer to work in partnership with the informal sector to take back cell phones and accessories in various parts of Delhi. The mutual success of this partnership will shape future recycling channels.

CHINTAN'S CHALLENGES 2.0

In the last four years, Chintan's key challenges have been related to enabling and facilitating the informal sector to embed itself in the fast-changing policy landscape. A second challenge has been to ensure not only inclusive policy but also to create a general consensus that the informal sector has significant value to offer in implementing policy, particularly EPR. It is premature to evaluate the degree to which Chintan's work has been able to meet these ends as the e-waste recycling scenario in India is still fluid. But already, the next set of challenges are becoming clearer.

One of the first steps is to engage with producers to deepen their linkages with the informal sector. Currently, producers and NGOs, or organizations of or acting on behalf of, wastepickers are partnering with each other for the first time to begin implementing take-back schemes. Such partnering is linked with capital investment that will help stabilize what should become a viable business run by the informal sector. But these are only pilots. In order to hold more relevance, there must be a wider strategy. According to the law, producers are not only required to engage in demonstrating the efficacy of take-back schemes, but they must also do so at a reasonable level. The proposed guidelines are likely to suggest 20 percent take back each year. Only further investment in newer schemes can ensure these standards are met. Along with this, a continuous interest in being part of the solution by producers is essential. The point is how best to shift from a pilot level initiative to an institutionalized system across India.

A second challenge is scale, particularly for the informal sector. Consider the top ten e-waste producing cities in India: Delhi, Bangalore, Chennai, Kolkata, Ahmadabad, Hyderabad, Pune, Surat, and Nagpur. Five years after the first initiatives around collection, there are active projects only in four of these cities. How other cities will set up adequate collection systems and scale these up is unclear. Nagpur offers a clue. Here, a few key players from Delhi control the e-waste trade. These are aggregators, persons who purchase e-waste from a number of smaller buyers and send it back to Delhi when they have three tons or more.[8] The players here are well organized, active in a number of cities, and do not seem to sub-contract their work to anyone outside their existing family and close business associates. They also have first player advantage. Chintan is already working with one of them to understand how he can upgrade and protect his work, be legally compliant, and scale up further. It is likely that replicating the work with the informal sector will require working with key actors and nodes. Otherwise, there will always be adequate leakage for toxic smelting.

The informal sector is only one aspect of scale. Another is municipal and other capacity to set in place the infrastructure and systems for e-waste recycling. Here, two types of solutions kick in. One relies on the companies themselves, including those with large dismantling facilities, or facilities to recover metals. In order to work to capacity, they require specific types of e-waste. In some cities, the business interests of such companies may drive capacity, to some extent. In this case too, an organized informal sector will be able to take advantage of the demand for a well-organized collection system. A second way to scale up will be through companies that are likely to specialize in collection. Where the informal sector is not well organized, or backed by other organizations, this may not be in its interest. Previous experience in the solid waste sector shows that the playing ground becomes uneven and the informal sector finds it hard to compete when large companies come in before it is organized enough to negotiate its own space in a city or locality.

Chintan sees many roles for itself in this scenario, including an agency monitoring the inclusion of the informal sector by both policy makers and collection companies. It also sees itself as tracking and advocating for more innovative Extended Producer Responsibility (EPR), which is able to respond to new realities. One of the key issues EPR practitioners must resolve is the price differential between what recycling companies and informal actors offer for any item of e-waste. Since the informal sector offers more, most waste continues to go for toxic recycling. A solution is for funds from EPR to bridge this gap, or enable a minimum acceptable price that consumers sell their e-waste to formal collectors. This must be backed by awareness programs, also possibly funded by EPR.

Chintan is also working with the informal sector to be a collection agent. By doing this, it is helping wastepickers and itinerant buyers in particular stake their claim as legitimate collectors and participants in the e-waste space. These roles apart, Chintan sees a role for itself in peer-sharing, where it will be able to share its resources and information with other organizations to help them push an upgraded informal sector ahead as an optimal collection system that is legally entrenched in the city and able to meet the required standards and needs.

The moral dilemma of children cannot be ignored. Children are an essential area of deep concern in the e-waste recycling world. In some cases, children are hired to dismantle and assist in handling e-waste.[9] They are not only exposed to hazardous chemicals, but are also unable to access an adequate education. But many other children, who may go to school and lead a normal life outwardly, are also impacted by the pollution. Burning copper wires results in dioxin emissions, and acid fumes cause respiratory distress. While poor environmental conditions are known to impact children, the case of e-waste is more complex, because it is handled at home, either where a child lives or in his or her neighborhood. Many such operations are in areas where there is poor infrastructure or facilities in general, making the space even less healthy for children.

Chintan's next level of work will include children more proactively. Already, the No Child in Trash program enables children who either pick trash or who are most likely to pick trash to access education. Apart from education, Chintan hopes its work with e-waste dismantlers and collectors will help to create the understanding that clean and green livelihoods are vital for children's health. A sizable portion of the work in this context will relate to consensus building around children's health, education, and other rights. Organized informal sector actors will also be involved in such work to serve as peers building perspectives around the need to protect children and organize for green jobs. The key barrier in Chintan's work in this area is related to the financial resources required for five years to demonstrate a viable impact.

But Chintan is already facing a fourth challenge: What to do with low value e-waste that most people want to give away for safe disposal? The best example is CDs and DVDs. These are not on the official list of e-waste, but they can be considered e-waste in the broadest sense and many consumers dump them into collection systems. Most recyclers accept these only if they come along with substantial quantities of e-waste to compensate. There is no recycling possible for many such items and they are likely to be dumped in landfills. They will also eat into the business plans of e-waste collectors. The only solution we see is to revise the list of what comprises e-waste and to compel the producers to set up a take-back scheme for these.

Given the volumes of electronics projected to be discarded in the future, recycling is clearly not the only approach. Refurbishing, a thriving business, must be encouraged as a means of reuse. Already, at least one recycling company is being able to refurbish computers in agreement with the producer, and passing these on to children without access to computers through nonprofits.[10] Apart from companies, creating strategic markets for repaired goods and second-hand goods is an excellent way for cities to encourage reuse.

Recycling electronic waste is a complex business in India, because it is not merely about reclaiming metals and plastics. It is equally about livelihoods, green jobs, poverty alleviation, and asserting the right of informal sector entrepreneurs be a part of every city's new thinking and practice. But any idea in this landscape can only expect to be successful if it is based on partnerships that listen to and are led by the visions of the informal sector players for their own future.

NOTES

1. A significant portion of this paper is based on my personal understanding of the issue. This has been shaped by several informal sector actors, their perspectives, ideas and openness in sharing these. The paper does not try to represent their point of view, but many issues have been gleaned from discussions with them, particularly in Delhi and Western Uttar Pradesh. I am particularly grateful to the members of Safai Sena and 4R. Thanks are also in order to Leena Buddhe, whose generosity enabled me to meet with several e-waste actors in Nagpur. I am grateful to my colleagues in Chintan for their ideas and more tangibly, their help in producing diagrams, maps, etc. for use in this paper. In particular, thanks are in order to Supriya Bhardwaj and Imran Khan. Some parts of this paper were previously described in a manual Chintan brought out to share experiences in the e-waste sector. The names of some of the informal sector actors have been changed to protect their identities.

2. This statistic was obtained from the website, www.weeerecycle.in. This project is co-financed by the European Commission under its SWITCH ASIA programme and the German Ministry for Economic Cooperation and Development (BMZ). The Deutsche Gesellschaft fuer Internationale Zusammenarbeit (GIZ) GmbH, the lead implementing agency, works on behalf of the BMZ. The Indian partners are the Manufacturers' Association for Information Technology (MAIT) and Toxics Link while the European partner is Adelphi Research gGmbH (Germany).

3. This term was first used by Elizabeth Grossman in her book, "*High Tech Trash : Digital Devices, Hidden Toxics, and Human Health*," Island Press, 2006.

4. This is approximated from the data that in 2010, Indians replaced their cell phones once in 7 years and 9 months. This was of course, a shorter cycle compared to previous years, and also compared to countries like the United States. From: *International Comparisons: The Handset Replacement Cycle.* By Roger Entner, analyst and founder, *Recon Analytics.* Date not available.

5. Examples of this are to be found in campaigns by several organizations, including Greenpeace India.

6. This data is derived from a survey undertaken by Chintan for the Delhi Pollution Control Committee to determine the extent of informal sector recycling in Delhi. The survey data is from October 2010 to September 2011.

7. E-Waste (Management and Handling) Rules, 2011.

8. The author makes this statement based on visits in 2011 and 2012 to Nagpur and detailed discussions with a range of actors in the e-waste informal sector, NGOs and individuals trading in e-waste.

9. This has been observed several times by the author, during site visits across North India.

10. While there may be other such formal sector companies undertaking refurbishing, the author personally has seen this practice only at the premises of Attero Recycling, in Rourkee, in Uttarakhand, a state in North India. Refurbishing is a common practice in the informal sector.

REFERENCES

Chaturvedi, Ashish, Rachna Arora, Vivek Khattar, and Jaspreet Kaur, 2007. "E-waste Assessment in India—Specific Focus on Delhi." German Technical Cooperation (GTZ)—Manufacturers Association of Information Technology (MAIT) study.

Grossman, Elizabeth, 2006. *High Tech Trash: Digital Devices, Hidden Toxics, and Human Health.* Island Press.

MEDIndia, 2007. "Greenpeace demands complete ban on import of e-waste into India," last accessed 27 August 2013. http://www.medindia.net/news/Greenpeace-Demands-Complete-Ban-on-Import-of-E-waste-in-India-27422–1.htm.

UNHABITAT, 2010. *Solid Waste Management in the World's Cities:Water and Sanitation in the World's Cities.*

Vaidyanathan, Rajini, 2012. "Is 2012 the year for India's internet?" BBC news. Last accessed 27 August 2013. http://www.bbc.co.uk/news/business-16354076.

Chapter Five

Social Justice as Fairness in the Global Food System

Michael Heasman and Ralph Early

It is accepted across political divides that the global food system faces fundamental challenges now and in the future regarding its sustainability and ability to provide healthy food for all. These challenges fall into two broad categories: (1) in relation to diet and human health, and (2) in relation to the need to address environmental concerns and the use of natural resources; both of which impact on the world's capacity to provide food (Lang and Heasman 2004).

The headline figures relating to these challenges are stark and often quoted. For example, in 2013 it was estimated that 12.5 percent of the world's population (868 million people) were undernourished in terms of energy intake. Yet these figures represent a fraction of the global burden of malnutrition if they were to also include the estimated 26 percent of the world's children whose growth is stunted or the 2 billion people who it is estimated suffer from one or more micronutrient deficiencies (FAO 2013).

A majority of nation states are now coping with multiple types of malnutrition which may coexist within the same country, household, or individual (FAO 2013). In addition, chronic non-communicable diseases (NCDs) such as cardiovascular disease, diabetes, and some cancers, have become the leading cause of morbidity, disability, and mortality in the world today. The prevention of NCDs are strongly linked to diet and particular types of food consumption patterns (Popkin 2009; Cecchini et al. 2010).

It is also increasingly well documented that the natural environment that comprises the entire basis for food production is under continuing duress from loss of soils, lack of fresh water, and nutrient depletion, through to threats to the insects that pollinate crops and control infestations. Added to this there is growing evidence of the impact of climate change on global food production. It is estimated that environmental factors such as these might cause yields to be 5–25 percent short of demand by 2050 to feed a population that will increase by a further 2.7 billion mouths from the 7 billion people alive in 2013 (UNEP 2009).

Many solutions are proposed to address these twin crises of human health and environmental sustainability in relation to food and agriculture. These range from what might be termed top-down technology fixes such as the genetic modification of core agricultural crops, including soy and corn (maize), which it is claimed are able to "feed the world" and address environmental sustainability at the same time, through to practices such as agroecology which are advocated to enable a smallholder or community-led path toward a food secure future (Altieri 1995; Foresight 2011).

Scratch beneath the surface of whatever approach advanced to "feed the world" and a fundamental chasm is exposed: we live in a food world that is deeply divided through food poverty, health inequalities and access, and control of the natural resources to produce food. The result is that some people are able to live in a food-rich world of a kind never before seen in history while, at the same time, in many countries and regions of the globe large numbers of people suffer food poverty and diet-related sickness and poor health—often within regions which are abundant in food.

CONFRONTING THE FOOD-RICH AND THE FOOD-POOR WORLD

The key aim of this chapter is to explore a number of the divisions that create and perpetuate the global divide between the food-rich and food-poor worlds, and to conceptualize the problem as a failure of social justice and fairness throughout the global food system. Increasingly better-off consumers throughout the world are becoming concerned and vocal about wanting to know how their food is produced, where it comes from, and what the environmental and human costs might be of creating and maintaining sustainable agri-food supply chains.

One response to such concerns, and a response shaped particularly over the last decade, has been the way food business has developed and implemented wide-ranging corporate social responsibility (CSR) strategies. The goal of CSR is to engage with the range of stakeholders that corporations need if they are to be successful in today's global marketplaces and to provide reassurances about the ethical and environmental credentials of food businesses from production through to marketing (Ionescu-Somers and Steger 2008; Zadek 2001).

However such attempts can be seen as piecemeal and fragmented. They involve individual corporations rather than fundamental structural change to the food system and many such initiatives have been criticized as "greenwash"—that is, corporate claims that are demonstrably fake or that risk misleading intended audiences such as claims about the environmental benefits of a product or service—rather than getting to the heart of the current dysfunctional food system with respect to human health and environmental protection and sustainability.

It is proposed here that a broader conceptual framework will be needed to address the chasm of inequalities and food poverty underlying many parts of today's global food system, and that the concept of *social justice as fairness* can provide a powerful analytical tool with which to develop the framework. But this is not new. Social justice as fairness has been and is the cornerstone of the battles fought by civil society, food campaigners, and grassroots activists for generations. For this reason—and against the backdrop of challenges facing the global food system as represented by issues of diet, health, and environmental sustainability—the focus of this chapter will be the struggle of food movements, non-government organizations (NGOs), and activists, in both developed and developing countries, to achieve social justice and fairness in relation to food supply.

In this context, NGOs and food movements play a crucial role, since even where there is a more conventional international establishment response—such as global institutions and governments working to address world hunger—this often takes on the mantle of "top-down" solutions that rarely seek out the perspectives of, or even include, those at the receiving end of such solutions. All too often difficult issues are bracketed into separate silos and the holistic notion of social justice as fairness as a guiding principle embodying decision making informed by a sense of compassion and humanity, is lost (Lang and Heasman 2004).

Confronting problems in the global food system can seem like an overwhelming task, especially as many of these are complex and multi-layered. To help cut through this complexity and to investigate a particular challenge within global food systems, the focus here is on a relatively neglected area of social justice as fairness in mainstream discourse, namely the working conditions and wages of the workers and smallholders who produce, harvest, process, and manufacture our food.

Problems such as a "living wage" or fairness for workers and smallholder producers integrated into the agri-food supply chain are at times marginalized by the headline issues of the environmental or nutritional crisis within the food system—important as these are—even though poverty wages, poor working conditions, and cost-cutting are often intimately linked. Examples will be drawn from "fair trade" labeling schemes and studies undertaken by

NGOs to highlight the employment conditions of workers throughout the food supply chain.

NGOs and workers' organizations are often the first to raise awareness among consumers about the issues that some politicians, policy makers, and businesses with vested interests would prefer to conceal from the public gaze. But before food and farm workers can be considered in detail, the concept of social justice as fairness must be discussed briefly and together with the broader, contextual "big picture" through which it might be applied.

WHAT IS SOCIAL JUSTICE AS FAIRNESS?

The concept of social justice as fairness is used in this chapter in the manner developed by the moral philosopher John Rawls. It is not the purpose here to engage in abstract philosophical theories of social justice and fairness, although this was the task Rawls set himself, but rather to use his work to suggest a pathway into what constitutes "fairness." Using Rawls' abstract concept to provide the basis for social justice as fairness it can be argued that a fair and socially just food system should be grounded in fundamental notions of how a human society is structured and the part that food plays in causing human health and well-being.

In his seminal work *A Theory of Justice*, Rawls argues that social justice as fairness must be regarded as the basic structure of society (Rawls 1971) enabling the main political and social institutions of society to combine as one system of social cooperation (Rawls 2001). He is concerned with how principles of social justice can provide a way of assigning the rights and duties in the basic institutions of society and that these can then define the appropriate distribution of the benefits and burdens arising from social cooperation.

Extrapolating from Rawls' work (he did not write about food systems), it becomes an imperative that for a food system to be socially just and fair there is the requirement for social justice as fairness to be instigated at a structural level rather than, say, manifesting at the level of individual consumer choice, although consumer behavior has a role to play in influencing the nature and dynamics of the food system.

Interpreting Rawls' abstraction of social justice as fairness in relation to the food system, it is clear that the social and economic arrangements and structures that influence and shape our food supply system are for many people in the world deeply unjust. They are unjust not only in terms of human suffering and misery caused by hunger, malnutrition, and overconsumption but also in the economic arrangements and inequalities in power existing within food supply chains. But Rawls cautions it is not always easy to come to an agreement about what is just or unjust in society. This is the critical challenge when it comes to figuring out how to share the "value" in food economies, or how to address the deepening dilemmas over who gets what with respect to natural resources to produce food, or who is simply paid a "living wage" to grow, process, serve, or sell the world's food.

The problem of fairness in food systems is not new. We only have to remember the struggle over the abolition of slavery in the production of sugar or other agricultural crops such as cotton and tobacco (Mintz 1985). Today however the notion of social justice and fairness is squarely on the corporate agenda and for those in government because the campaigns of food activists and NGOs continue to raise consumer awareness of the injustices that exist in food supply chains.

Examples of this new consumer awareness include today's successful marketing of Fairtrade branding (with a capital "F") and the policy and political rise of the justice-based "food sovereignty" movements epitomized by La Via Campesina ("the way of the peasant") which provides a voice in international advocacy on food justice (Pimbert 2009). A further important step toward the path of social justice as fairness has been the re-statement of the right to food through the ongoing work of the latest United Nations Special Rapporteur on the Right to Food, Olivier de Schutter (De Schutter 2013). All of these point to increasing successes of NGOs and food campaigners to have fairness in our global food system placed on the international political agenda.

SOCIAL JUSTICE IN FOOD AS A GLOBAL PROBLEM

The challenge of social justice in the food system is global. It unites problems in both rich and poor countries, especially with respect to globalized agri-food supply chains. For example, Lang (1997) shows how in the UK (a rich-world country) from the 1980s onward, a new generation of food activists and organizations were needed to inject different perspectives into food policy discourses not only by focusing on particular topics such as food adulteration, food poverty, or the poor state of school meals, but also through its language, themes, and methods of working, to challenge injustices and unfairness in food systems. Through charting a number of high profile food scandals in the UK, Lang argues NGOs played a critical role in becoming the mediators of public opinion and provided a counterbalance to the voices of establishment viewpoints, whether from government or from food business (Lang 1997).

Back in the 1970s critiques from civil society were already emerging that food policy could not be left to "free markets" and that there was a public need to address the health and environmental consequences of industrial food production. Part of this battle was to enable consumers to make informed choices. This notion has become more mainstream through the rise in ethical consumerism—a prominent example being Fairtrade and other certified product labeling schemes.

There are also wider political and policy implications about the role of the public and the private in food systems. As the neoliberal economic agenda gained ascendency from the 1980s onward, the state increasingly became portrayed as the enemy of "markets." With respect to the new food movement, in contrast, campaigners appealed to the public to force the state to help protect people and communities from the excess of food markets and corporate activities throughout food systems. Re-assessing the relationships between state, industry, and the public is central to the new food policy debate over social justice as fairness.

Food and beverage corporations are also being forced to respond to the twin challenges of human health and environmental sustainability for very practical reasons. This manifests itself in the form of CSR strategies which address the concerns of consumers and other stakeholders, and often makes good business sense, for example by cutting costs through decreasing a corporation's environmental footprint such as reducing waste, energy, water, and packaging use and consumption.

Food business leaders now recognize that they must address the environmental issues they face with regard to their supply chains security. For example, their businesses might fail in the future to obtain the raw materials and ingredients they need to operate. They also need to control costs and ensure the reliability of raw material supply in the face of increasingly volatile and risky global markets, which was brought into a sharp focus by the global food price crisis starting in 2007/2008 (Clapp 2012). For reasons such as these food businesses today are forced to reckon with a range of changing social and environmental risks existing in our food system.

What is emerging is a new, but often muddled, messy, and fragmented globalized social engagement throughout the food system. This engagement includes different stakeholders setting out or pursuing contrasting agendas with competing narratives concerning the future of food. However, responses to the many crises that arise in relation to global food supply rarely start from the consideration of social justice as fairness and a framework setting out duties and responsibilities as a first step in defining solutions. In many instances there is still a reliance on vociferous, often established grassroots activism driven by necessity, such as a response to poor working conditions, a specific food crisis, or driven by concerned citizens coming together to support or campaign on food related issues. Such activity once again brings the matter of social justice and fairness in global agri-food supply chains to the fore. Policy responses have often been reactive (or are perceived to be) to specific crises rather than proactive in building a food system built on the principles of social justice as fairness.

POWER IN FOOD SYSTEMS

It would be incorrect to suggest the human and environmental crises facing the global food system go without political, policy, or business responses. In fact global food security is high on the political agenda these days due to the almost universal recognition of the sustainability challenges facing the future of food (Foresight 2011). However it is the nature of these responses that expose major gaps in understanding between those at the "top" to those at the "bottom" or on the receiving end of solutions (IF Campaign 2013). An example is seen in the work emerging from the G8 Summits—the very cauldron of global power—on nutrition and food security which serves to illustrate the need for a nuanced approach to understanding global food-related problems.

The G8 Summits bring together the leaders from the most powerful economies in the world, namely Canada, France, Germany, Italy, Japan, Russia, the United States and the United Kingdom. At the June 17–18, 2013 G8 Summit, held under the UK Presidency at Lough Erne, Northern Ireland, global leaders again made a commitment to respond to the urgent need to achieve sustainable global food and nutrition security (HM Government 2013). This commitment was set out as part of the work of the New Alliance for Food Security and Nutrition.

The New Alliance was established during the G8 in 2012 under the US presidency and aims to increase agricultural production through private sector partnerships. The aims of the initiative are laudable: to accelerate responsible investment in African agriculture and lift 50 million people out of poverty by 2022 (DFID 2013, 2). In 2012 six African countries signed up to the New Alliance process—Burkina Faso, Cote d'Ivoire, Ethiopia, Ghana, Mozambique, and Tanzania—and it was announced at the 2013 G8 meeting that a further three had come on board—namely, Nigeria, Benin, and Malawi.

Critics argue that the money attached to the New Alliance needs, however, to involve more closely the people who are meant to be lifted out of poverty, and that many of the private sector partnerships will mean, in practice, that deals will involve and benefit multi-national agri-business corporations rather than smallholders (Monbiot 2013; Fairtrade Foundation 2013). The funding is important since it is a large sum and the New Alliance expects to leverage around $3.75 billion of private sector investment.

Further weaknesses of the New Alliance approach were highlighted in a thoughtful commentary written by Robinson and Humphrey (2013). They asked: How does the New Alliance link agriculture to nutrition and will the promised agricultural investment necessarily translate to improved nutrition by making nutritious foods more accessible for the people who need them?

In their analysis of the promised private sector investment projects relating to the first six African countries to sign up, they found that out of 111 projects more than half focus on non-food or export-only crops such as cocoa and cotton or on activities that are not crop specific (such as providing credit or for agro-chemicals). The second largest group of investments target staple crops (such as rice or maize) that do not provide important micronutrients unless they are fortified. Robinson and Humphrey (2013) argue, " . . . if we want to make combating undernutrition an important goal, then the New Alliance needs to invest in the right crops and activities, and make sure these are targeted to the populations who suffer most from undernutrition . . . " They highlight the mismatch between the stated goals of the program and the activities that are actually being funded (Robinson and Humphrey 2013).

While the G8 New Alliance is important in that it achieves high level political and policy status for food security as well as committing significant resources to food security, the voices and views of smallholders and those which the New Alliance claims to be helping are not effectively heard in the process. Further it is not clear in what ways the New Alliance initiative sets out to achieve social justice as fairness. For example, will the initiative enable poor producers to access markets at fair prices or help them toward land rights or the fair use of natural resources and seeds? By framing questions around social justice as fairness many NGOs, activists, and scholars are able to challenge the motivations of the powerful and offer alternative voices to the dominant narratives.

It is also interesting to note what the G8 leaders at the 2013 Summit identified as the three critical generic issues facing the world today, namely: advancing trade, ensuring tax compliance, and promoting greater transparency. They also stated that "promoting growth and jobs is our top priority" (UK Government, G8 Lough Erne 2013, 2). Such critical issues might also be framed within the concept of social justice as fairness, but unfortunately they might also be seen as more of the same neo-liberal agenda that has been highly damaging to food security such as promoting trade and export crops over localized food systems or community nutritional needs (Bello, 2009; Lappé 2008, 27–57).

The topic of jobs and work in food systems is taken up below to show how the focus on economic development and growth in food systems is inadequate—the mantra of economic growth at all costs does not necessarily include fairness and social justice in terms of either paying a living wage or enhancing the quality of jobs while achieving positive "growth" outcomes.

SOCIAL JUSTICE AS FAIRNESS IN FOOD— A BROADER CONTEXT

Trying to cut through the complexity of challenges facing the global food system is a daunting task, especially when it comes to providing workable solutions. A unique attempt at getting to grips with such a task in relation to fairness was made by the UK's Food and Fairness Inquiry formally launched in 2009 by the UK charity the Food Ethics Council (FEC 2010). The FEC's Food and Fairness Inquiry set out to investigate why and in which ways the problem of social justice is being downplayed in food policy debates. All too often the FEC saw these debates tending toward a focus on economic and environmental issues at the expense of the social. The Inquiry called upon expert witnesses to provide oral evidence in a series of hearings and received more than 100 pieces of written evidence from across different food sector interests.

The Inquiry tackled both UK and international issues of fairness. In assessing the written and oral evidence from experts in the well-fed country of the UK, Helen Browning, chair of the Inquiry, was moved to write in the foreword to the Inquiry's final report: "The sheer scale of unfairness across all aspects of the food system demands urgent attention in its own right. We also saw how a fairer food system is a prerequisite for meeting our wider sustainability and health goals" (FEC 2010, 7).

The Inquiry provides a useful starting point to examine in greater depth a more applied or practice-based approach to the notion of fairness in food systems. To this end the Inquiry adopted a framework for social justice that embraced three core topics which are useful to detail here. The first was what it called "equality of outcomes (fair shares)" which aims to capture how the food system distributes gains and burdens among different people. The second part of the Inquiry framework described fairness in terms of "equality of opportunity (fair play)" in that everyone had equal access to the means to bring about favorable or desired outcomes. The final strand was fairness as "autonomy and voice (fair say)" where the Inquiry sought to explore the process and involvement of people in the decisions that affect how they lead their lives with respect to food systems so they are able to have a meaningful voice in the process of developing food policies and a say in how to build their long-term food security (FEC 2010, 31–32).

The Food and Fairness Inquiry was wide-ranging and its final report presented a large number of recommendations and key messages to address the complexity of the topics they covered. The Inquiry's findings can be seen as documenting the depth and breadth of unfairness in the food system. It is clear that enabling a socially just and fair food system is beyond the capacity of individuals, consumers, or single companies. This then puts a lot of emphasis on the need for a public response that must manifest itself through mechanisms of governance to address the structural roots of unfairness in food systems. A key challenge in achieving this will be how to articulate such a "public voice" and how this is used to shape food policy and food politics to implement social change.

The Inquiry report does bring attention to the notion of "responsibilities" for government, business, and civil society. In the latter case, as food citizens, we are urged to do our share through our consumption choices by making purchases that can cause the changes required to bring about social justice as fairness. In short, the Inquiry seems to be suggesting that the fight for social justice as fairness in the food system will be a long and continuing struggle, but it is not clear how our respective responsibilities will need to be played out. In other words: Can we "eat" our way to social justice through buying habits alone?

With regards to individual consumption the Inquiry identified paths forward which might prove difficult and painful for many, including rich world consumers if they have to accept higher food prices or adopt consumption behaviors that reflect the full social and environmental costs of production—often referred to in economics as "externalities" which in the case of food might be the "external" costs of, say, water pollution from the application of agri-chemicals or the health care costs brought about as a result of poor diet. Some big picture structural challenges, including accounting for social and environmental costs in our food system, are explored in more detail below as well as examples of broad-based responses to address these policy issues in practice.

SOCIAL JUSTICE AS FAIRNESS IN GLOBAL FARMING

It can be very problematic to attempt to define what a "farm" is given the diversity of agricultural, food, and non-food production enterprises that utilize land for production and there is a tendency among some to talk about "farming systems" instead. Agriculture has been defined as the cultivation of land and a farm as an area of land used for growing crops and keeping animals to provide food and the buildings associated with it (DEFRA 2010). Even though definitions may appear to make clear what agriculture and farming are, when the terms "farming" and "agriculture" are used as generic terms there is the need for care in explaining what is actually being talked about and what kind of agriculture or farming are being indicated, as terminology can have profound implications when it comes to understanding and applying social justice as fairness. Much is made of the need to keep on increasing agricultural productivity and enhancing efficiencies to feed the world and to use selected scientific tools, such as genetic engineering, to address food security and food system sustainability (Mazoyer and Roudart 2006). Yet this refers to a very specific type of farming or agricultural system, often applying the tools and technologies of industrial farming which in itself raises many concerns about animal welfare, negative impacts on agricultural biodiversity, environmental damage, and the reduction of ecosystem services, let alone concerns about social justice as fairness.

Long before the environmental realities of industrial farming were properly understood, seminal works such as *Silent Spring* by Rachel Carson (1962), and *Animal Machines* by Ruth Harrison (1964), were sounding the alarm about the threats to environment sustainability, species preservation, and animal welfare presented by industrial farming; and hence the entailed issues of justice. Although much progress has been made in improving animal welfare in industrial agriculture systems, for example through the work of the Farm Animal Welfare Council in the UK and its development of the "Five Freedoms" defining the welfare needs of farmed animals, there can be no doubt that industrial agriculture, among other economic activities, has caused and is causing significant environmental degradation and loss of species. This is confirmed in reports such as those of the Millenium Ecosystem Assessment (World Resources Institute, 2005) and the investigation into Ecosystems and Human Well-Being. Although not covered here, the harms suffered by farmed animals for human benefit represent issues of justice as fairness and have been explored by numerous thinkers (see for example Regan 2004; Singer 1995). The harms to the environment also represent issues of justice, but in this context such issues are more difficult to frame, though a number of environmental ethicists have risen to the challenge (Rolston 1987).

In spite of the undoubted economic and political might that the combined forces of industrial agriculture represent and their apparent value to world food production, industrial agriculture and its associated agri-food supply chains produce only 30 percent of the world's food. Smallholder agriculture and food producers still account for around 70 percent of the world's food production. Breaking this figure down this includes 50 percent of the world's cultivated foods being produced by smallholders/peasants, another 12.5 percent still coming from hunting/gathering, and a further 7.5 percent derived from urban food produced by city dwelling peasants (ETC Group 2009, 1).

In terms of the total labor force employed in agriculture again we need care about who are the food and agricultural workers and their significance to the wider economy. In 2000 just 2.1 percent of the working population was employed in agriculture in the United States and 4.3 percent in the European Union (for 15 Member States at the time). By way of contrast in the same year, in countries such as India and Africa around 60 percent of their economically active population was growing food. In transition economies the figures were still substantial but declining, for example, 16.5 percent in Brazil, 21.5 percent in Mexico, and about half of China's work force was still engaged in agriculture (Bernstein 2010, 2). Part of the ongoing debate and struggle over the future of the global food system is whether industrial agriculture and big business will feed the world or if the millions of smallholders can be mobilized to produce more food, and what should the balance should between such "farming systems" be?

The distribution of agriculture and food producers that these figures suggest would seem to indicate that very different strategies and policies are needed to address wider issues of social justice and fairness in ensuring the world's ability to feed itself sustainably. Such market, business, and employment structures are not adequately integrated into many policy responses to the problems facing the global food system as illustrated by the earlier example of the G8 New Alliance for Nutrition and Food Security.

The minimum necessary social conditions for farming are access to land, labor, tools, and seeds and it is by nature a very localized activity and way of life. The industrial agricultural sector, on the other hand, has emerged in conjunction with other modern industrial sectors and technologies, utilizing very specialized services such as plant and animal science, post-harvest processing, sophisticated logistics and marketing with significant reliance on commodity production and markets and the achievement of economies of scale (Bernstein 2010; Mazoyer and Roudart 2006). A consequence of the shift from farming to industrial agriculture has been the marginalization of many smallholders and small-scale food industry workers.

In the West this has resulted in a substantial loss in the number of farms, especially family farms, as they have become unviable in the face of globalized, capital-intensive commodity production often supported by large sums of taxpayers' money through government policies that divert public monies through subsidies and other support measures to enable large-scale industrialization to become a reality. Even food aid policies to developing countries were devised as part of this government support for large-scale rich-world industrial agriculture monocultures (Friedmann 1993). In many poorer countries an imposed shift from smallholder farming to agriculture for export markets has had a devastating impact on many smallholder farming communities and other localized food producers and economies (Bello 2009).

GRASSROOTS RESPONSES TO INDUSTRIAL AGRICULTURE

In the face of dominant political narratives and the concentration of power among corporate players in the global food system a number of grassroots movements have emerged to challenge these forces, often grounded in narratives of social justice and fairness. An important social justice movement in this respect is La Via Campesina, which has sought to reassert the role of "peasant" farming and has developed the powerful concept of "food sovereignty" as an alternative to that of industrial agri-business. La Via Campesina grew from grassroots activism from the early 1990s (it was officially founded in 1993) to a position in which it is a movement that embraces 200 million people across the globe under its "food sovereignty" umbrella. La Via Campesina includes small-scale producers, fisherfolk, women, youth, the landless, migrants, indigenous peoples, and farm and food workers (Rosset et al. 2011).

The concept of "food sovereignty" was launched at the 1996 World Food Summit in Rome and goes further than traditional concepts of food security to not only include issues of access and affordability of food, but also questions who has power and control over the resources to produce food. The concept aims to ensure that food is culturally appropriate and is produced using ecological and sustainable methods. Importantly the movement fights to ensure that people have the right to define and own their food and agricultural systems. It demands to put those who produce, distribute, and consume food at the heart of global food systems and policies rather than the demands of markets and corporations (Pimbert 2009).

In its 2013 meeting held in Jakarta, La Via Campesina called for rural and urban organizations and social movements to transform and build a new society based on food sovereignty and justice. The method of agroecology pioneered in Cuba, but extending much more widely, is the preferred method put forward as an alternative to industrial agriculture methods. Agroecology is practiced as an ecologically based alternative and although definitions vary, it is seen as a system that applies a set of ecological principles drawn from biology and is knowledge intensive, often building on traditions going back many generations (Rosset et al. 2011).

Social justice and fairness movements such as those caught under the broad La Via Campesina canopy illustrate the fundamental differences in the narratives pursuing social justice as fairness in global food systems. This includes the global private sector partnerships with global agri-business corporations favored by the G8 leaders at one extreme and at the other end, the food sovereignty movement that explicitly rejects the food capitalism which is characterized by aggressive flows of financial and speculative capital into industrial agriculture, land, and nature (Holt-Gimenez 2009; La Via Campesina 2013).

SOCIAL JUSTICE AS FAIRNESS AND FOOD WORKERS

A neglected and difficult area for dialogue in the world of food politics is that of ensuring social justice and fairness for the workers who grow and produce food, whether they are smallholder producers, especially those who rely on trade in global markets, or wage laborers or workers on plantations, or in food factories and processing plants, as well as those in the retail and food-service sectors. This section uses both developing and developed world examples to explore the working conditions of food workers and shows that this is a topic that cuts across food geographies. The issue becomes much more complex when it involves the many workers in poor, economically underdeveloped countries who produce food (and non-food products) for wealthy consumers in economically developed countries.

The global food supply system allows products such as "fresh" vegetables (and flowers) to be produced in Africa and flown daily to European supermarkets, and seafood and chicken prepared in Southeast Asian countries for consumption in Europe and the United States. In a sense this kind of business is an extension of the more familiar trade in commodities between the rich and poor countries of the world, such as that involving sugar, tea, coffee, cocoa, and bananas that has occurred for generations. Indeed the transfer and types of foods produced in low-income countries for rich-consumer food markets is truly global and ubiquitous.

A classic example in food studies is to be found with respect to the fishing and seafood industries. John Wilkinson, in a seminal paper, documents the impacts of different factors such as the introduction of technologies or new production methods, in the global fish value chain and how this has transformed the market relationships between developed and developing world markets (Wilkinson 2006). He shows that over a 20 year period from the 1970s onward trade flows for fish as food had completely reversed with the developed world shifting from being a net exporter of fish in 1973 to a substantial net importer by 1997 (Wilkinson 2006, 141). This resulted in the net revenue from fish exports by developing countries becoming more than the net value of their rice, coffee, tea, sugar, and banana exports combined. Hence developed world consumption patterns, often driven by supermarket and food service marketing practices, have transformed global fish and seafood geographies, which has also resulted in serious environmental challenges including the over-exploitation of fish stocks. This has also affected the diets of people in developing countries who have traditionally relied on fish as an important source of dietary protein.

"FAIRNESS" AND FOOD WORKERS IN THE GLOBAL FOOD SYSTEM

We now turn to describe some of the specific challenges facing workers producing food and agricultural products with respect to social justice as fairness as they engage in the global food system. There is one caveat to what follows: because of the scale and diversity of global food markets this section can only highlight a small number of selected case studies as examples of research into the working conditions of food workers. It should be noted around 2.5 billion people worldwide are dependent on agriculture for their livelihoods (Vorley 2003). In making the selection of case studies to highlight we focus on examples of the work of NGOs or worker organizations active in recent years in trying to address wages, working conditions, and fairness for food workers and communities. But it must be emphasized these cases are simply an ad hoc selection from an endemic problem within the global food system.

There are also wider structural changes to agri-food supply chains that impact working conditions and food workers which are not discussed in detail here. For example, Best and Mamic (2008), writing about global agri-food supply chains for fruit and vegetable value chains, demonstrate the impact on workers of key modern trends such as value chains becoming buyer-driven, the imposition of tough quality standards by major retailers, increasing concentration at all stages of the supply chain, and the increased risks and costs of highly integrated value chains to producers. They cite that such trends—while having the potential for some benefits for workers and smallholders such as increased export income from horticultural products—also carry serious risk for workers not only through incomes being squeezed but by increasing work intensity and producers cutting to more flexible employment arrangements to meet buyer demands (Best and Mamic 2008).

THE FAIRTRADE MOVEMENT

There is a positive story about fairness and food workers involved in the supply of food from the developing world to the food markets in developed countries and this is to be found in the growth and success of the Fairtrade labeling movement. Fairtrade labeling schemes were founded to reform global trade in favor of social justice as fairness and are playing an important role in helping to inform consumers so that they can exercise ethical choices in their food buying behaviors.

The first Fairtrade label, called Max Havelaar, was launched in 1988 in the Netherlands and was used on coffee from Mexico sold through Dutch supermarkets. From this beginning the labeling concept has spread to many Western countries, sometimes under the Max Havelaar label, but also in other versions such as Transfair and the Fairtrade Mark. In 1997 the Fairtrade Labelling Organizations International (FLO) was set up in Bonn, Germany to unite the labeling initiatives under one umbrella and to harmonize such worldwide standards and certification.

Put simply, the scheme works by paying producers in developing countries a "fair" price for their products. This is especially important for export crops like coffee and cocoa which are subject to volatile global markets and are controlled by major processing corporations. The fair price paid to producers guarantees an economically sustainable price for production, regardless of how low world prices might be. It also pays the market price if it goes beyond the set "fair" price. The labeling scheme sets standards that Fairtrade producers must adhere to in order to ensure certification and there is a Fairtrade "premium" that can be earned which goes into a communal fund for workers and farmers to use to improve their social, economic, and environmental conditions.

The Fairtrade movement model engages directly with consumers through their buying behaviors to make a difference for producers. The success of engaging consumers through the different labeling schemes is evident in the way it connects to large numbers of developing world producers: the numbers of farmers and workers participating in Fairtrade grew to 1.24 million by the end of 2011 through 991 Fairtrade producer organizations. Around 60 percent of the farmers and workers in the Fairtrade system are located in Africa and the Middle East (Fairtrade Labelling Organizations 2012). Additionally, Fairtrade sales revenues and Fairtrade Premium receipts continued to grow despite the global recession. Between 2009/10 and 2010/11 these increased by 22 percent and 19 percent respectively to EUR 673 million and EUR 61 million. Volumes of certain products also rose significantly during this period, particularly for cocoa and sugar (Fairtrade Labelling Organizations 2012).

In Fairtrade International's 2013–15 Strategic Framework it is recognized that even though the Fairtrade labeling movement is pioneering in its objectives and has a model that works, this needs to be scaled up and taken much further. One area highlighted was that there is still much to be done to provide a living wage for workers as distinct from the separate challenges faced by smallholders. This is especially so in relation to bananas, tea, and flowers, and producer businesses need to work with the international labor movement to negotiate improved terms of employment.

THE WAGES OF TEA WORKERS

An example of this need to negotiate improved terms of employment for workers and the complexity of the issues is shown by research undertaken on wages in the tea industry by the Ethical Tea Partnership (whose members include many of the world's leading tea companies) and the development NGO Oxfam (Ethical Tea Partnership and Oxfam 2013). This study points out that while statutory minimum wages are established in 90 percent of countries in many cases wages paid to workers fail to comply with statutory requirements. Where there is compliance, minimum wages may not meet the basic needs of workers and their families.

In this research the workers' wages on both certified estates (such as Fairtrade, Rainforest Alliance, and UTZ Certified) and non-certified estate were assessed (that is, waged workers on tea estates, as opposed to smallholders). In the tea industry "wages" are often made up of a paid wage and the provision of in-kind benefits such as food, fuel, and accommodation. Through three case studies in West Java (Indonesia), Malawi (Africa), and Assam (India) the research team calculated a total wage based on adding cash wages and converting in-kind benefits to a cash value.

The conclusions of the research make difficult reading for certifying bodies such as Fairtrade, since one of the major findings was that wages of tea workers were found to be no higher on certified estates than on those that were not certified. The report says this is because for the wages element of certification, Fairtrade standards only required that wages do not fall below the legal minimum. This issue is a problem faced by many low-paid food workers (and for workers in other industries as well) in that the legal minimum wage falls short of providing a "living wage."

In theory minimum wages are set to enable workers to provide basic needs for themselves and their families, but these are often below that needed for a "living wage." One calculation, based on other industries, found the gap between a minimum wage and a "living wage" in countries such as Bangladesh and India to be 62 percent and 47 percent respectively. However, there is no generally agreed-upon method of calculating a "living wage," even though it can be defined as a low cost but acceptable family budget; definitions also vary from country to country.

The United Nations (1948) states among other things in Article 23 of the Universal Declaration of Human Rights that "Everyone who works has the right to just and favourable remuneration ensuring for himself and for his family an existence worthy of human dignity." Manifesting this objective in practical terms is tricky and it is likely to be subject to political relativism, even so, campaigners argue that the implementation of living wage regulations is a means toward reducing poverty levels.

The Ethical Tea Partnership and Oxfam researchers found that while total benefits for tea workers, who are also mainly women, were above the applicable national poverty line (in Assam, West Java, and Malawi), in all three regions the poverty line is below the World Bank definition of extreme poverty of US$1.25 a day in local prices at the time of the study. The researchers therefore concluded that certification is no guarantee that workers' wages will meet their households' basic needs. But it must be pointed out—as the researchers do—that assessing the wages of tea workers is complex and much more work is needed to make an accurate assessment (Ethical Tea Partnership and Oxfam 2013).

In fact this is one of the report's three major recommendations. The report suggests that more work is needed involving tea companies, standards bodies (such as Fairtrade), and auditing firms to ensure consistency of approaches in assessing and auditing wages to see that they meet basic household needs. Related to this the researchers also recommend improving the understanding and measurement of wages in the tea sector and improving the dialogue about wages between different stakeholder groups, including trade unions.

A GLOBALIZED PROBLEM OF FOOD WORKING CONDITIONS

Tea is not an isolated example. A study, again produced by Oxfam (Oxfam and IPL 2013), but this time in conjunction with a private business, International Procurement and Logistics (IPL), looked into the export produce sector in Kenya specifically in relation to the production of beans and flowers. The study found that wages were insufficient to enable a decent standard of living for workers and their dependents.

This study, like the tea study, actively engages business in tackling what at face value are hugely problematic issues for them, including wage levels and their competitiveness in international markets. It is interesting to note that IPL is the largest importer of fresh produce into the UK and is owned by the UK's second largest supermarket ASDA (which in turn is owned by Walmart, the world's largest retailer). In the report, IPL writes that it is committed to focusing on a number of areas identified by the research. Their responses include partnering with IPL suppliers to build strategies that achieve improved living standards for workers.

The managing director of IPL is quoted as saying: " . . . We have taken important learning from this work and are committed to ensuring that the value that we create is shared across our supply chain, especially benefitting the standards of living for farm and packhouse workers and the livelihoods of small holders" (Oxfam and IPL 2013, 2).

Again and again NGOs or activist groups point to the unfairness and unjust working conditions of global food supply chains. However, NGOs are increasingly engaging with the businesses they spotlight to work with them to improve conditions. NGOs recognize that having businesses close factories or plantations or relocating them is no help to already struggling workers.

The challenge of securing social justice as fairness in terms of worker rights and ensuring environmental sustainability is evident in numerous industries including the shrimp processing industry. In June 2013, for example, the activist NGO, International Labor Rights Forum, published a brief report on a shrimp processing company based in Thailand that is a long-time supplier to Walmart, which is perhaps unsurprisingly the largest retailer of shrimp in the United States. The report alleged this shrimp processing company used underage workers, practiced the nonpayment of wages, and charged excessive fees for work permits (International Labor Rights Forum 2013).

This report brings to attention one of the hidden aspects of social injustice in food supply chains. That is the large reliance on migrant labor to produce our food. In this case the Thai company was using almost entirely migrant labor from Burma, Cambodia, and Laos.

MIGRANT WORKERS IN AGRI-FOOD SUPPLY CHAINS

Many agri-food supply chains have become reliant of migrant labor to grow, harvest, or process food. It is a global problem and one that rarely reaches wider consumer recognition or even sympathy. This dependency on migrant labor is an issue for both the developed and developing world. Apart from the transport of food materials and products from regions where production methods challenge the notion of justice as fairness, the global food system and market competitiveness encourage the migration and use of people to enable the operation of low-cost production systems.

This practice as a social and political issue was crystalized in 2004 in the UK with the Morcambe Bay cockle pickers disaster. At least twenty-three Chinese workers, all illegal immigrants to the UK, were drowned while collecting cockles (shellfish) from the Morcambe Bay beach at low tide (HSE 2006). The incident brought into being a new agency The Gangmasters Licensing Authority and legislation (the Gangmasters [Licensing] Act 2004) the function of which are to ensure the safety and to protect the rights of temporary and migrant laborers. The Gangmasters Licensing Authority's mission is to prevent worker exploitation, protect vulnerable people, and deal with unlicensed/criminal activity and ensure that those licensed to operate under the law actually do so (GLA 2013). This mission coheres with the concept of justice as fairness in the food supply system and the existence of the Gangmasters Licensing Authority is further evidence that without such agencies or initiatives such as Fairtrade Labelling, the rights of the weakest actors within the food system would count for nought. In essence, the weakest actors are made the means to the ends of the strongest, in contradiction of the Kantian principle that people should be made ends in themselves and not solely the means to ends (Kant 2007).

The use of migrant workers is also a growing issue for the food industry as was highlighted, briefly, in the UK during 2013. When the British government acted to tighten immigration rules for the country as a whole, a side-effect of its policy quickly became apparent when food businesses expressed concerns that tighter immigration policies could restrict seasonal migrant labor, which has become essential to harvesting the UK's seasonal vegetable and fruit crops.

The government minister responsible was warned this might lead to a rise in labor costs and a 10–15 percent rise in supermarket prices (Travis 2013). The problem arose when the British government proposed the closure of the UK's seasonal agricultural workers scheme at the end of 2013 which had allowed an annual quota of 21,250 Bulgarian and Romanian workers to come to Britain for a maximum of six months. These workers account for a third of Britain's seasonal agricultural workforce. The scheme was seen as crucial for the supply of strawberries, salad, apples, and other soft fruit to UK supermarkets (Travis 2013).

But the problem of migrant and low paid labor in Britain's food industry is not a recent occurrence. The UK has a highly concentrated food retail sector and a competitive "low price" consumer market. As a result the supermarkets are accused of passing cost-savings down their supply chains. One consequence of this is a restructuring of labor markets including the use of migrant workers who are often employed as low-paid, temporary pickers, packers, and processors in food and agricultural production.

The vulnerability of migrant workers in food and agricultural business is rarely documented so a report published in 2009 by the UK's Ecumenical Council For Corporate Responsibility (ECCR 2009) is something of a rare insight. The EECR is a church-based investor coalition working for economic justice, environmental stewardship, and corporate and investor responsibility. In their report *Vulnerable Migrant Workers: The Responsibility of Business*, the precarious life of migrant workers is documented in areas of the UK domestic economy where low-skilled flexible labor is concentrated including in care, cleaning, construction, hospitality, and catering, as well as food production, manufacturing, and retailing.

The research focused on the food sector in the UK and Ireland and compared at the time of the research the policies and practices of nine prominent food production, manufacturing, and supermarket companies toward migrant workers, particularly in their supply chains. The companies investigated at the time were: Associated British Foods, Greencore Group, Kerry Group, Morrisons, Northern Foods, Premier Foods, Sainsbury's, Tesco, and Unilever.

The report found that few of these food companies are explicit about the potential vulnerability of migrant workers or the additional support they might need. Although the report said most recognize some responsibility for workers in their supply chains, few appear to have established considerations about labor conditions into their core business practices.

The study detailed a wide range of findings, but generally found that the monitoring of labor conditions throughout the supply chain was weak among the companies and at times there was a failure to translate a company's stated labor policy into practice. In the case of three companies the report finds evidence of exploitation of migrant workers in their supply chains. Among a series of recommendations, the report highlighted the need for companies to: recognize the potential vulnerability of migrant labor, temporary and agency workers; implement effective codes of conduct for suppliers; increase awareness of rights among workers; and strengthen monitoring and audits.

ECCR researcher Sunniva Taylor wrote in the report: "Many companies' profits benefit from the use of flexible labor in the supply chain. Companies and investors therefore have a moral responsibility to reduce the incidence of vulnerable work throughout their business and supply chain."

WORKING CONDITIONS OF TOMATO PICKERS IN THE UNITED STATES

While it might be assumed many of the more disgraceful examples of food and agriculture worker exploitation are found in the developing world, it would be wrong to assume this is a simple "developing" versus "developed" world issue as the examples in the next section illustrate.

In the Disneyworld and retirement paradise of Florida, USA, is to be found one of the more prominent examples of farmworker exploitation and, in the most extreme cases, modern-day slavery. This has led to a ground-breaking fair food campaign organized by the Coalition of Immokalee Workers (CIW) who harvest tomatoes for the US retail food industry.

Florida and California are the two largest producers of tomatoes in the United States (producing around 940 million pounds in each state in 2012) which represents two-thirds of US fresh tomato commercial acreage (USDA 2013). Fresh tomatoes from Florida go to major food corporations such as fast food groups and large retailers. To supply these corporations, Florida tomato harvesters are paid by the "piece," typically 50 US cents for every 32 lb bucket, which leads to poverty-level wages and workers being subjected to poor working and living conditions (such as long hours and overcrowding).

The origins of the CIW is as a community-based organization of mainly Latino, Mayan Indian, and Haitian immigrants working in low-wage jobs throughout the state of Florida including harvesting Florida's tomatoes. CIW began organizing in 1993 and through a series of hard fought campaigns (including a hunger strike and a 200-mile march) by 1998 they had won a 13 to 25 percent industry-wide pay raise (but this still meant average wages were below the US poverty level). The CIW campaigns targeted the customers of the Florida tomato corporations including the food service and retail giants buying Florida tomatoes.

In 2001 the CIW began its Campaign for Fair Food and launched a national farmworker boycott of a major fast-food company, Taco Bell, calling on the company to take responsibility for human rights abuses where its produce is grown and picked. Over a period of four years the Taco Bell boycott gained support from student, religious, labor, and community groups that culminated in March 2005 with Taco Bell agreeing to improve wages and working conditions for the Florida tomato pickers in its supply chain.

From this campaign an Alliance for Fair Food was created and other corporations were pressured to improve their supply chain practices with respect to tomatoes. In April 2007, after a two-year campaign, McDonald's and the CIW reached a similar and expanded agreement to that with Taco Bell. Other corporations have subsequently followed such as Burger King, Whole Foods Market, and Subway in 2008. In 2009–2010 agreements were made with food service providers/caterers Bon Appetit Management Co. (part of Compass Group), Aramark, and Sodexo.

Following a 2010 agreement with the Florida Tomato Growers Exchange, the CIW's Fair Food Principles were extended to 90 percent of the Florida tomato industry. The principles include a code of conduct, a cooperative complaint resolution system, a participatory health and safety program, and a worker-to-worker education process. From this the CIW's Fair Food Program was created together with the Fair Food Standards Council as an independent auditing and oversight body. In 2012 a further agreement was made with food retailer Trader Joe's and in October of the same year Chipotle Mexican Grill also signed up to the Fair Food Program (following a six-year campaign). But the major supermarkets (except Whole Foods and Trader Joe's) have yet to join the Fair Food Program at the time of writing. As CIW state this is: "the one remaining obstacle in the way of long-awaited, sustainable change in the fields" (CIW 2013).

The CIW campaigning work has now been widely recognized through being presented with a number of prestigious social justice awards for its innovative work on food justice and fairness. CIW continues to extend its campaigning work for fair food and food justice for food and agriculture workers.

CONCLUSION: THE IMPLICATIONS OF *SOCIAL JUSTICE AS FAIRNESS* FOR THE GLOBAL FOOD SYSTEM

The focus here has been on NGOs and food movements that are active in bringing about structural change in food systems, mainly drawing on examples of actions aimed at improving living and working conditions for the men, women, and children who grow, harvest, and produce agricultural and food products in the agri-food supply chains of major food corporations. These examples highlight the ongoing and significant challenges that remain in ensuring "living wages" for workers and producers often caught in supply chains starting from poor countries, but leading to food markets in wealthy, developed countries.

It is interesting to note that in many of the cases cited it is NGOs or activist groups working in conjunction with food businesses who together are investigating how to address poor working conditions and labor practices in supply chains. In this manner major stakeholders are working to redefine the duties, benefits, and responsibilities within food production which would fit with Rawls' social justice as fairness framework. However, it would be wrong to suggest that poor working conditions and wages in food agri-food supply chains are being widely addressed—the examples reported here are often the exception—and this is an area of on-going conflict and dispute. But by adopting more formally a "social justice as fairness" framework this could serve as a means to speed-up and scale-up the dialogue and find the resolve to tackle this difficult and contentious area that might engage audiences in a process of change from consumers, policy-makers to business and activist groups as well as workers and their communities.

There is a pressing need to widen the debate about work and working conditions of those who produce our food from the field to the retail and food service sector and to develop evidence on the consequences of not addressing this element of food supply chains with respect to the use of natural resources, sustainability, and human health and well-being.

This will require difficult debates around the politics of food not least because of the endemic nature of inequalities and unfairness in global food systems. There is a structural chasm at the heart of agri-food supply chains that goes beyond simply the developed world-developing world dichotomies of political rhetoric around food security or "feed the world" policies. A more detailed analysis of this structural chasm is not possible here and is situated in the nature of global food capitalism itself—a topic extensively documented (see for example, Bello 2009, Fine et al. 1996, McMichael 2009, Oosterveer and Sonnenfeld 2012, Patel 2007, Weis 2007).

In re-framing challenges facing global food systems through social justice as fairness new perspectives on the structures of food in society can be set out and solutions can be developed. Rawls' work suggests we need to develop a set of principles to achieve this that might define duties and benefits. In the selected examples documented in this chapter the size of this task is apparent. It would raise difficult and extremely far-reaching questions about how as individuals and societies we might need to interact and re-connect with our food sources to enable food for all that addresses both human health and environmental sustainability and the future security and sustainability of food production.

The escalating global food crisis and related issues such as climate change or the use of water, has the potential to bring about a tipping point—forcing us to confront how we feed ourselves and what it means to be part of humankind and yet at the same time seeing ourselves as part of our planet's global biodiversity. Implementing policies and business models built on social justice and fairness offers a means of enabling the future of food that is both fair and sustainable. But whether this is possible or the political will is there, not least in reforming the structure of the global food system or to even developing food policies and implementing them to enable meaningful and long-term change to ensure a fair distribution of social benefits, currently remains a moot point.

REFERENCES

Altieri, Miguel A. 1995. *Agroecology: The Science of Sustainable Agriculture*. Boulder: Westview Press.

Bello, Walden. 2009. *The Food Wars*. Brooklyn, NY: Verso.

Bernstein, Henry. 2010. *Class Dynamics of Agrarian Change*. Halifax and Winnipeg: Fernwood Publishing.

Best, Sarah and Ivanka Mamic. 2008. *Global Agri-food Chains: Employment and Social Issues in Fresh Fruit and Vegetables*. Employment Working Paper No. 20. Geneva: International Labour Office.

Carson, Rachel. 1962. *Silent Spring*. Boston: Houghton and Mifflin.

Cecchini, Michele, Franco Sassi, Jeremy A. Lauer, Yong Y. Lee, Veronica Guajardo-Barron, and Daniel Chisholm. 2010. "Tackling of Unhealthy Diets, Physical Inactivity, and Obesity: Health Effects and Cost-effectiveness." *The Lancet* 376: 1775–84.

CIW. 2013. This section is written using the resources available at the Coalition of Immokalee Workers (CIW) website. Accessed July 9, 2013. http://www.ciw-online.org.

Clapp, Jennifer. 2012. *Food*. Cambridge: Polity Press.

De Schutter, Olivier. 2013. *Report of the Special Rapporteur on the Right to Food. United Nations General Assembly*. Human Rights Council, 22nd Session, Agenda item 3. A/HRC/22/50/Add.3. Geneva.

DEFRA. 2010. *Definition of Terms Used in Farm Business Management*. London: Department for the Environment, Food and Rural Affairs.

DFID. 2013. *New Alliance for Food Security and Nutrition. 2013 Progress Report Summary*. London: Department for International Development (DFID).

ECCR 2009. (The Ecumenical Council for Corporate Responsibility). *Vulnerable Migrant Workers: The Responsibility of Business*. Oxford: ECCR.

ETC Group. 2013. *Who Will Feed Us?* Ottawa, Canada: ETC Communique, No. 102, 2009. Accessed July 10, 2013. http://www.etcgroup.org/sites/www.etcgroup.org/files/ETC_Who_Will_Feed_Us..

Ethical Tea Partnership (ETP) and Oxfam. 2013. *Understanding Wage Issues in the Tea Industry: Report from a Multi-stakeholder Project*. London: ETP.

Fairtrade Foundation. 2013. "G8 Food Security Initiative Needs to Include Smallholder Farmers." *Fairtrade Foundation Press Release* June 9, 2013. Accessed June 20, 2013.http://www.fairtrade.org.uk/press_office/press_releases_and_statements/june_2013/

Fairtrade International. 2013. *Unlocking the Power of the Many: Fairtrade International's 2013–15 Strategic Framework*. Bonn: Germany.

Fairtrade Labelling Organizations International. 2012. *Monitoring the Scope and Benefits of Fairtrade*. Fourth Edition. Bonn, Germany: Fairtrade International.

FAO. 2013. *The State of Food and Agriculture*. Rome: Food and Agriculture Organization of the United Nations.

FEC (Food Ethics Council). 2010. *Food Justice: The Report of the Food and Fairness Inquiry*. Brighton: Food Ethics Council.

Fine, Ben, Michael Heasman, and Judith Wright. 1996.*Consumption in the Age of Affluence: The World of Food*. London: Routledge.

Foresight. 2011. *The Future of Food and Farming. Final Project Report*. London: Government Office for Science.

Friedmann, Harriet. 1993. "The Political Economy of Food: A Global Crisis," *New Left Review* 197: 29–57.

GLA. 2013. Gangmasters Licensing Authority. Accessed August 18, 2013. http://gla.defra.uk/Who-We-Are/Mission-Statement/.

Harrison, Ruth. 1964. *Animal Machines*. London: Vincent Stuart Publishers.

HM Government. 2013. "G8 Events: Hunger Summit. London: UK Government, 2013." Accessed July 9, 2013. https://www.gov.uk/government/news/g8–events.

Holt-Gimenez, Eric. 2009. "From Food Crisis to Food Sovereignty: The Challenge of Social Movements," *Monthly Review*, 61: 142–56.

HSE. 2006. "Cocklers Tragedy Highlights the Need for Safety Standards." *Health and Safety Executive Press Release.* March 24, 2006. Accessed August 18, 2013. http://www.hse.gov.uk/press/2006/c06005.htm.

IF Campaign. 2013.*Enough Food For Everyone: The Need for UK Action on Global Hunger*. Oxford: www.enoughfoodif.org.

International Labor Rights Forum. 2013.*Briefing Paper: The Walmart Effect: Child and Worker Rights Violations at Narong Seafood, Thailand's Model Shrimp Processing Factory*. Washington D.C.: International Labor Rights Forum.

Ionescu-Somers, Aileen and Ulrich Steger. 2008. *Business Logic for Sustainability: A Food and Beverage Perspective*. Basingstoke: Palgrave Macmillan.

Kant, Immanuel. 2007. *Critique of Pure Reason*. London: Penguin.

La Via Campesina. 2013. *The Jakarta Call. Call of the VI Conference of La Via Campesina, June 9–13, 2013*. Accessed July 17, 2013. http://viacampesina.org

Lang, Tim. 1997. "Going Public: Food Campaigns During the 1980s and Early 1990s." In *Nutrition in Britain: Science, Scientists and Politics in the Twentieth Century*, edited by David F. Smith, 238–260. London: Routledge.

Lang, Tim and Michael Heasman. 2004. *Food Wars: The Global Battle for Mouths, Minds and Markets*. London: Earthscan.

Lappé, Frances Moore. 2008. "World Hunger: Its Roots and Remedies." *A Sociology of Food & Nutrition. Third Edition*, edited by John Germov and Lauren Williams, 27–57. Melbourne: Oxford University Press.

McMichael, Philip. 2009. "A Food Regime Analysis of the 'World Food Crisis,'" *Journal of Agriculture and Human Values,* 26: 281–295.

Mazoyer, Marcel and Laurence Roudart. 2006. *A History of World Agriculture*. London: Earthscan.

Mintz, Sidney. 1985. *Sweetness and Power: The Place of Sugar in Modern History*. Harmondsworth: Penguin.

Monbiot, George. 2013. "Africa, let us help—just like in 1884," *The Guardian*, Monday June 10, 2013. Accessed June 10, 2013. http://guardian.co.uk/commentisfree/2013/ju/10/african-hunger-help-g8–grab/print.

Oosterveer, Peter, and David A. Sonnenfeld. 2012. *Food, Globalization and Sustainability*. London: Earthscan.

Oxfam and IPL (International Procurement and Logistics). 2013. "Exploring the Links Between International Business and Poverty Reduction: Bouquets and Beans from Kenya." *Oxfam Press Release May 15, 2013.* Accessed July 9, 2013. http://www.oxfam.org/en/grow/pressroom/pressrelease/2013–05–15/oxfam-and-ipl-release-joint-report-investigating-poverty-issues-supply-chain-kenya#sthash.d2gUMfql.dpuf

Patel, Raj. 2007. *Stuffed and Starved: Markets, Power and the Hidden Battle for the World Food System*. London: Portobello.

Pimbert, Michel. 2009. *Towards Food Sovereignty: Reclaiming Autonomous Food Systems*. London and Munich: CAFS, IIED and RCC.

Popkin, Barry. 2009. *The World is Fat: The Fads, Trends, Policies and Products that are Fattening the Human Race*. New York: Avery / Penguin.

Rawls, John. 1971. *A Theory of Justice. Revised Edition.* Cambridge, Massachusetts: Harvard University Press.

Rawls, John. 2001. *Justice as Fairness: A Restatement*. 2nd Edition. Edited by Kelly, E. Cambridge, MA: Harvard University Press.

Regan, Tom. 2004. *The Case for Animal Rights. Revised Edition*. Berkeley, CA: University of California Press.

Robinson, Ewan and John Humphrey. 2013. "How Much is the New Alliance Doing for Food Security and Nutrition?" Institute for Development Studies (IDS), University of Sussex,

UK, blog, 2013. Accessed July 9, 2011. http://www.globalisationanddevelopment.com/2013/06/how-much-is-new-alliance-doing-for-food.html

Rolston, Holmes. 1987. *Environmental Ethics: Duties and Values in the Natural World*. Philadelphia, PA: Temple University Press.

Rosset, Peter M., Braulio Machín Sosa, Adilén Maria Roque Jaime, and Dana Rocío Ávila Lozano. 2011. "The Campesino-to-Campesino Agroecology Movement of ANAP in Cuba: Social Process Methodology in the Construction of Sustainable Peasant Agriculture and Food Sovereignty," *The Journal of Peasant Studies* 38: 161–191.

Singer, Peter. 1995. *Animal Liberation. Second Edition*. London: Pimlico.

Travis, Alan. 2013. "Agricultural Workers from Ukraine May be Needed in Future, May Told." *The Guardian*, May 14, 2013. Accessed May 14, 2013. http://guardian.co.uk/uk/2013/may/14/agricultural-workers-ukraine-future-may/print

UK Government. 2013. "UK Presidency of G8." Accessed June 21, 2013. http://www.gov.uk/government/topical-events/g8–2013.

United Nations. 1948. *Universal Declaration of Human Rights,* 1948. Accessed August 18, 2013. http://www.un.org/en/documents/udhr/.

UNEP. 2009. *The Environmental Food Crisis: The Environment's Role in Averting Future Food Crises. A UNEP Rapid Response Assessment.* United Nations Environment Programme / GRID-Arendal Arendal, Norway.

USDA. 2013. "North American Fresh-Tomato Market, Economic Research Service." Accessed July 10, 2013. http://www.ers.usda.gov/topics/in-the-news/north-american-fresh-tomato-market.aspx.

Vorley, Brian. 2003. *Food Inc. Corporate Concentration from Farm to Consumer*. London: IIED and UK Food Group.

Weis, Tony. 2007. *The Global Economy: The Battle for the Future of Farming*. London: Zed Books.

Wilkinson, John. 2006. "Fish: A Global Value Chain on the Rocks." *Sociologia Ruralis* 46: 139–153.

World Resources Institute. 2005. *Millenium Ecosystem Assessment, Ecosystems and Human Well-Being: Synthesis*. Washington, DC: Island Press.

Zadek, Simon. 2001. *The Civil Corporation: The New Economy of Corporate Citizenship*. London: Earthscan.

Chapter Six

Challenging Labor

Working Conditions in the Electronics Industry

Marisol Sandoval and Kristina Areskog Bjurling

The growing importance and availability of electronics products has transformed the lives of people around the globe. According to estimates by the International Telecommunication Union (ITU), today one-third of the world's population is using the Internet, the global penetration of mobile phone subscriptions has reached 87 percent and 74 percent of all households in developed countries and 25 percent of households in developing countries own a computer (ITU 2011, 1–2). New information and communication technologies have the potential to connect people around the world, to facilitate communication and cooperation, to assist political protest and to foster participation as well as to alleviate work. However, at the same time the production of these electronics products often takes place under unacceptably burdensome conditions. This chapter aims to focus attention on the darker side of the electronics boom. It builds on the results of a number of empirical studies conducted by the European makeITfair project, which is presented below. In this chapter we provide insights into the working reality in the electronics manufacturing sector and point at specific challenges. Based on research results of the makeITfair project we argue that corporate self-regulation is unlikely to lead to sustainable improvements. By building a better understanding of the causes and effects of labor rights violations in the electronics production sector the project highlights the necessity for structural reforms. Fostering such long-term transformations requires raising awareness regarding labor rights, exposing corporate social irresponsibility, and increasing public pressure on corporations. This chapter makes an important contribution to that task.

In the following we will give an overview of market leading companies in the sector (section 1) and introduce the makeITfair project (section 2). In the next section we briefly describe some common characteristics of four major electronics production countries (section 3), before we provide more detailed evidence regarding several work-related problems in the electronics manufacturing sector (section 4). Finally, in the conclusion we point toward some starting points for improving the situation of workers (section 5).

DO ELECTRONICS COMPANIES MEET THEIR SOCIAL RESPONSIBILITIES?

The electronics industry is characterized by a great expansion. Consumers engage in ever-increasing consumption of new electronic devices such as laptops, mp3 players, smart phones, and iPads. The production and sale of electronic products is a profitable business sector. However, it is also very competitive and fast moving, where labels can win and lose market share rapidly. In 2011, five electronics companies were among the 100 biggest public companies in the world: Apple (ranked 22), Samsung Electronics (ranked 26), Hewlett Packard (ranked 67), Intel (ranked 85), and Cisco (ranked 91) (Forbes 2012). As figure 6.1 shows, Apple has taken the lead. Between 2005 and 2011 Apple's annual profits grew by 62 percent.

The major electronics companies acknowledge that the protection of labor rights in their supply chain is part of their corporate social responsibility (CSR). In their CSR communications they highlight that they are committed to protecting workers' rights in their supply chain. Apple, for example, in its latest "Supplier Responsibility Report" writes: "We require that our suppliers provide safe working conditions, treat workers with dignity and respect, and use environmentally responsible manufacturing processes wherever Apple products are made" (Apple 2012, 3). Similarly, HP makes a strong commitment to the protection of workers' rights in its supply chain: "As our supply chain develops, our priorities remain constant: to protect workers' rights and dignity, ensure strong health and safety standards, reduce environmental impacts, and uphold high standards of business ethics" (HP 2011). Cisco commits to "embedding sustainability into routine business practices at every stage of the value chain product lifecycle" (Cisco 2011, A6), while Samsung promises to "address the social issues throughout the supply chain." Likewise Intel highlights that it "is working to continuously improve transparency and promote corporate responsibility throughout the global electronics supply chain" (Intel 2010, 79). Through these public statements, the companies indicate that they are committed to socially and environmentally responsible practices in their supply chains.

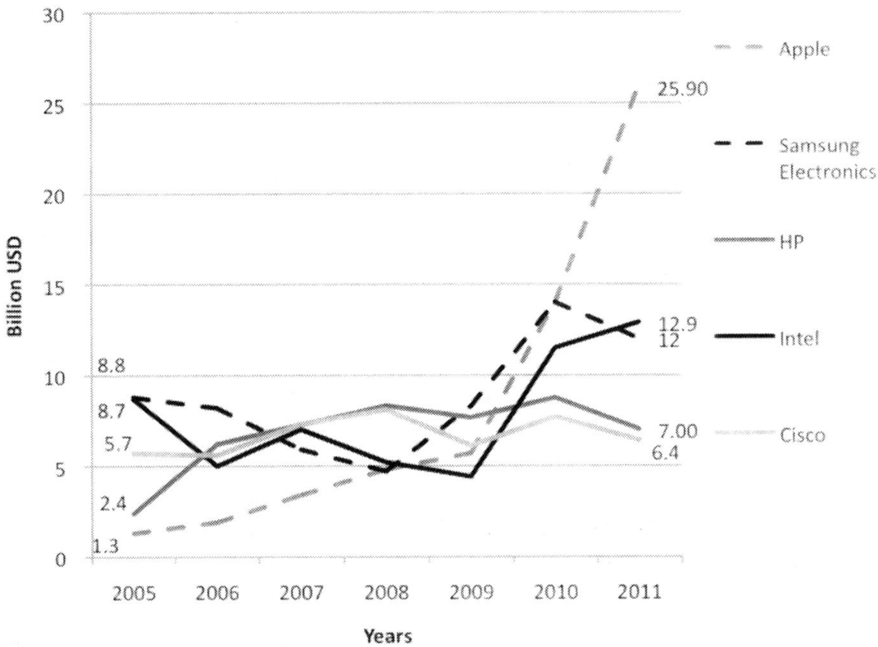

Figure 6.1. Profits of the five largest electronics companies, 2005–2011. Source: Apple (2012), HP (2012), Samsung (2012), and Cisco (2012).

However, CSR has often been criticized as being mainly a marketing tool that changes corporate rhetoric but does not affect actual business practices. Critics stress that CSR obscures the negative effects of corporate operations and functions as a marketing strategy that does not challenge the imperative of profit maximization and leaves the core business model untouched (Sklair and Miller 2010, 492; Hanlon and Fleming 2009, 938; Boje 2008, 8, 19; Roberts 2003, 257; Hanlon 2008, 159; Shamir 2004, 684; Banerjee 2008, 64). These critics fear that CSR remains limited to a rhetorical strategy and "that all this talk of ethics is just that—talk" (Roberts 2003, 250). Sklair and Miller for example argue that CSR might be used as "a deliberate strategy to mystify and obscure the reality of capitalist globalization" (2010, 492). Similarly Hanlon and Fleming point out that CSR can function as "an ideological 'smoke screen' designed to either soften the image of firms engrossed in the rampant pursuit of profit [. . .] or a way to deflect attention away from an unsavoury core business model" (2009, 938). Boje describes CSR as a "shield to hide unethical practice" (2008, 8). In order to hold companies accountable and review whether they comply with their strategies and goals, independent, critical counter-assessments are indispensable. As indicated above, large electronics companies publicly state their commitment to protecting workers' rights in their supply chain. The makeITfair project looks behind these statements and monitors actual corporate practices, evaluating whether the discourse of CSR matches the reality.

MAKEITFAIR: THE NEED FOR INDEPENDENT MONITORING

MakeITfair is a project funded by the European Union that aims to raise awareness about social and environmental consequences of the production and the disposal of consumer electronics.[1] Since 2007 the member organizations of makeITfair have documented working conditions and corporate behavior throughout the manufacturing networks of IT companies. The manufacturing factories included in the research have been identified either by local partners or based on publicly available information.

MakeITfair has conducted original research about the situation of employees in the game console, mobile phone, computer parts, and camera production industries in China, India, the Philippines, and Vietnam: the mobile phone, game console, and mobile music player production in China is the subject of *Playing with Labour Rights* (Finnwatch, SACOM and SOMO 2008).[2] *Silenced to Deliver* (SOMO and Swedwatch 2008) summarizes the findings of a study conducted by SOMO and Swedwatch about working conditions in six mobile phone factories in China and the Phillipines.[3] The situation in the Philippines was also the focus of SOMO's study *Configuring Labour Rights* (2009), which examines working conditions in the production of computer parts.[4] In *Out of Focus* Swedwatch and SOMO (2011) describe the results of their research on camera manufacturing in Vietnam.[5] *Phone Equality* (Finnwatch, Cividep and SOMO 2011) documents the findings of a recent study of mobile phone production in China.[6]

In the following section we will present the main results of makeITfair's research by giving an overview of the situation regarding labor rights in four major electronics production countries: China, India, the Philippines, and Vietnam.

ELECTRONICS MANUFACTURING IN CHINA, INDIA, THE PHILIPPINES, AND VIETNAM

The work situation in the electronics manufacturing sector in China, India, the Philippines, and Vietnam is similar in various respects. In this section we highlight its basic characteristics regarding workforce composition, the location of electronics factories, the formal protection of worker rights, as well the situation of labor unions in the electronics supply chain. These findings are based on research conducted by makeITfair between 2008 and 2011.

Labor Force: Employees in the Electronics Sector

The workforce in electronics manufacturing mostly consists of young, often female, workers who have left their homes in rural areas and migrated to towns and special economic zones in order to find work and be able to make a living. For example, the average age in the Indian mobile phone manufacturing industry is 22 years. As the labour supply exceeds the demand, factories require 10 years or more of school education. Thus, many employees are overqualified for the work they are doing. The workforce consists in large part of migrant workers, many of them female (Finnwatch, Cividep and SOMO 2011). Despite the fact that they are overqualified, many workers depend on their factory jobs in order to be able to support their families. This economic necessity often leaves workers no choice but to accept bad working conditions such as long hours of overtime work, low pay, or threats to health and safety.

A majority of female and migrant workers also characterizes the workforce structure in electronics manufacturing in Vietnam. Statistics from the Vietnamese government show that in 2008, 90,746 workers were employed in the electronics sector and three out of four were female (GSO 2010). Most of these workers are migrant workers who live in rented rooms close to the factory (Swedwatch and SOMO 2011). The fact that many workers need to leave their hometowns and families in order to find work means that they often are isolated and lack a social network, which makes them easier to control.

The situation in China is similar. Research conducted by SOMO and Swedwatch (2008) reveals that most workers in the mobile phone production in China are young, female migrants, who try to financially support their families in rural areas. The situation for migrant workers is particularly difficult as they often are socially isolated. The separation of workers that have migrated from similar areas by assigning them to separate dormitories or assembly lines is a common management practice (SOMO and Swedwatch 2008, 11). Estimates show that in the Chinese Guangdong province, for example, 65 percent of the workers in the manufacturing sector are migrant workers (Finnwatch, SACOM and SOMO 2009, 17). As employees tend to be young, many of them have no previous work experience. They therefore lack standards of comparison and have a low degree of awareness regarding their rights (Finnwatch, Cividep and SOMO 2011, 4).

The lack of experience, social networks, and awareness regarding their rights makes these workers vulnerable. Furthermore most workers are highly dependent on their work in order to be able to make a living and to support their families. Due to these dependencies workers are perceived to be easily controllable and are often forced to accept poor working conditions including low pay, forced overtime, and unsafe work practices.

Labor Spaces: Special Economic Zones

Electronics production mostly takes place in so-called special economic zones (SEZ). Governments have installed such zones in order to attract foreign direct investment (FDI). Companies that are located in these areas benefit from tax reductions and sometimes less strict labor regulations. In China for example, SEZ were first established in 1980 (Yeung et al. 2009, 223). The first four SEZ were located in the coastal areas of southeast China: Shantou, Shenzhen, and Zhuhai in Guangdong province and Xiamen in Fujian Province. In 1984 the entire Hainan province was added as a fifth SEZ (Yeung et al. 2009, 224). In addition to traditional SEZ, several further areas with special regulations exist today: among them are 69 economic trade and development zones (ETDZ), 54 high-tech industrial development zones (HIDZ), 15 free trade zones (FTZ), and 61 export processing zones (EPZ) (Zeng 2011, 10–12). The creation of special economic zones for attracting foreign companies through providing investment incentives is not unique to China.

Some of the oldest SEZs are located in India, where so-called "export processing zones" have existed since 1965. Companies located in these areas were required to achieve a certain minimum export performance. As a strategy to boost foreign investment, in 2000 the Indian government started an initiative to establish SEZ (Finnwatch, Cividep and SOMO 2011, 11). SEZ in India offer several benefits for companies such as duty free imports and duty free domestic procurement of goods for development, operation, and maintenance for units within a SEZ, a 100 percent tax exemption on income from exports for the first five years and a 50 percent exemption for the next 5 years, exemption from minimum alternate tax, central tax sales and service tax, the possibility for external commercial borrowing up to 500 million USD (Ministry of Commerence and Industry, 2012). Significant tax reductions are also common in other countries such as Vietnam and the Philippines.

In Vietnam the regular corporate income tax is 28 percent. Companies can be granted up to eight years of tax holidays starting from the first year in which profits are made, further tax reductions of between 5 and 10 percent after the end of tax holidays, as well as exemptions from value added tax (VAT) and duties for the import of certain goods (Botman, Klemm and Baqir 2010, 168f). The regular corporate income tax in the Philippines is 35 percent. However, the Philippine Economic Zone Authority (PEZA) can grant substantial tax benefits to companies located in SEZ. Companies outside SEZ can apply to the Board of Investments (BOI) to receive similar benefits. Companies can, for example, receive between 3 and 8 years of tax holidays. After the end of tax holidays the PEZA can grant further exemptions from national and local taxes if companies instead pay a 5 percent tax on gross income. Furthermore, companies receive exemptions from taxes on imports of supply and machine parts (Botman, Klemm and Baqir 2010, 170–172).

These facts show that SEZs in China, India, Vietnam, and the Philippines provide incentives to encourage foreign investment into the country. This development strategy—luring foreign investors by offering special tax concessions in SEZs—has been effective in developing manufacturing hubs in the SEZs described above. However, working conditions in these manufacturing hubs are often harsh, creating a new set of problems for workers.

Labor Rights: The ILO Core Conventions

While governments create new rules to provide financial incentives to multinational corporations, regulation to protect labor rights is often insufficient. A look at ratification figures for conventions of the International Labor Organization (ILO), for example, reveals that in several areas the commitment of governments to protect human rights is missing. Among the countries that are included in this overview, only the Philippines have ratified all eight ILO core conventions on fundamental human rights (see table 6.1).

This overview shows that India has not yet made a commitment to abolish child labor. The Vietnamese and Chinese governments have until now not officially condemned forced labor. China, India, and Vietnam have not ratified the conventions on freedom of association and collective bargaining. In states that have not ratified the core conventions, there is no legal obligation to uphold these basic labor rights. However, even in countries which have ratified all core conventions and which have laws in place to protect these rights, there is no guarantee that these will be upheld. Labor laws are routinely breached in many countries manufacturing electronics in Asia. At the very least, ratification provides tools that workers can use to hold governments accountable and sourcing companies cannot hide behind claims that they are "just following the national law."

Labor Associations: Unions in the Electronics Supply Chain

Among the countries discussed in this chapter, only the Philippines have ratified the ILO core conventions on the right to unionize. According to the Philippine constitution all workers have the right to collective bargaining as well as peaceful and concerted activities, including strikes. Nevertheless, union activists often have to face police brutality and repression by factory management. Local unions have reported dismissals, intimidations, and killings of union activists (SOMO 2009, 26). Despite the ratification of the ILO conventions on freedom of association and collective bargaining and the existence of corresponding national laws, the International Trade Union Con-

Table 6.1. Ratification of ILO core conventions

		China	India	Philippines
Freedom of association and collective bargaining	C-87: Freedom of Association and Protection of the Right to Organise Convention	not ratified	not ratified	ratified
	C-98: Right to Organise and Collective Bargaining	not ratified	not ratified	ratified
Elimination of forced and compulsory labor	C-29: Forced Labor Convention	not ratified	ratified	ratified
	C-105: Abolition of Forced Labor Convention	not ratified	ratified	ratified
Elimination of discrimination in respect of employment and occupation	C-100: Equal Remuneration Convention	ratified	ratified	ratified
	C-111: Discrimination	ratified	ratified	ratified
Abolition of child labor	C-138: Minimum Age Convention	ratified	not ratified	ratified
	C-182: Worst Forms of Child Labor Convention	ratified	not ratified	ratified

Source: ILO (2012).

federation (2011) reports that among all Asian countries the situation of union activists is "most deadly" in the Philippines.[7]

Similarly, the Indian constitution guarantees citizens the right to freedom of association, which includes forming and joining a labor union. Furthermore the Indian Trade Union Act prohibits discrimination against trade union members. However, employers are not legally obliged to recognize a union or to engage in collective bargaining (Finnwatch, Cividep, and SOMO 2011, 39, 41). Furthermore, the right to strike is limited in India. The Essential Services Maintenance Act (ESMA) allows governments to ban strikes in "essential services," which are not clearly defined. According to the ESMA for Tamil Nadu, where the mobile phone companies that makeITfair studied are located, strike organizers as well as participants can be punished with three years imprisonment or fines. What is particularly problematic is that even the "refusal to work overtime" or to "continue work or to accept work assigned" as well as "any other conduct which is likely to result in, or results in, cessation or substantial retardation of work in any essential services" is prohibited (Finnwatch, Cividep, and SOMO 2011, 43). The case of India illustrates that even if laws to protect workers' rights exist, they are often not sufficiently implemented and enforced at the factory level.

In China and Vietnam the legal situation is different. In both countries only one official trade union exists. This means that workers do not have the right to free association. In China the All China Federation of Trade Unions (ACFTU) holds a monopolistic position. Investigations of four Chinese electronics supplier factories showed that workers either do not know about the existence of a union or think it would be loyal to the factory management (Finnwatch, SACOM and SOMO 2008, 8; Finnwatch, SACOM and SOMO 2011, 5). Therefore, organizing workers in China is particularly challenging since workers are unable to form independent trade unions to advocate on their behalf.

The Vietnam General Confederation of Labour (VGCL) is the only legal union in the country. Trade union elections are held at the factory level. However, many union representatives are managers and therefore loyal to management. In 75 percent of all union meetings factory managers are present. According to Vietnamese law holding a strike is only possible under highly restrictive conditions: strikes are only legal if they are related to legal worker rights (as codified in law) and not to workers' interests (Swedwatch and SOMO 2011, 14). This regulation makes it nearly impossible for workers to fight for an improvement of worker rights, without risking punishment.

A young, largely female, inexperienced, and highly dependent workforce, lax regulatory standards regarding the protection of worker rights, and poor union representation constitute the context in which electronic production takes place in China, India, the Philippines, and Vietnam. In the following section we will take a closer look at the situation of those workers who supply consumers all over the world with mobile phones, computers, mp3 players, game consoles, photo cameras, and other electronic goods.

BEHIND THE GADGET—WORK IN ELECTRONICS PRODUCTION

In this section we give an overview of the most pressing problems regarding working conditions in the electronics supply chain: wages, working hours, precarious labor, discrimination, risks for occupational health and safety, low living standards, and threats to freedom of association and the right to collective bargaining. The evidence is based on research conducted by makeITfair between 2008 and 2011. All makeITfair research is based on interviews with workers, managers, trade union representatives, and external experts. In order to ensure that employees dare to speak freely it is important that all interviews are confidential, held outside the factory area, and without the presence of management.

Wages

A general problem throughout the electronics manufacturing sector in China, India, Vietnam, and the Philippines is the low wage level. Even if minimum wage standards are met, the wages workers receive for full time employment are often barely enough to allow workers to cover basic living expenses for themselves and their families. In other words, legal minimum wages are not adequate living wages.

In China, despite some recent increases in the official minimum wage level, employees in the electronics sector have to work hard to cover their basic living expenses. In 2010 minimum wages in all but one Chinese province increased on average by 24 percent. This was the first major increase since the national introduction of minimum wages in 2003. Despite these increases, minimum wages in China are still far from sufficient. Workers report huge gaps between their actual wages and what they consider necessary for a decent life (Finnwatch, SACOM and SOMO 2011, 10). The fact that electronics companies fail to ensure that workers in their supply chain receive adequate wages raises questions regarding the sincerity of their commitments to CSR.

A factory that received significant media attention in 2011 is the Shenzhen-based production facility of Hon Hai Precision Industry Co. (Ltd), better known under its trade name Foxconn. A series of suicides at the Foxconn production facility in Shenzhen, at which, for example, Apple's iPhone is produced, directed public attention to the working conditions at the electronics manufacturer. As a reaction to these events and the resulting media attention, Foxconn in June 2010 increased monthly wages from 900 Yuan to 1,200 Yuan (EUR 137). In October 2010 wages were further raised to 2,000 Yuan (EUR 229), but only for workers who had been working at the factory for more than six months. It therefore remains unclear how many workers actually benefited from the wage increase (Finnwatch, SACOM and SOMO 2011, 28). Workers who receive the basic wage of 1,200 Yuan reported having difficulties with covering their basic food and housing expenses.

Basic wages at other factories in the electronics sector are comparable to the wages at Foxconn. This includes Multak, another electronics manufacturer located in Shenzhen, which produces LCDs for Sony and mp3 players for Motorola, Phillips, and other companies. It pays new hires a basic monthly wage of 1,100 Yuan (EUR 126). At a Flextronics production facility in Zhuhai city, which produces the Xbox game console for Microsoft, newly hired workers receive 1,100 Yuan (EUR 126). Microsoft's Xbox is also produced in the Dongguan-based facility of Celestica. Basic monthly wages at the Celestica campus in 2010 were 1,080 Yuan (EUR 124). Workers can increase their basic wages by working overtime (Finnwatch, SACOM and SOMO 2011.) Table 6.2 gives an overview of minimum wages as well as actual basic and total wages at different electronic manufacturing facilities in China.

The situation in the Philippines is similar. In 2008 SOMO's study of computer parts manufacturing in the Philippines revealed that legal minimum wages were too low. Even if both parents worked, minimum wages were not enough to cover basic living expenses of a family (SOMO 2009, 24f). Another study conducted by SOMO and Swedwatch showed similar results. For example, in May 2008 the minimum wage in one main export processing

Table 6.2. Wages in the Chinese electronics manufacturing industry

	Celestia Dongguan campus, Songshan Lake	**Multec** Henggang town, Longgang district, Shenzhen	**Flextronics** Xin Quing Science & Technology Industrial Park, Doumen, Zhuhai city	**Hon Hai Precision Industry** Co (Foxconn) Shenzhen
Main customers	Microsoft (until January 2010), IBM, Whirlpool, ZTE	Sony, Motorlola, Phillips	Microsoft	Apple
Legal monthly minimum wage in the region	Dongguan: 920 Yuan	Shenzen: 1,100 Yuan	Zuhai: 960 Yuan	Shenzen: 1,100 Yuan
Basic monthly wage	1,080 Yuan (124 EUR)	Newly hired: 1,100 Yuan (126 EUR) After probation period: 1,298 Yuan (149 EUR)	Newly hired: 1,100 Yuan (126 EUR) After 3 months: 1.165 Yuen (133 EUR) After 18 months: 1,335 Yuan (153 EUR)	Newly hired: 1,200 Yuan (137 EUR) After 6 months: 2,000 Yuan (229 EUR)
Total monthly wage (including overtime, food and housing allowances, shifts subsidies)	Average: 1,800–2,500 Yuen (206 to 286 EUR)	Average during peak season: 1,900–2,100 Yuan (217–240 EUR) Average during low season: 1,300–1,400 Yuan (149–160 EUR)	Average 2,000–2,500 Yuan during peak season (229–286 EUR)	At maximum during peak season: 3,000–4,400 Yuan (340-500 EUR)

Source: Finnwatch, SACOM and SOMO (2011).

zone in the Philippines was EUR 120, while the basic living expenses for an average family in this region were EUR 320 (SOMO and Swedwatch 2008, 8). Legal minimum wages that are below the living wage help attract foreign direct investment. This is however highly problematic as low legal minimum wages provide companies with an excuse for not paying their employees' living wages.

Likewise, research into camera producers in Vietnam showed no violations of minimum wage laws, however due to high inflation rates it is becoming increasingly difficult for workers to save money or sometimes to cover living expenses. From the four supplier factories that were included in this study, workers from two factories reported that their wages were not enough to cover their living expenses (Sanyo DI Solutions Co. Ltd. and Samsung Electronics), while in the other two factories workers confirmed that wages cover their basic needs (Olympus Vietnam Co. Ltc. and Pentax Vietnam) (Swedwatch and SOMO 2011, 40). Similar issues were also found in India. Recent research conducted by Finnwatch, Cividep and SOMO (2011) shows that wages in mobile phone production, despite complying with legal minimum wages, are far too low. In 2011 wages in Indian factories of Nokia, Flextronics, Foxconn, and Salcomp were between Rs 4,130 and 5,500 (EUR 66–88), which is around half of what workers themselves considered a decent living wage, that would allow them to rent a room and to start a family (Finnwach, Cividep and SOMO 2011, 5). The fact that electronics companies fail to ensure adequate wages in their supply chain reveals that they, despite commitments to CSR, do not meet their responsibility toward those workers that produce their products. The labor of these workers is the source of the profits of electronics companies. However, workers themselves only receive a minimal share of the wealth they are creating, while most of this wealth is turned into private profit of company owners.

Research conducted by makeITfair shows that even when electronics manufacturers in China, the Philippines, Vietnam, and India comply with minimum wage regulations, these wages are insufficient. Minimum wages in these countries are far from enough to allow workers and their families to live a decent life. This makes it particularly difficult for workers and activists to campaign for higher wages when simply adhering to minimum wages is insufficient to provide for decent living standards for workers and their families. On the one hand increasing minimum wages thus seems crucial. On the other hand, it is important to raise public awareness regarding the problem of low wages and to pressure companies to pay living wages. Furthermore manufacturing countries are competing with each other and often struggle with the fear that western companies will relocate their production to another country if minimum wages are raised. Electronics companies thus should be considered responsible for ensuring adequate wage levels. A living wage should cover expenses for food, housing, clothes, education, social security, and health care for a family, and allow for some savings.

The Asia Floor Wage Campaign (2009) suggested a method for calculating the living wage. According to this calculation a living wage needs to cover the costs for food, equivalent of 3,000 calories per adult family member multiplied by two, in order to cover also other basic need such as clothing, housing, education, healthcare, and savings. The living wage should provide for a family of two adults and two children. It thus should cover the cost for food worth 3,000 calories for three consumption units (two adults and two children) multiplied by two. It is thus calculated as follows: price for food worth 3,000 calories x 3 x 2 (Asia Floor Wage Campaign 2009, 50). A worker should be able to earn a living wage within a working week of a maximum of 48 hours. This calculation of a living wage was developed with specific regard to the garment sector, but is also be applicable for other sectors such as electronics manufacturing.

Since it is evidently very difficult for workers to challenge the minimum wages structures in all countries, from consumers and NGO-movements such as Asia Floor Wage Campaign, are important awareness-raising which can help put pressure on companies to affect the low wages.

Working Hours

Connected to the problem of low wages is the issue of excessive overtime. For many workers, overtime is the only possibility for increasing their otherwise low wages. Furthermore workers often feel that they cannot refuse overtime either because overtime is compulsory or because they fear not being given any additional shifts in the future if they refuse to work overtime once. Excessive overtime of between 80 and 120 hours a month is not uncommon in the electronics manufacturing sector.

In 2008, in an investigation of four Chinese electronics suppliers, makeITfair found that in three of four studied factories (Flextronics, Celestica, and Multec) 80 to 90 hours of monthly overtime were common during peak season. In the fourth factory (Foxconn), monthly overtime amounted to up to 120 hours (Finnwatch, SACOM, and SOMO 2008, 7). A follow-up study in 2010 showed that after the tragic suicides in 2010, overtime at Foxconn was reduced. However, although workers were granted one day off per week, they were still working 75 to 80 hours overtime per month. The study again revealed overtime of up to 120 hours per month in one factory, this time at the factory of Celestia at Dongguan campus. Overtime between 60 and 100 hours a month was also found at Flextronics in Zhuhai city and Multec in Shenzhen (Finnwatch, SACOM, and SOMO 2008, 7). In another study SOMO and Swedwatch found that in one Chinese factory that supplies chargers for Nokia, Samsung, Motorola, and LG, 80-hour working weeks were common (SOMO and Swedwatch 2008, 9). These practices violate Chinese labor law, which permits overtime of 36 hours per month at most (Finnwatch, SACOM, and SOMO 2008, 7). The situation of excessive overtime is not unique to China.

Similar conditions exist in the Philippines. Workers who are producing for Motorola and LG reported working weeks of more than 60 hours and having to continuously work 25 days of day shifts followed by 25 days of night shifts (Swedwatch and SOMO 2008, 9). Likewise, an investigation of eight factories in the Philippines in which computer parts are manufactured showed that usual working times were 12 hours per day for six days a week and even seven days a week during peak seasons. Workers were scared that refusing overtime would have negative consequences (SOMO 2009, 26). This shows that also in regard to working hours, electronics companies fail to meet their social responsibility.

Workers are also heavily affected by up and down turns in demand: excessive overtime during peak season results in exhaustion, while low demand and little overtime during the low season leads to reduced wages which makes it difficult for many workers to cover their living expenses. Even if overtime is officially labeled voluntary, low wages often force workers into working excessive overtime. While companies comply with legal minimum wage standards, compliance with regulations for maximum working hours is often insufficient. The fact that minimum wage levels are too low makes compliance relatively easy for companies and at the same time creates the need for workers to work overtime to earn extra money. The research conducted by makeITfair over the last couple of years shows no clear improvement regarding the issue of overtime. The relationship between low wages and high overtime rates is a basic structural characteristic of contemporary electronics manufacturing. It allows companies to keep their payroll low at the expense of workers, and at the same time meet high production targets.

Precarious Labor

Despite low wages and long working hours, employees in the electronics manufacturing sector often have to face precarious and insecure working conditions. In the Indian mobile phone manufacturing sectors, for example, the workforce is split into two types of employees: permanent employees and contract workers. At the four factories that were investigated by Finnwatch, Cividep, and SOMO (2011), the percentage of contract workers ranged between 10 and 60 percent. Contract workers receive fewer security benefits as well as lower wages, and their possibilities for career advancement are fewer (Finnwatch, Cividep and SOMO 2011, 5). In three of the four Indian mobile phone factories studied, most workers start as trainees. Workers keep the status of trainees for 15 to 18 months, although the actual training period does not last longer than one month. At the end of the training period, workers have no right to claim a permanent employment contract. Apart from the insecurity contract workers and trainees are facing, they often receive significantly lower wages than permanent employees (Finnwatch, Cividep and SOMO 2011, 30). High job insecurity puts workers under pressure as their contracts can be discontinued at any time. Different types of contracts within one factory also creates divisions among workers, which hampers the joint struggle against poor working conditions that, to different degrees, affect all of them.

Swedwatch and SOMO's (2011) latest research into camera production in Vietnam confirms that job insecurity is a major problem in electronics manufacturing. At a Pentax factory in Vietnam workers who were interviewed only had one-year contracts although they had been working in this factory for six years already. Similarly, at the Olympus factory studied, workers complained about job insecurity. They reported that the company published lists with names of workers whose contracts will be renewed just one week before the old contracts expired. The decision about whether contracts are renewed or not depended on the workers' performance and attitude (Swedwatch and SOMO 2011, 36).

Also in the Philippines another makeITfair partner, SOMO (2009), found a trend toward "contractualization" of workers in the electronics industry. Many workers receive only six-month contracts either directly from the electronics company or from work agencies. This type of employment not only reduces job security but also workers' rights and benefits such as paid vacations, paid sick leave, and wage bonuses (SOMO 2009, 30).

A practice that is particularly common at Chinese electronics supplier factories is the employment of student interns. Students are cheap labor since they do not receive regular social security benefits. They however have to work night shifts and overtime like regular workers. In 2008 makeITfair researchers found this practice at all four Chinese electronics manufacturers studied. Large numbers of 16- to 18-year-old students were employed for up to one year. Reductions in labor costs can also be achieved through hiring contract or dispatch labor. In one factory producing for Microsoft 20 percent, and in another factory even 50 percent of the total workforce consisted of this kind of cheap labor (Finnwatch, SACOM, and SOMO 2008, 7). A follow up study in 2010 showed that while one company significantly reduced the amount of student labor, other factories, such as Foxconn, still employed large numbers of 16– to 18–year-old students for periods of three to six months (Finnwatch, SACOM, and SOMO 2011, 5).

The practice of giving workers only short-term contracts makes long-term life planning difficult. Contract workers are not only suffering from the fear of losing their job, but often also receive lower wages and fewer security benefits. Furthermore, this practice increases factory management's power over workers. Threatening workers with the refusal to renew a contract can be used as an instrument for controlling workers' behavior, such as forcing them to meet higher production targets or to work overtime. Short notice times furthermore give workers hardly any chance to rearrange their lives and to find new employment if their contracts are not renewed.

Discrimination

Discriminatory recruiting practices occur throughout the electronics manufacturing sector. Often, job applicants need to undergo medical check-ups during the hiring process. For female applicants pregnancy tests are common. A 2008 makeITfair study of four electronics supplier factories in China, for example, showed that medical checks were used at all four investigated factories. Applicants had to pay for the check-ups themselves, regardless of whether they were employed or not. Hepatitis B was a reason for rejection in three out of four investigated companies (Finnwatch, SACOM, and SOMO 2008, 7). In a 2010 follow-up report Finnwatch, SACOM, and SOMO found that discrimination on Hepatitis B decreased (Finnwatch, SACOM, and SOMO 2011, 4). This could partly be due to the public criticism makeITfair and others raised in investigation reports (see for example Finnwatch, SACOM, and SOMO 2008, 7).

Apart from discrimination due to illness, gender discrimination is common in many electronics factories. A study by Swedwatch and SOMO (2011) on camera production in Vietnam revealed structural discrimination against female workers at an Olympus factory. Interviewees reported that female workers would initially receive only a six-month contract. After this six-month period they would receive a one-year contract while male workers would receive a one-year contract after just one month of training. Workers furthermore reported that pregnancy was used as a reason for not renewing contracts (Swedwatch and SOMO 2011, 30). In general, however, women are often preferred as employees. This can be seen in the hiring adverisements for the Vietnamese Olympus factory, which explicitly target women between 18 and 35 years of age. Only hiring young workers constitutes a form of age discrimination (Swedwatch and SOMO 2011, 33).

Gendered hiring practices also prevail in China. Many workers in the electronics industry are young women. In China they often leave their families in the countryside to find work in an industrial area and provide some financial assistance for their relatives. Often factories prefer to hire female workers because they are considered to be good at performing detail-oriented work and to be more obedient and less likely to engage in protests (Swedwatch and SOMO 2008, 11). These gendered stereotypes make it easier for women to be hired, but their positions are often precarious in the factories. In the Philippines for example wages for women in the electronics industry are often higher and jobs there guarantee more social security than jobs in the informal sector. However women are still suffering from poor working conditions and are often endangered by sexual harassment and violence (Swedwatch and SOMO 2008, 11).

Risks for Occupational Health and Safety

Various occupational health and safety risks are common in the electronics manufacturing sector. The problems are partly related to generally exhausting working conditions due to long hours of standing and shift work. Workers in many cases also have to work in dangerous environments and are exposed to toxic chemicals, often without proper safety equipment.

One basic problem for many workers is the exhaustive and repetitive work at the assembly line. Often workers have to meet high production targets and therefore feel stressed due to the fast work pace. Most often workers also have to stand for their whole shifts, which many of them consider to be very exhausting (Swedwatch and SOMO 2008, 33). An investigation of the working conditions in Chinese electronics supplier factories in 2008, for example, revealed that workers were suffering from having to stand during entire shifts of 11 hours, exhausting month-long night shifts, and long queues to use the toilet (Finnwatch, SACOM, and SOMO 2008, 6). A 2010 follow-up study showed that these problems had basically not improved (Finnwatch, SACOM and SOMO 2011, 5).

Similar issues were found in Vietnam. Workers at a Vietnamese Olympus factory, for example, complained about exhaustion due to many hours of standing during work and restrictions in using the toilet (Swedwatch and SOMO 2011, 29). Likewise workers in the Indian mobile phone production considered long hours standing combined with a high working tempo as problematic (Finnwatch, Cividep and SOMO 2011).

Apart from being stressful, repetitive, and exhaustive, work in electronics manufacturing often brings about serious safety risks. As the production of electronics is chemically intensive, workers risk being exposed to hazardous toxic substances and fumes (Finnwach, SACOM and SOMO 2009, 18). In many factories health and safety training as well as protection equipment are insufficient. In 2008, in an investigation of a Chinese manufacturer for printed circuit boards for mobile phone companies Nokia, Samsung, Motorola, and LG, makeITfair found that employees in the departments for painting, spraying, panel cleaning, and oxidizing were not provided with chemical-resistant gloves and therefore suffered from itches and pain. Swedwatch's and SOMO's investigation into mobile phone manufacturing in China and the Philippines also showed that workers in both countries were suffering from health issues such as muscle strains, eye problems, allergies, dizziness, exhaustion, burn injuries, cutting, chest pains, and weight loss and were concerned about bad ventilation and the fear of getting seriously ill due to the exposure to chemicals (Swedwatch and SOMO 2008, 10, 33). Often workers do not even know which chemicals they are exposed to at their workplace. Workers interviewed for a recent makeITfair report on the Chinese electronics manufacturing sector complained about insufficient knowledge about health risks associated with the use of certain chemicals (Finnwatch, SACOM, and SOMO 2011, 5).

Similarly, workers in digital camera factories in Vietnam report the use of unknown chemicals during their work. At Samsung Electronics Vietnam Co. Ltd. (SEV) and Sanyo DI Solutions Co. Ltd. workers were concerned because of the strong chemical smell and bad air quality but did not know which chemicals exactly were in use (Swedwatch and SOMO 2011, 30). Chinese workers furthermore reported that even if protection equipment is provided, it often is not used. Tight schedules and high production targets require workers to work as quickly as possible. Workers are afraid that they will be slowed down and unable to meet their production targets if they use protective equipment such as gloves (Swedwatch and SOMO 2008, 33).

The combination of a risky work environment and a lack of training and safety equipment regularly results in serious accidents: between July 2009 and early 2010, 47 workers at United Win in Suzhou, China, a subsidy of Wintek Corporation that produces Apple products, were hospitalized because of n-hexane poisoning (SACOM 2010, 2). Eighty-five cases of industrial injury were reported between August 2009 and July 2010 at the Flextronics campus in Zhuhai (Finnwatch, SACOM and SOMO 2011, 22). In 2010, a female worker at an Indian Nokia factory got stuck in a machine and died while attempting to remove a jammed piece (Finnwatch, Cividep and SOMO 2011). In July 2010 a pesticide incident occurred at a Foxconn campus in Sriperumbudur, India. A pesticide that was used on the factory campus got into the factory's faulty ventilation system and caused symptoms like fainting, breathlessness, and coughing for 200 workers (Finnwatch, Cividep and SOMO 2011). In May 2011 three workers were killed in an explosion at the polishing department at a Foxconn factory in Chengdu, China (SACOM 2011, 1).

In addition to these serious threats to the physical health of workers, mental health problems also occur. Sometimes workers suffer from psychological problems due to social isolation. Many workers left their families in the countryside to find work in special economic zones. An investigation after the culmination of suicide tragedies at the Foxconn campus in Shenzhen revealed that workers who are working in the same shifts or who have migrated from the same region are often assigned different dormitory rooms. As they are also not allowed to talk to each other during work, it is difficult for them to establish social contacts (Finnwatch, SACOM and SOMO 2011, 30; earlier research found similar results, see: SOMO and Swedwatch 2008).

These results show that in many factories meeting high production targets is more important than the health of workers. Furthermore the inhumane working environment in many factories ignores the human need for social contacts and reduces workers to appendages of the machines they are operating.

Disciplinary Measures

Another common strategy in many electronics factories is to control the behavior of workers through various disciplinary measures. In some factories, fines and wage deductions are used as punitive measures. In a study of Chinese electronics suppliers, makeITfair found that in three out of the four studied factories, workers were punished with wage reductions if they made mistakes or fell asleep during work (Finnwatch, SACOM and SOMO 2008, 8). A follow up investigation in 2010 showed that strict disciplinary measures remained in place. For example at Celestica's Dongguan-based production facility workers had to pay a fee for falling asleep during work or making mistakes. They were also fined if they could not keep to the monthly tolerance of 30 minutes for arriving late to work or leaving early (around one minute per day). Flextronics abolished fines and wage deduction as disciplinary measures but a strict discipline system remained in place. If workers violate the company's rules they receive "points." A regular worker who receives six points will be fired, while for workers who are on probation two points are enough to be fired (Finnwatch, SACOM, and SOMO 2011).

The practice of using fines and wage reduction to punish workers who make mistakes or fall asleep was also found in all of the studied supplier factories of leading international mobile phone companies. In a factory producing for Nokia, Motorola, Samsung, and LG investigators found that workers were fined if they fell asleep although they had to work 12 to 13 hour shifts six days a week (SOMO and Swedwatch 2008, 9).

Workers in the Indian mobile phone production sector reported that having to clean the shopfloor in front of colleagues was used as a punitive measure for not meeting production targets (Finnwatch, Cividep, and SOMO 2011, 37). Such humiliating measures demonstrate the often inhumane working conditions and the power the factory management has over workers.

Low Living Standards

Many workers migrate from the countryside to find work in electronics factories in the hope of securing decent living conditions for themselves and their families. In reality, however, the living standards of most workers in the electronics manufacturing industry are low. As discussed earlier, wages are low and working hours are long. Most workers need to financially support their families in the countryside. In order to be able to send part of their wages home to their families they try to keep their own living expenses as low as possible. In China workers often live in dormitories inside factory campuses because those are cheaper than other accommodation. Often the rooms are small and shared by many workers, which mean there is very little privacy. Sometimes hygiene problems exist in dormitories because workers themselves are responsible for housekeeping, but have little time and energy for cleaning due to long working hours (Finnwatch, SACOM, and SOMO 2008, 8).

The Vietnamese factories of Samsung, Olympus, and Pentax provide cheap shared dormitory rooms. Workers at Samsung reported that they prefer to live in the nearby village rather than in factory dormitories, because they want to avoid strict dormitory rules such as regulated bus times for going to the factory, strict meal times and having to report in. As housing in the village is more expensive, typically three workers share each room (Swedwatch and SOMO 2011, 41).

In India, workers often chose to live in the countryside, where living expenses are lower. In order to save costs five to seven workers commonly share one room. MakeITfair investigators visited one room that was shared by 25 women who were sleeping on the floor without furniture. Living in the countryside results in long commuting times. Most workers travel between two and four hours each day. The average travel time to the home of their parents was four hours. As workers can only take limited leave, occasions to visit their families are rare and their stays short (Finnwatch, Cividep and SOMO 2011, 20). These results also show that in their free time it is hard for workers to find relief from work. Many of them spend their limited free time in small shared dormitory rooms, or commuting to visit their families and to escape the social isolation of small and shared dormitory rooms.

Freedom of Association and the Right to Collective Bargaining

MakeITfair research found that workers' rights to unionize and collective bargaining are limited in the Philippines, Vietnam, China, and India. Despite the fact that the Philippines have signed the ILO core conventions on labor unions, Philippine workers often fear joining a union due to the threat of losing their employment as well as violent repression. In 2008 only 3 to 5 percent of the Philippine labor force was organized. Especially in export processing zones, in which most large electronics factories are located, "no-union, no-strike" practices are common. Workers know that participating in union activism can be dangerous. Interviewed workers reported dismissals of union members and reported that factory management would not allow workers to organize. They furthermore reported that during the application process they were questioned about their knowledge about and sympathy for unions. Workers at Fujitsu reported that if applicants said that they would like to join a union they were not hired (SOMO 2009, 28).

As in the Philippines, in India workers officially have the right to free association. However, in practice several obstacles exist that hamper union activities. Employers follow different strategies for preventing workers from joining unions, such as filing false criminal charges against union members, undesirable transfers, violence, threats, or even murder of union activists (Finnwatch, Cividep, and SOMO 2011, 39). In India the workforce in electronics manufacturing is divided into regular employees and contract workers. This situation weakens the collective power of workers. Contract workers fear losing their jobs and therefore do not want to join a union (Finnwatch, Cividep, and SOMO 2011). MakeITfair has studied the union situation at Indian mobile phone factories and found that after worker strikes at the Chennai Nokia and Foxconn factory campuses in 2009 and 2010, unions were introduced. Nokia recognized the Labor Progressive Federation (LPF) as a trade union. However, after a while an independent union, the Nokia Employees Union, was formed. As this union is not connected to any larger union or political party its strength is limited to the Nokia workers that join the union (Finnwatch, Cividep and SOMO 2011, 40). In April 2010, Foxconn also recognized the LFP as a trade union at the factory. A three-year wage agreement was achieved between the union and Foxconn. However, workers were not satisfied with the union's activity, which was affiliated to the then-ruling party Dravida Munnetra Kazhagam, and therefore instead joined the Centre of Indian Trade Unions (CITU), which is connected to the Communist Party of India. In October 2010, 200 workers were arrested when participating in a strike for higher wages and recognition of CITU (Finnwatch, Cividep and SOMO 2011, 42). Limitations to the right to free association are not specific to India and the Phillipines but are also common in other electronics production countries.

In China and Vietnam, union activity is also restricted. MakeITfair investigations of four Chinese electronics manufacturers in 2009 and 2011 revealed that most workers were not aware of the existence of unions. Workers at Celestica in Dongguan, Flextronics at Zhuhai industrial park as well as at Foxconn's Shenzhen-based production facility were not aware of the existence of a union. Only at Vista Point Technologies did workers know that a union exists, but reported that it would favor management interests (Finnwatch, SACOM, SOMO 2009, and 2011). Limitations of the right to free association are also common in Vietnam. Swedwatch and SOMO conducted an investigation of four digital camera factories in Vietnam and found that freedom of association is not guaranteed and that opportunities for collective bargaining and complaint systems are missing. In three out of four factories unions were only organizing social events: protecting workers' rights was not part of their agenda. One factory, Samsung, even refused to install a labor union until May 2011, even though Vietnamese labor law requires it (Swedwatch and SOMO 2011, 37). Workers at Sanyo DI Solutions Co. Ltd. reported that they achieved a wage raise through a sit-down strike in January 2011, but at the same time criticized union representatives taking sides with management. Workers participating in the strike feared repression from management or the police. Workers at Pentax VN in Vietnam argued that union representatives are loyal to factory management and complained that they are only concerned with social events instead of protecting worker rights (Swedwatch and SOMO 2011, 38). Electronics companies claim to be socially responsible, however fail to ensure conditions that allow workers to associate freely and to establish adequate forms of worker representation.

Despite different official legislation regarding the right to unionize and to collective bargaining, makeITfair research shows that these rights are limited in all four countries. Often freedom of association, the right to collective bargaining as well as the right to strike and protest are limited. In China and Vietnam only one official trade union exists, which does not allow workers to form independent unions. In both countries, workers often are not aware of the existence of unions or are not satisfied with the union's activities and criticise their loyalty to management. In the Philippines, workers fear violence and repression and therefore do not dare to join a union. In India, factory management often deters workers from forming or joining a union. Adequate complaint systems are missing in the electronics factories in all four countries. This situation makes it difficult for workers to collectively fight for the protection of their rights and improve their working conditions.

CONCLUSION

While workers in the electronics sector manufacture products that represent progress, prosperity, and a modern lifestyle, electronics companies continue to fail to respect human rights in their supply chain. For most workers even the most basic work qualities—such as wages that cover their basic needs and working hours that allow for a minimum amount of free time—are not guaranteed. This is a contradiction that reveals a separation between workers and the fruits of their labor. In one recent investigation at Foxconn's Chengdu production line for the iPhone, a worker told SACOM: "Though we produce for iPhone, I haven't got a chance to use [an] iPhone. I believe it is fascinating and has lots of function. However, I don't think I can own one by myself" (Worker quoted in SACOM 2011a, 19).

Improving the situation of workers requires structural changes. Today, workers have to meet high production targets while receiving low wages. Market driven capitalism promotes low cost products and high profit margins. At the same time international norms on corporate social responsibility demand respect for human rights. This implies cost, investment, dialogue, sustainable sourcing, and shared value. For example, according to Forbes Magazine (2007), in 2011 Apple was the second most profitable company in the world, only superseded by the oil corporation Exxon Mobil. As long as companies are not willing to accept higher production costs, doubts need to be raised about the sincerity of Apple's and other companies' commitments to the protection of labor rights in the supply chain.

An important starting point for improving working conditions in the electronics sector is empowering workers. Assisting workers in their own struggle for an improvement of their working conditions is essential. This, first and foremost, requires the protection of the freedom of association and the right to collective bargaining. Unions have the important role of informing workers about their rights and organizing collective actions. Today, in many electronics production countries, union are not allowed to operate freely and union activists often face repression, which makes it difficult for them to adequately inform, represent, and protect workers.

MakeITfair's research revealed that in many cases workers were not even aware that the companies they were producing for had a code of conduct that is supposed to protect their rights. However, as long as workers have to fear being punished for engaging in union activities and in protest actions the impact of unions will be limited.

Secondly, it is of utmost importance to raise public awareness in order to gain support for the struggle of workers regarding their situation. Mobile phones, cameras, mp3 players, and computers are omnipresent in the lives of most people in developed countries. Often the miserable conditions under which these products were produced are not visible. Informing the public about the situation of workers in the electronics supply chain also requires independent research that monitors the actions of electronics companies and documents corporate wrongdoing. Creating public awareness about this issue is important for increasing pressure on companies and states. This is one of the main goals of makeITfair. One of makeITfair's awareness raising campaigns was called "Time to Bite into a Fair Apple" which culminated in a global action day on May 7, 2011. Another example for successful awareness raising was that Change.org and SumOfUs.org collected almost 400,000 signatures between January and May 2012 in order to protest against labor rights violations in Apple's supply chain.[8] In January 2012 Apple responded to increased public pressure by being the first electronics company to publish a list of suppliers and join the Fair Labor Association. While these steps signal that Apple is concerned about its reputation, they do not guarantee an actual improvement of the situation of workers. Nevertheless, these actions are important for companies to know that the public is watching and that their sourcing practices are under scrutiny. After all, their profits are connected to their public image, particularly for electronics companies like Apple that rely heavily on promoting a certain image of the company in order to sell their products. With all of these campaigns, ongoing independent monitoring is crucial to ensure that companies are adhering to local and international labor standards and their own stated codes of conduct.

It is necessary to strengthen legal frameworks for the protection of worker rights; legal mechanisms are a necessary element for fostering the protection of worker rights. The need for action exists both in regard to improving as well as enforcing existing legal standards. With regard to minimum wage regulation, for example, the major problem is that legal minimum wages are too low and do not allow workers to cover their basic needs. On the contrary, in regard to maximum working hours, regulations exist—such as a maximum of 36 hours overtime per month in China—but their enforcement is inadequate. Especially with regard to the most severe issues such as child labor and forced labor, companies need to be held legally responsible for their wrongdoings. The makeITfair campaign has been working with its partners between 2007 and 2012 to address these concerns by networking between Asian and European civil society groups, through disseminating information to consumers and by having a dialogue with and about the electronics industry worldwide.[9] Out of this work, as well as the work of trade unions and consumer groups, and because of increasing media attention, the view of the IT industry is changing and people are starting to demand greater corporate accountability.

NOTES

1. makeITfair is co-ordinated by the Dutch organisation SOMO (Centre for Research on Multinational Corporations). Project partners are Swedwatch and Fair Trade Center from Sweden, Finnwatch and Pro Ethical Trade Finland from Finland; DanWatch from Denmark, Germanwatch from Germany, Association of Conscious Consumers (ACC) from Hungary, ACIDH from the DR Congo, CIVIDEP from India, Workers Assistance Center (WAC) from the Philippines, and Civil Society Research and Support Collective (CSRSC) from South Africa.

2. In 2008 Finnwatch, SACOM, and SOMO investigated working conditions at four Chinese supplier factories of Apple, Microsoft, Motorola, Philips, and Sony. The four factories under investigation were Celestica Technology, Flextronics International (incl. Vista Point Technologies/Multek), and Hong Fu Jin Precision's Foxconn. For the initial study interviews with 110 workers were conducted between April and August 2008. In a follow-up study on *Game Console and Music Player Production in China* (Finnwatch, SACOM and SOMO 2011), 100 workers from the same factories were questioned between July and September 2010.

3. Those six factories are suppliers of the five largest mobile phone companies: Nokia, Samsung, Motorola, LG, and Sony Ericson. For this report 102 workers were interviewed. The Hong-Kong based NGO Students and Scholars Against Corporate Misbehaviour (SACOM) conducted interviews with Chinese workers during 2007 and 2008. Interviews with workers from the Philippines were conducted by the Workers Assistance Center Inc in 2007.

4. For this report 106 workers from 12 factories were interviewed. This included eight factories in the Cavite Export Processing Zone (CEPZ) in Rosario, Cavite, two factories in Laguna Techno Park, one factory in Carmelray Industrial Park I-Special Economic Zone and

one factory in First-Cavite Industrial Estate. In addition 12 NGOs and trade unions and six management representatives were interviewed.

5. For this study, which was conducted in cooperation with the consulting group Global Standards and the Vietnamese NGO Center for Development and Integration (CDI), 84 workers form Olympus, Pentax, Samsung, and Sanyo factories were interviewed.

6. Finnwatch, Cividep, and SOMO studied factories of Nokia, Salcomp, Flextronics and Foxconn, that are located in Sriperumbudur around Chennai, Tamil Nadu. Between February and May 2011 the local partner Cividep interviewed 100 workers at these four factories.

7. International Trade Union Confederation. 2011.Anti-union repression increases in Asia-Pacific. Retrieved from http://www.ituc-csi.org/press-release-anti-union.html on April 18, 2012.

8. Until May 16, 2011 Change.org collected 256,425 signatures for its petition "Protect Workers Making iPhones in Chinese Factories." Retrieved from http://www.change.org/petitions/apple-protect-workers-making-iphones-in-chinese-factories-3 on May 16, 2011. SumOfUs.org collected 137,986 signatures for its petition "Apple: Make the iPhone 5 ethically." Retrieved from http://sumofus.org/campaigns/ethical-iphone/ on May 16, 2011.

9. In late August 2012, EU declined the application for a 3–year continuation of the makeITfair project, envisioning studies on the electronics industry's challenges and opportunities based on the UN Guiding Principles for Corporations and Human Rights, among other activities. However, the participating organizations will continue cooperate within the makeITfair.

REFERENCES

Apple. 2012. *Supplier Responsibility Report, Apple*. Modified April 25, 2012, http://www.sec.gov.

Asian Floor Wage Campaig. 2012. "Stitching a Decent Wage across Boarders." http://www.cleanclothes.org/component/docman/doc_download/25–stitching-a-decent-wage-across-borders.

Banerjee, Subhabrata Bobby. 2008. "Corporate Social Responsibility. The Good the Bad and the Ugly," *Critical Sociology* 34: 51–79.

Bojc, David M. 2008. "Contributions of Critical Theory Ethics for Business and Public Administration." In *Critical Theory Ethics for Business and Public Administration*, edited by David M. Boje, 3–28. Charlotte: Information Age Publishing.

Botman, Dennis, Alexander Klemm and Reza Baqir. 2010. "Investment Incentives and Effective Tax Rates in the Phillipines: A Comparison with Neighbouring Countries," *Journal of the Asia Pacific Economy*, 15: 166–191.

Cisco. 2012. Financial Statements 2005–2011, last modified on 25 April 2012, http://www.cisco.com/web/about/ac49/ac20/ac19/ar2005/index.html.

Cisco. 2011. Corporate Social Responsibility Report, last modified on 25 April 2012, http://www.cisco.com/web/about/ac227/csr2011/docs/CSR2011_full_report.pdf.

Forbes. 2012. "The Biggest Public Companies." Accessed April 25, 2012. www.forbes.com/global2000/list/.

GSO. 2010. "The Electronics industry in Vietnam," ILO unpublished report commissioned to EconomicaVietnam, the General Statistics Office.

Hanlon, Gerard and Peter Fleming. 2009. "Updating the Critical Perspective on Corporate Social Responsibility." *Sociology Compass* 3: 937–948.

Hanlon, Gerard. 2008. "Rethinking Corporate Social Responsibility and the Role of the Firm," In *The Oxford Handbook of Corporate Social Responsibility*, edited by Andrew Crane, Abagail McWilliams, Dirk Matten, Jeremy Moon and Donalod S. Siegel, 156–172. Oxford: Oxford University Press.

HP. 2012. "HP SEC-filings 2005–2011," modified April 25, 2012, http://www.sec.gov/.

HP. 2011. "HP 2011 Supply Chain Responsibility." Accessed 25 April 2012, http://www.hp.com/hpinfo/globalcitizenship/society/supply_chain_responsibility.html.

Intel. 2012. "Intel SEC-Filings 2005–2011." Accessed on April 25, 2012, http://www.sec.gov.

Intel. 2010. Corporate Responsibility Report. Accessed April 25, 2012, http://csrreportbuilder.intel.com/PDFFiles/CSR_2010_Full-Report.pdf.

International Labour Organisation. 2012. Ratification of the Fundamental Human Rights Conventions by Country. Retrieved from http://www.ilo.org/ilolex/english/docs/declworld.htm on March 7, 2011.

ITU (International Telecommunication Union). 2011. *Facts and Figures*." Accessed April 25, 2012, http://www.itu.int/ITU-D/ict/facts/2011/material/ICTFactsFigures2011.pdf.

Ministry of Commerce & Industry. 2012. Special Economic Zones in India. Retrieved from http://sezindia.nic.in/about-fi.asp.

Roberts John. 2003. "The Manufacture of Corporate Social Responsibility." *Organization* 10: 249–265.

Samsung. 2012. "Samsung Financial Statements 2005–2011," Accessed 25 April 2012, http://www.samsung.com/us/aboutsamsung/ir/financialinformation/auditedfinancialstatements/IR_AuditedParent.html#t2010.

Samsung. 2011. "Samsung Sustainability Report 2011." Accessed April 25, 2012, http://www.samsung.com/us/aboutsamsung/sustainability/sustainabilityreports/download/2011/2011%20Samsung%20Electronics%20SR%20report%20final.pdf.

Sklair, Leslie and David Miller. 2010. "Capitalist globalization, corporate social responsibility and social policy." *Critical Social Policy* 30: 472–495.

Shamir, Ronan. 2004. "The de-radicalization of corporate social responsibility." *Critical Sociology* 30: 669–689.

Yeung, Yue-man, Joanna Lee and Gordon Kee, "China's Special Economic Zones at 30." *Eurasian Geography and Economics* 50(2004): 222–240.

Zeng, Douglas Zhihua. *How Do Special Economic Zones and Industrial Clusters Drive China's Rapid Development?* Policy Research Working Paper, 5583, The World Bank.

makeITfair Reports on Working Conditions in the Electronics Supply Chain

Finnwatch, SACOM & SOMO. 2009. *Playing with Labour Rights*, MakeITfair Report.

Finnwatch, Cividep & SOMO. *Phone Equality. MakeITfair Report.*

Finnwatch, SACOM & SOMO. 2011. *Game Console and Music Player Production in China.* MakeITfair Report.

"Foxconn and Apple Fail to Fulfil Promises: Predicaments of Workers after the Suicides." Accessed on October 20, 2011, http://sacom.hk/wp-content/uploads/2011/05/2011–05–06_foxconn-and-apple-fail-to-fulfill-promises1.pdf

SOMO. 2009. *Configuring Labour Rights. Labour Conditions in the Production of Computer Parts in the Philippines*,MakeITfair Report.

SOMO & Swedwatch. 2008. *Silenced to Deliver.* MakeITfair Report.

Swedwatch & SOMO. 2011. *iSlave Behind the iPhone. Foxconn Workers in Central China.* MakeITfair Report.

All makeITfair reports are available here: http://makeitfair.org/en/the-facts/reports.

Chapter Seven

Global Supply Chains

Struggle Within or Against Them?

Sanjiv Pandita and Fahmi Panimbang

Jayanti is worried and she never felt like this before. Working as a garment worker for more than 18 years in Sri Lanka, she thought she had seen the worst. At 17, she moved out of her village to help her family out of poverty by working in garment factories near Colombo. Life has never been easy for her. It has been marked by very low wages, excessive overtime and filthy and crowded living conditions. She was called "Juki girl" and abused many times both inside and outside the factory.[1] Over the years she has changed jobs, but the conditions have hardly changed. Her body gave up many times but she always came back as there were no other jobs available. Yet she tolerated it, hoping for a better life for her children. Padma, her 16 year-old daughter, has been unable to finish school due to the financial burden and may have to join Jayanti as a garment worker. Jayanti is desperately trying to hold back her tears for the fear it may spoil the shirt she is sewing, yet one can see the rage in her eyes—nothing has changed for her over two decades and her children may have to face the same.

Jayanti's story exemplifies the condition of millions of garment workers spanning dozens of developing countries in Asia and across the world. Jayanti's story reverberates with Fatma, working in Ashulia, near Dhaka, Bangladesh, and Tevy, a garment worker from Phnom Penh, Cambodia, and all those workers at the lowest tier of the multi-billion dollar garment supply chain. Global garment production takes place through an intricate web of supply chains spread around the globe. This process of production, which has been in existence for more than three decades, is carried out by workers, predominantly young migrant women, in workplaces better identified as "sweatshops," in conditions that have been proven over the years to be inhumane.

Just as this chapter was being written, it was announced that Amancio Ortega, the founder and Director of Spanish clothing giant the Inditex group—better known for its brand Zara—became the third richest person in the world with an estimated wealth of about US$46 billion.[2] Ironically his wealth is more than three times the GDP of Cambodia (estimated at US$ 12.9 billion),[3] where many of the 300,000 garment workers stitch garments for Zara earning a meager US$60–80 a month, working for more than 10–12 hours a day. There is more irony to this, reflective of the nature of the garment supply chain. This rise of Amancio Ortega also comes at a time when Spain is reeling under one of the worst economic crises in its history; workers in Spain are struggling, the unemployment rate has reached 25 percent and is still spiraling. In an extreme contrast with Jayanti's story and those of millions of workers in many countries, including in his own country, Ortega's accumulation of wealth reflects the injustice and exploitative nature of the global supply chain system.

This chapter discusses the global supply chain system and analyzes it as a symbol of exploitation and capital accumulation in the era of the "global factory." It describes the impact of the global supply chain system. In particular, the chapter describes uneven development and unequal relationships between countries in Asia, and elaborates on how the supply chains model of growth has impacted upon working populations and the environment. It argues that global supply chains cannot be reformed by Corporate Social Responsibility (CSR), since CSR is a form of charity rather than representing any meaningful structural change. The chapter concludes with a proposed agenda for labor movements.

UNDERSTANDING THE CONCEPT OF GLOBAL SUPPLY CHAINS

Global supply chains are systems of capital accumulation through the coordination of international trade. As systems that connect technology-intensive economic activities and organizational networks including supply chain management, global supply chains have allowed companies to develop, manufacture, and market certain commodities with maximum profit. In the transnational production system that characterizes global capitalism, economic activity is not only *international* in scope but also *global* in its organization. While the "internationalization" refers to the geographical spread of economic activities across national boundaries, "globalization" indicates a degree of functional integration between these internationally dispersed economic activities (Gereffi 1994). Like the theory of global commodity chains, the concept of global supply chains not only considers the significance of the geographical spread of economic activities, but also their organizational scope i.e., the linkages of various economic actors, including raw material suppliers, factories, manufacturers, traders, and retailers (Gereffi 1994).

Although the two concepts of global commodity chains and global supply chains are related, they differ slightly. The notion of global supply chains refers to a broader analysis than commodity chain theories introduced by scholars such as Wallerstein, Hopkins, and Gereffi.[4] Wallerstein's World System Theory includes analysis of the emergence of a new global manufacturing system in which economic integration goes beyond international trade in raw materials and final products, to cover the centrally co-ordinated but internationally dispersed production of many of the activities along the chains of certain commodities or manufactured products.[5] Supply chains are the most important dimensions of the commodity chain in terms of governance structures that include the authority and power relationships that determine how financial, raw materials, and other resources, including labor, can be organized, allocated, and managed within a chain to produce a certain commodity. There are two important types of structures within global supply chains: supply chains driven by the manufacturer, and those driven by the buyer or brand.[6] Currently the networks of both types of supply chains are increasingly spreading to all corners of the world. These networks involve natural resources, raw materials and components, and labor in numerous countries. For example, a certain brand of clothing can be designed in the United States, made of raw materials from Pakistan and components from Bangladesh, partly manufactured in Thailand and Indonesia, and then shipped to Cambodia or China to be finished, and marketed primarily in the United States and Europe. In fact, there is nothing new about the phenomenon of the linked global supply chain, as it has been in existence at least since the 19th century when cotton from Asia was supplied to the British textile industry during the colonial period. However, in the last three decades the spread and complexity of global supply chains have developed more rapidly than ever before.

Global Supply Chains as Capital Accumulation

For corporations, global supply chains are seen as trade relations between the buyer/brand companies and suppliers that are not restricted to domestic markets, but that are also connected to each other "upstream to downstream" and from local to global levels. Corporations recognize that a logistical system that is integrated internationally can create more effective processes of capital movement and market integration (Banomyong 2010). The emergence of the flexible labor market system is linked to this effort where corporations view labor as a production factor that should be bent to facilitate and smooth the connected processes of industry, trade, and markets in order to maximize profits.

Though the issues and problems of global supply chains are familiar to labor movement activists, global supply chains remain under-analyzed. Some labor groups limit their responses to the system by seeking to make a particular company respect workers' labor rights. This response is often triggered by the exposure of high-profile cases that involve multinational companies violating workers' rights or causing environmental pollution. Emerging issues in global supply chains will never be adequately addressed by focusing on a particular issue within a particular company, or even by focusing on a particular industry. The problems arising from global supply chains should be addressed in a way that acknowledges and focuses on the root problem, which is the complex capitalistic system that involves various actors including states and global capital.

A recent case illustrates the challenges activists face in addressing specific issues in one particular factory at the expense of addressing the root causes of the problem. The campaign and lobbying effort was coordinated by a US-based NGO, *Educating for Justice*, which successfully dismantled the hidden sweatshops run by Nike subcontractor, PT Nikomas, in Serang, Banten province, Indonesia. Activists demanded an investigation and eventually urged Nike to pay US$1 million for two years of unpaid overtime to thousands of workers (although the sweatshop had been operating for 18 years).[7] Urging Nike to pay US$1 million to the workers is an important step, yet this does not end the sweatshops in the factory, let alone in many other factories. Campaigning and lobbying is necessary but obviously not sufficient, as the sweatshop continues and Nike's business continues to run as usual. The investigation in PT Nikomas does not change workers' fate and the practice of unpaid work continues because there is not an adequate mechanism in place to ensure that factories are inspected. Even after the investigation, workers at PT Nikomas are still working 30–60 minutes longer than their official working day. They are obliged to start their work 15–30 minutes earlier, reduce the time for a break, and go home later than the official workday. A union leader said that most of the workers did not get their unpaid wages; Nike's obligation to pay US$1 million is still unchecked. There is no union engaged in the process and the management is not transparent. One of the major problems is that there is not an adequate supervisory role for the state to monitor companies' activities. For example, at present in Indonesia there are only 2,384 inspectors to handle 216,547 companies, and labor activists claim that inspectors are not doing their job (Lembaga Informasi Perburuhan Sedance 2011).[8] This clearly reflects an anti-labor regime that prioritizes the interests of corporations over workers. CSR projects further engender corporations to states by allowing corporations to engage in voluntary mechanisms such as Codes of Conduct, which undermine and in some cases nullify instruments of state supervision.

Global supply chains require the exploitation of capital against labor and beyond. The disregard for workers' rights and dignity is pervasive. For example, Nike paid the basketball legend Michael Jordan 20 million US dollars for advertising Nike products, equivalent to the amount of wages received by thousands of workers in four of Nike's big supplier factories in Indonesia. The majority of these workers are women who earn only 15 US cents per hour (LaFaber 2002). It is, therefore, important to see global supply chains—as evidenced by the production network of corporations such as Nike—as symbols of the expanded capacity and mobility of global capital.

Transnational corporations such as Nike have been in constant motion across the globe in search of capital accumulation. The number of transnational corporations has grown dramatically over the past four decades. In 1971 there were 1,337 transnational corporations based in the United States. In 1983, this number increased to only 1,339 companies but by 1998 it was 2,901 companies. Transnational corporations from Japan totaled 13 in 1971, 64 in 1983, and by 1998 increased to 2,296. There were 80 transnational corporations from Germany in 1971, up to 241 in 1983, and increased further to 1,764 in 1998 (Hart-Landsberg 2011). Those corporations do not work alone, but are connected to each other in a complicated web of networks. Today, the multinational corporations that are most influential, and control global networks, are primarily from the United States (163), Germany (101), the United Kingdom (59), France (53), Canada (38), Japan (35), Italy (34), China (34), the Netherlands (33), and Sweden (18) (Vitali et al. 2011).

The expansion of global supply chains has changed peoples' mind-sets, norms, and their views on how they work i.e., how they earn a living. Today, almost all ways to labor and make a living are determined by capital movement and transnational corporations. In other words, in this current system of global supply chains corporations accrue huge benefits through their exploitation of society and the environment. The logic and model of laboring in the era of global capitalism has expanded into everyday life of societies in many countries. Previously, these forms of labor exploitation were limited to factories, particularly inside industrial zones in developed countries.

STATES AND UNEVEN DEVELOPMENT

In Asian countries, the expansion of global supply chains in the region has been closely linked to the still-dominant paradigm of export-driven development that forces governments to mold labor to meet the needs of global consumption and capital interest. The dynamics of the supply chain system in Asia have been rapidly changing since the 1980s, when Japan and other developed countries started their Foreign Direct Investment (FDI) in developing countries such as Indonesia, Malaysia, Thailand, and the Philippines. Globalization and the expansion of global supply chains have forced the governments of developing countries to leave the development model oriented toward meeting the needs of domestic industries through import substitution and protectionism. Global capital has been forcing governments in developing countries to implement an export-driven development model that relies on FDI. Taking the United States as an example, this has contributed to the decrease of the US share of manufacturing in GDP from around 28 percent in the 1950s to 12 percent in 2010 (Bellamy-Foster et al. 2011), as factories and jobs have been relocated to countries with cheaper labor. Developing and transition economies continued to account for half of global FDI in 2011 as their inflows reached a new record high, at an estimated US$755 billion (UNCTAD 2012).

The dynamics of this development model have resulted in unequal relations, even among Asian countries themselves, i.e., capital-sending countries (developed countries, such as those in East Asia) and the capital-receiving countries (developing countries, such as South and those in Southeast Asia), with the former holding greater power over the latter. On the one hand, this is made possible by the increasing ease of moving capital, and on the other hand, it is driven by developments in technology, communication, finance, and transportation. The global supply chain system is so pervasive that ultimately it has turned even non-industrial workplaces into part of a "global factory." This is part of a broader effort to coordinate global production in order to accumulate capital. Developing countries are the source of labor-intensive production and must suffer the social and environmental impact. Meanwhile the production control and benefits remain predominantly in the hands of transnational corporations, especially among those based in developed countries. For example, thousands of young laborers in factories in the Pearl River Delta areas in the Guangdong Province, China, work to manufacture goods for buyer/brand companies, the transnational corporations from the developed countries including Japan, US, and Europe. Foreign investors are constantly demanding just-in-time supply for the lowest possible production costs, which require minimum labor costs.[9] In essence, these transnational corporations have considerable control over how, when, and where manufacturing will take place and how much profit accrues at each stage of the chain (Fernandez-Stark et al. 2011).

Yet, global supply chains are not only limited to factory production, but are also engaged in exploiting large numbers of people in many countries–including in Latin America and Africa with an abundance of natural resources—who engage in producing components and raw materials for the world's consumption. In this context, home-based workers are integrated into the global supply chain system by being outsourced to do unprotected jobs.[10]

In the end, global supply chains have affected vulnerable people around the world and contributed to the destruction of the environment in developing countries.

As mentioned above, the dynamics of global supply chains have contributed to unequal relations between the capital-receiving and capital-sending countries. Figure 7.1 below illustrates the hierarchy in which the developed countries invest and transfer power to the middle-income countries that then subcontract to the developing countries in order to meet the world's consumption needs, especially from developed countries. In this hierarchy, the main actors are transnational corporations that have complex relations with the state.

The above mentioned hierarchical relation is also called the "triangle manufacturing" process. It is the mechanism used by the inner-circle countries in the production structure and global trade i.e., developed countries and newly industrialized economies during the transition period to the higher-valued economic activities. The process happened in the 1970s and 1980s when exports from Asian countries to the Middle-East were increasing. The essence of "triangle manufacturing" is that the buyer/brand countries from the developed economies give their orders to the manufacturing companies of the newly industrialized economies (Taiwan, South Korea, Singapore, Hong Kong) that have cooperated before—for example the garment companies in Hong Kong or Taiwan—that in the end move some or all of their production to the countries with low-wage labor (such as Indonesia, Cambodia, or Bangladesh). Offshore or supplier companies can be a branch, joint-venture, or contractors/sub-contractors. Thus, this "triangle manufacturing" model has changed the status of the manufacturing companies in the newly

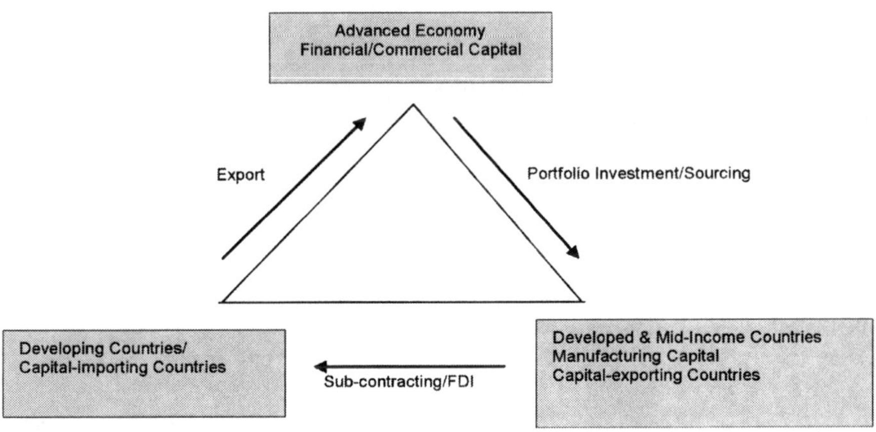

Figure 7.1. Globalized circuit of capital. Source: Chang, D. (2011).

industrialized countries in East Asia, which were previously viewed as the main contractors of the production, to be "middle-men" in the commodity chain driven by the buyer/brand companies (Gereffi 1994:224–25).

The newly industrialized economies in East Asia do have important assets in that the companies in this sub-region have long relationships with the buyer/brand companies in the United States and Europe that were built on trust through successful export transactions for years. Since the buyer companies (especially from Japan, the United States, and Europe) often do not have experience with production—hence the term "production without factories"—these companies prefer to rely on manufacturing companies of the newly industrialized countries in East Asia that are well-experienced to ensure that the standards set by the buyer companies on price, quality, and delivery schedules are met by the factories in the developing countries(Gereffi 1994).

Many corporations in East Asia have benefitted from their status as "middle-men." Together with the other corporations in developed countries, these corporations have forced political agenda of economic liberalization in the region. Developing countries are urged by the developed economies to engage in free trade by deregulating their policies of investment, trade, and finance. The result is that developing countries in South-East Asia have adopted policies that are "market-friendly," considered among the most liberal in the world. The Association of Southeast Asian Nations (ASEAN), for example, is a group of countries in South East Asia that developed a free trade agreement in 1992 (ASEAN Free Trade Agreement/AFTA), one of the first regional trade agreements in the world. Increasingly, developed countries are using free trade agreements in order to secure favorable trade relations with various developing countries (Hart-Landsberg 2011).

In addition, developing countries' reliance on FDI from developed economies—both states and the private sector—is the result of deliberate efforts by global corporations and national governments. This has happened through several stages including the integration of developing countries into the global capitalist system since the 1980s. Developed countries promote free trade policies that aim to eliminate all restrictions on trade and finances. These policies are in their favor since they are well positioned to take advantage of these asymmetrical policies as they apply to developing countries (Chang, D. 2009, 122). This condition is not natural, nor is it an inevitable process due to technological advances and the rapid flow of global information. Rather, the result is a political agenda involving active intervention by both global corporations and national governments that have imposed a set of new regulations and mechanisms in their favor.

Today, developed countries hypocritically espouse a free trade agenda, while condemning protectionist policies that those same countries benefited from in the past. Developed countries experienced rapid economic growth due to the same types of protectionist policies they now criticize. Now that they are well positioned to benefit from so-called free trade, they are pushing the free trade agenda on the rest of the world.[11] In the context of East Asia, newly industrialized countries such as South Korea, Taiwan, and Singapore have adopted a model whereby a developmental state relies on state intervention and regulation to effectively promote capitalist development.

IMPACT OF THE GLOBAL SUPPLY CHAIN SYSTEM

Though the main purpose of receiving FDI that is often given by government bureaucrats in developing countries is the need to create jobs and employment opportunities for their citizens, most FDI does not create much new employment. This is because most FDI in developing countries is in brownfield investments i.e., they take the form of acquisitions or mergers of two or more companies rather than new investment or greenfield investments. Such brownfield investments actually contribute to an increase in unemployment in developing countries rather than creating new jobs. Since the 1990s, the total brownfield investment in developing countries reached half of the total global FDI. At the peak point of FDI in 2001, FDI in developing countries reached 80 percent of total global FDI (Chang and Grabel 2004, 108–9; Chang, H. 2010; Ietto-Gillies 2005, 202). These mergers and acquisitions were accompanied by mass dismissals of workers. This was done through the informalization of employment as a rationalization process and through privatization of state-owned enterprises. The section below provides an example of outsourced or agency workers in Indonesia who were treated unfairly by an unloading services company. The company was formerly a state-owned enterprise, which was privatized through a take-over process by foreign capital.

The Voices of Workers in the Global Supply Chain: Alliance of Outsourced Workers at Jakarta International Container Terminal (APOJICT), Jakarta, Indonesia

> The privatization of Jakarta International Container Terminal through the process of acquisition by global capital in international logistic and supply management has resulted in the workers' suffering, rather than bringing any benefit to them.

In a meeting in early May 2011 with several unionists from an alliance of outsourced logistics workers' unions at Indonesia's largest container port, Jakarta International Container Terminal, we asked the unionists about their stories of working at the "bottom" of the global supply chain—in this case providing logistics services for a global multinational—which happens to be based in Hong Kong. The unionists related that they have been suffering from the unjust decision taken by the company last year, as most of the outsourced workers were unlawfully dismissed from the company after joining a protest. The national Labour Court legitimized the company's wrongful decision, demanding only that the dismissed workers be paid their due severance payments, rather than challenging the dismissals themselves. However most of the dismissed workers have decided to appeal this Labour Court ruling and demand reinstatement.

Jakarta International Container Terminal used to be a state-owned enterprise, but the privatization of the company through the process of acquisition by global capital in international logistic and supply management—Hutchison Port Holdings/Hutchinson Whampoa Limited—has resulted in the workers' suffering, rather than bringing any benefit to them by this "brownfield" investment. The capital controls 75 percent of the container market in Jakarta's Tanjung Priok Port through its cross-shareholding. Below is the workers' story:

> We worked as outsourced workers for a logistics company at Jakarta International Container Terminal since 1991, but now we have been unlawfully dismissed from our jobs. Our situation got worse when Jakarta International Container Terminal, formerly a state-owned company named PT PELINDO II, was privatized in 1999 and a Singapore-based company Grosbeak Pte Ltd gained 51 percent of the company's shares. Grosbeak Pte Ltd is a subsidiary of Hutchinson Port Holding Ltd, which is one of the business units of Hutchinson Whampoa Ltd based in Hong Kong.
>
> We have been through unfair treatment: our employment status never changed, even though we worked there for two decades. Outsourced workers like us comprised 60 percent of the total workers but all of us had the same tasks as all the permanent workers. As outsourced workers we could not join the JICT union which exclusively organized only the 40 percent of workers who had permanent status. We were employed by three different labor agencies and we signed our contracts from time to time with those agencies. That was certainly not fair and, in fact, was against the labor law. Such a situation made us become organized and we began to establish a coalition of outsourced workers to fight for our rights. The coalition is called the Alliance of Outsourced Workers at Jakarta International Container Terminal (Aliansi Pekerja Outsourcing—Jakarta International Container Terminal—APOJICT). APOJICT had begun raising its grievances in 2009, to no avail. We consolidated our efforts and, together with a national coalition of unions, the Committee for National Solidarity or KSN (Komite Solidaritas Nasional), have been actively taking up a nation-wide campaign against union-busting, privatization, and labour market flexibility. On February 1, 2010, more than 500 outsourced workers participated in a two-hour lock-out which caused an enormous loss for the company; this has proven that we, outsourced workers, actually played a vital and strategic role in the company's overall performance. The management came to appease us and promised to enter into negotiation. However, the

permanent workers' union (which had been fighting for only their own union members' rights) had impeded the settlement.

In the following days we were intimidated, our families got a lot of threats, and some of us were forced to leave our jobs. We reported the case to the Labour Department, House of Representatives, and Ministry of State-owned Enterprises. However, the company only neglected our demands, and systematically intimidated and unlawfully dismissed most of us, even though we got the recommendation from the Labour Office to grant permanent status to us. The Labour Court had further endorsed the dismissals and required the company to provide severance pay. Due to the economic hardship, a few of us took the severance payment while most of the others of us have gone for appeal to the Supreme Court. We need decent work and we have the right to employment.

Through all this, we realized that privatization had been worsening our working environment and people's livelihoods. We came to know that the giant multinational corporations such as Hutchinson have been playing a pivotal role in dragging workers into the "race to the bottom."

A recent ILO Report has pointed out that workers who lost their jobs are increasingly working as contract workers or in the informal sector with little or no protection for their normative rights. In the ASEAN Region, the number of poor (living on less than US$2 per day) has risen in the past two years, from 140 million to 158 million people, or from 51 percent to 57 percent of total workers in the regions (ILO 2010). To ensure that the investment climate remains conducive to FDI, states continue to make investment-friendly policies, or find ways to manipulate the constitution. In collusion with businesses, states have engaged in egregious acts including the seizure of land, industrialization of agriculture, and commoditization of natural resources and public facilities. For example, since the 1960s, gold mining in West Papua has been under virtually complete control by US-based TNCs, including Freeport Mc-Morran Copper & Gold Inc., which holds 2.6 million hectares and has expelled people from their land. Recently at least 60 people were killed and 148 people were imprisoned for obstructing Indonesia's mining investment (Mufakhir 2012). In the Philippines, unionists were murdered. Recently, in Indonesia, peasants in Lampung Province were brutally murdered by a company, with assistance from the local police that was trying to grab their land for palm oil and rubber production (Kompas 2011). Not long ago, a labor activist in Bangladesh who exposed a case of exploitation was murdered (Global Post 2012). In China, workers at Foxconn—a Taiwan company that assembles and supplies products for one of the most profitable companies in the world, Apple—experienced physical and mental depression causing dozens of them to commit suicide. In South Korea, workers for Samsung, a company which for years has openly declared itself as anti-union, suffered from blood cancer and leukemia due to a toxic chemical contamination in its factories.[12] A report of the Asian Network for the Rights of Occupational and Environmental Victims stated that recently in the Asian region 1.1 million workers died every year from their work, which equates to 30,000 workers per day or 125 workers per hour or 2 per minute (ANROEV 2012). This list illustrates the extent of exploitation and collusion between states and capital. Instead of serving people who elect them, democratic institutions such as local authorities tend to repress citizens and conspire with business interests. People have lost their sovereignty and their livelihood and are deprived of their basic rights. The deeper the integration of the global supply chain is in their lives, the more pressure it puts on people.

The detrimental effects of the global supply chain system include environmental damage and the social cost paid by society (i.e., the separation of families due to migration, the loss of rights to health care, and loss of rights to land). Companies continue to take maximum profits while the danger and risk are externalized to society and the environment. All of this is hidden from the public's eyes. In other words, the systems that made it possible for Asian-based supply chains to come up with considerably cheaper products (such as US$3,000 cars, US$300 computers, or US$30 mobile phones) also mean that these goods are produced at enormous costs which are borne by society and the environment.

THE GLOBAL SUPPLY CHAIN SYSTEM CANNOT BE REFORMED

Various groups have made efforts to "clean up" global supply chains and make corporations act fairly. For example, many groups have called for intensifying voluntary mechanisms of corporate accountability through Codes of Conduct or Corporate Social Responsibility (CSR) initiatives. However, these voluntary mechanisms have not brought about any significant changes. In fact, recent studies on the role of Codes of Conduct in improving workers' welfare in Indonesia showed negative results (Kjellgren 2010). Another study showed the same trend for CSR in Indonesia, India, China, and South Korea (AMRC 2012). Of course since the inherent nature of capitalism prioritizes capital accumulation, global supply chains cannot be reformed through these voluntary mechanisms.

The biggest problem with CSR is not that it has limitations, nor is it its questionable ability to sufficiently address the problems it intends to ameliorate. Rather, it is the fact that it takes people in completely the wrong direction. For many large corporations, CSR is primarily a strategy to divert attention away from the negative social and environmental impacts of their activities. The activities of CSR mostly concentrate on community development where the corporations focus on what they call "comprehensive development" where they provide health facilities and sanitation, schools, and housing, as well as entrepreneurship skills for villagers. Such corporate strategies have been effectively hegemonic, providing a strong legitimacy and license for corporations to sustain the exploitation of human and natural resources. More importantly, it leads people to wrongly assume that corporations, and not states, are responsible for citizens' basic rights to better education, clean water, healthcare, etc. It disciplines people and motivates them to behave in ways that make state regulation obsolete, while leaving them at the mercy of market forces.[13]

Corporations use CSR projects as a form of green-washing[14] and a marketing strategy rather than as genuine responsibility for workers' well-being. The rights of workers at shop floors have, in fact, been deliberately neglected and violated for the sake of higher profit, exposing the real corporate sense of responsibility. The most notorious case is the glossy CSR report of Hindustan Lever Limited (Hindustan Unilever), the Indian subsidiary of Unilever PLC, the country's largest packaged mass consumption goods company that deals in home and personal care products, food, and beverages. The CSR report of Hindustan Unilever on *Improving Health and Well-being of People* in India is in extreme contrast with the company's ruthless ways of dealing with workers.[15] In its Doom Dooma factory in Assam about 700 workers and union leaders have been attacked since 2007 for asserting their basic rights. Hindustan Unilever has been involved in a number of CSR initiatives by promoting programs such as Project Shakti of Unilever. The project is aimed at creating rural entrepreneurs by providing training to 13,000 underprivileged Indian women, who are trained to distribute the company's products to 70 million rural consumers. Working with women's self-help groups, the company teaches them selling and book-keeping skills and equips them with commercial knowledge (Muruganantham 2010).

The case clearly shows that CSR is merely a marketing gimmick and an effective exercise in greenwashing. On the one hand, the company deliberately neglects the rights of its own workers at the workplace, while, on the other hand, it builds a good image of contributing to the society. Exploiting a large number of women under the banner of CSR by involving them in selling and distributing Unilever's products, Hindustan Unilever in fact has increased its profits dramatically. The women participating in the project have been reaching out to the Indian domestic market that helped Unilever to get 30 percent more consumers in rural areas since the inception of the project in 2000.

Furthermore, by promoting CSR, corporations are trying to change the industrial relationship in a company to a harmonious one, so that they can violate workers' basic rights without any considerable resistance. In other words, the purpose of CSR is to entertain and to appease the labor movement and civil society. CSR initiatives are also designed to guard the interests of multinational companies within the international sub-contracting system. Through CSR initiatives, corporations pacify the labor movement by providing a basis for NGOs and trade unions to get involved in monitoring the manufacturing process of the multinational companies. As a consequence, many NGOs and trade unions participate and join the CSR bandwagon, engaging in monitoring activities and dialogue with shareholders, giving up their core work at the grassroots level (Leong and Chan 2006).

AGENDA FOR THE LABOR MOVEMENT

The mobility of capital and the consolidation of global supply chains is not a natural, unidentified process arising from finance and technological advancement or more rapid global information flows. Rather, it is a political project involving the active intervention of both global corporations and national governments by imposing an immense range of new legal mechanisms and regulations which serve their interests. This political project, therefore, should be the first and foremost agenda item for unions to dismantle. They should do this by promoting new legal mechanisms and regulations to subordinate capital to people and to the democratic requirements established in international human rights standards.

The rise of the global production and supply chain system has resulted in the shift of world manufacturing from industrialized countries to developing nations. This shift began in the 1970s and has escalated in recent decades. The economic architecture that created a global production and global supply chain system has had a tremendous impact on working people. The system has hurt workers both in the core countries and peripheries. In the core, such as the United States and Japan, economies receive less investment and fewer employment opportunities, and wages are being driven down through globalized competition. In the peripheries, the competition between countries for FDI and export markets is leading to the systematic establishment of anti-labor regimes to lock in developing countries' comparative advantages based on cheaper, more manageable labor.

Global supply chains present new challenges to labor movements. The supply chain has also divided the working class by scattering assembly lines to different places and by causing the informalization of labor. On the one hand, effective collective bargaining by workers and communities in the global supply chain needs broader working class solidarity, which should come from a unified cross-sectoral alliance of all working people, yet on the other hand the supply chain leads to difficulty in organizing workers. Organizing at the shop floor level itself has become difficult, but even where shop floor unionism is strong, relying only on shop floor unions turns out to be ineffective for collective bargaining with multinational employers and state authorities on workers' issues. Thus, workplace struggles need to be connected to, and reinforce, broader transformative national efforts to challenge the coordinated global production networks aimed at capital accumulation.

It is indeed crucial to regularly campaign against certain corporations or brands (one section of global supply chains) when they violate labor rights, damage the environment, or grab people's lands, as a way to challenge the system. However, the "naming and shaming" campaigns directed at particular corporations should not be considered as an endpoint on their own since they do not change the whole system. Rather, we need to go beyond such campaigns to the point where broader efforts to dismante neoliberal capitalism can take place. Naming and shaming campaigns are important and necessary, but they are obviously not sufficient. Global supply chains cannot simply be reformed.

The effort to challenge global supply chains needs a comprehensive strategy in addition to local level struggles. Given the deep divisions and competitions that easily arise among workers in global supply chains (of industry, employment status, race/class/gender), it is critical to articulate the commonalities for the working class as a whole, which may formulate the basis for broader solidarity and formation of common strategies and goals for collective bargaining. For example, the process of capital accumulation by dispossession (not only in terms of land acquisitions and displacements, but also dispossession in terms of denying various rights of the people and slashing expenditures in public welfare). that is marginalizing most of the people could become one such common platform for the struggle. However, this also requires reclaiming the sphere of politics as a legitimate object of people's struggle and above all, to reclaiming people's sovereignty.

NOTES

1. Derogatory term used for the garment workers in Sri Lanka. Juki is one of the earliest Japanese sewing machines being used in the country.
2. See http://fashion.telegraph.co.uk/news-features/TMG9461957/Zara-owner-is-worlds-third-richest-person.html (accessed on October 12, 2012).
3. See http://data.worldbank.org/country/cambodia (accessed on October 12, 2012).
4. See Raikes, Jensen, Friis, and Ponte, (2000) and Gereffi (1994).
5. Ibid.
6. In his analysis on global commodity chains, Gereffi (1994, 215) describes that global commodity chains have three main dimensions: first is an input-output structure, which is a set of products and services linked together in a sequence of value-adding economic activities. The second is territoriality that is a spatial dispersion or concentration of production and marketing networks, comprised of enterprises of different sizes and types. The third is governance structure, i.e., authority and power relationships that determine how financial, material and human resources are allocated and flow within a chain.
7. Based on interviews with a union leader from Nikomas factory. November 6, 2012. See also "Indonesian Nike Workers Win $1m in Unpaid Overtime," *Jakarta Globe*, January 11, 2012.
8. Based on Interviews with Sedane Labor Resource Center and a union leader from Nikomas factory, November 6, 2012.

9. See Gereffi (1994, p.224–25) for an explanation about the role of Newly Industrialised Countries as a "middle man" in the "triangle manufacturing."

10. Home-based work is a growing global phenomenon with over 100 million people working from their homes, in countries both rich and poor. With the rise of complex global chains of production over the past decades, home-based work has grown exponentially. For further study about home based workers, see Sinha (2006).

11. Countries that used to implement protectionist policies were, among others, the United States, Germany, Sweden, France, Finland, Austria, Japan, Taiwan, and South Korea. See Chang (2008).

12. For comprehensive research on Samsung and its anti-union behavior, see Chang (2006).

13. See AMRC (2012).

14. Greenwashing is an amalgam of "green" and "brainwashing." The term is generally used when significantly more money or time has been spent advertising being green (that is, operating with consideration for the environment), rather than spending resources on environmentally sound practices. This is often portrayed by changing the name or label of a product to evoke the natural environment or nature—for example, putting an image of a forest on a bottle containing harmful chemicals.

15. The report is available at http://www.hul.co.in (accessed on November 1, 2011).

REFERENCES

ANROEV. 2012. Asian Network for the Rights of Occupational and Environmental Victims campaign publication. http://www.amrc.org.hk/node/1247.

Asia Monitor Resource Centre. 2012. *The Reality of Corporate Social Responsibility: Case Studies on the Impact of CSR on Workers in China, South Korea, India and Indonesia*, Hong Kong: AMRC.

Banomyong, R. 2010. *Supply Chain Dynamics in Asia*. ADBI Working Paper 184. Tokyo: Asian Development Bank Institute.

Chang, Ha-Joon, and Ilene Grabel. 2004. *Reclaiming Development: An Alternative Economic Policy Manual.* London and New York: Zed Books.

Chang, Ha-Joon. 2008. *Bad Samaritans: The Myth of Free Trade and the Secret History of Capitalism*. New York: Bloomsbury Press.

Chang, Ha-Joon. 2010. *23 Things They Don't Tell You about Capitalism*. New York: Penguin Books.

Chang, Dae-oup. (ed.) 2006. *Labour in Globalising Asian Corporations: A Portrait of Struggle* Hong Kong: AMRC.

Chang, Dae-oup. 2009. *Capitalist Development in Korea: Labour, Capital and the Myth of the Developmental State*. London: Routledge.

Chang, Dae-oup. 2011. *Globalization and Development: States and Global Market* (lecture notes), Department of Development Studies, SOAS, University of London.

Gereffi, Gary. 1994. "Capitalism, Development and Global Commodity Chains." In *Capitalism and Development*, edited by Leslie Sklair, p. 215-231. New York: Routledge.

Global Post. 2012. "Bangladesh labor leader murdered two weeks after international rights victory." April 9, 2012.

Fernandez-Stark, Karina, Stacey Frederick, and Gary Gereffi. 2011. *The Apparel Global Value Chain: Economic Upgrading and Workforce Development,* Duke University Center on Globalization, Governance and Competitiveness, p. 12.

Foster, John Bellamy, Robert W. McChesney, and Jamil R. Jonna. 2011. "The Global Reserve Army of Labor and the New Imperialism." *Monthly Review*, 63:27–29.

Hart-Landsberg, Martin. 2011. "Capitalism, the Korea-US FTA and Resistance." *Critical Asian Studies* 43:319–348.

Ietto-Gillies, Grazia. 2005. *Transnational Corporations and International Production: Concepts, Theories and Effects,* Cheltenham: Edward Elgar Publishing Limited.

ILO. 2010. *Labour and Social Trends in ASEAN 2010: Sustaining Recovery and Development through Decent Work*, Bangkok: ILO Regional Office for Asia and the Pacific.

Kjellgren, Jessika. 2010. *Codes of Conduct—A Useful Remedy to Help Garment Workers Reach Quality of Life? A Study from the Perspective of the Indonesian Garment Workers, Union Representatives and Labor-NGOs Who are at the Heart of the Concern,* unpublished BA thesis, Gothenburg University *Kompas*, December 14, 2011.

Lembaga Informasi Perburuhan Sedane. 2011. *Annual Labor Update*. Bogor: LIPS, 2011.

LaFaber, Walter. 2002. *Michael Jordan and the New Global Capitalism*, New York: WW Norton.

Leong, Apo and Ka-wai Chan. 2006. "Critical Reflection on CSR: A Labour's Perspective," *Asian Labour Update*. 60.

Mufakhir, Abu. 2012. "The Case of Freeport Mc-Morran Copper & Gold Inc. in Indonesia's Extractive Industry," *Asian Labour Update*, 81:19–24.

Muruganantham, G. 2010. Case study on Corporate Social Responsibility of MNC's in India, International Trade & Academic Research Conference (ITARC), London.

Raikes, Phillip, Micahel Jensen, and Stefano Ponte. 2000. "Global Commodity Chain Ananlysis and the French *Filiére* Approach: Compariosn Critique." *Economy and Society* 29: 390-417.

Sinha, Shalini. *Rights of Home-based Workers*. New Delhi: National Human Rights Commission.

Vitali Stefani, James B. Glattfelder, and Stefano Battiston. 2011. "The Network of Global Corporate Control." www.plosone.org. Accessed February 12, 2012.

UNCTAD. 2012. *Global Investment Trends Monitor*, 8:24.

Chapter Eight

Increased Visibility for Marginalized Voices in the Production and Consumption of First Nations Media

Claire Litton-Cohn and Sky Croeser

Our communications and media shape, and are shaped by, broader social and political structures. Power is exercised in the production of media according to who is excluded, who has a voice, and how this affects the final product we consume. As technology impacts access to information and provides new platforms for people, we need to look more closely at who participates and how. Media designed for and by Inuit in Canada demonstrates the power of digital media for the continuation and preservation of Inuit culture and redefines how indigenous communities interact with the global economy.

Digital media have become a focal point for some indigenous communities in their efforts to retain their cultural identities and organize against racist policies and attitudes. Particularly relevant in the many digital options available is streaming radio, which is well suited to indigenous interaction styles and worldviews, and promotes the building of on- and off-line communities in ways which show a continuity with traditional structures. Isuma Distribution International has banded together with several other organizations, including the Municipality of Igloolik and Nunavut Independent Television Network, to develop DID. DID uses Internet, community radio, local and social media to amplify traditional Inuit decision-making skills (*angjqatigiingniq, or "deciding together"*). This project aims to provide needed information in understandable language, provide space to discuss concerns publicly and reach collective decisions with the power of consensus. DID was launched to deal with the Environmental Review of the $6 billion Baffinland Iron Mine at Mary River in north Baffin Island, and provided many opportunities for local community members to speak out. From May 2012 to

June 2012, DID media tools informed, consulted, and assisted Inuit to make decisions together within the seven impacted Inuit communities, and supported those communities in participating in the public hearings held by Baffinland and the Nunavut Impact Review Board in July 2013.

A *ngjqatigiingniq* is a necessary component of transparency and problem-solving for northern communities, and the potential for democratic participation by underserved minority communities is often ignored by multinational organizations. Nipivut Nunatinnii, an Inuit-run radio station that broadcasts primarily in Inuktitut, is a subsidiary of DID and is streamed on the IsumaTV website, as well as being accessible through various radio stations in northern communities (IsumaTV 2012a). The radio station has a bricks-and-mortar location in Igloolik, Nunavut, Canada, but occasionally broadcasts live from remote locations, as when they covered the RockinWalrus music festival in June 2012.

This chapter looks at the growing economic and social importance of online content, noting that while we often assume that the Internet creates "placeless" communities based purely around shared interests, there are important inequalities within the emerging knowledge economy and in online media. In particular, indigenous people are vastly under-represented, and frequently *mis*represented. Specific challenges exist for indigenous people using online media: these technologies are frequently built around hegemonic cultural frameworks, and online cultures often replicate and reinforce racist attitudes. The norms surrounding sharing content in online communities may also be problematic given indigenous cultures' desire to protect indigenous knowledge from commodification and inappropriate distribution. Nevertheless, by adapting analogue and digital technologies to meet indigenous needs, IsumaTV has been able to develop an important tool for social change.

IsumaTV's work takes place within the context of a global sense of "place" which has shifted with the advent of the Internet. Communities are no longer bounded by geographical location; "netizens" can theoretically live everywhere and nowhere, as Internet consumers declare allegiance to online personalities and lifestyles that are more closely identified with online communities than national or local identities. The vast scope of available information has allowed us to promote the following fallacies: that there is a free and easy exchange of information online; that free exchange of information is possible and preferable; and that netizens are more culturally aware than citizens (MacKinnon 2012, 202). This change in the way we view identity—that it is based more on the transfer of mutually agreeable information than geographic location, skin color, or cultural background—opens up new opportunities for social change, but it also creates new challenges.

In part, these challenges are rooted in the growth of the "knowledge economy," which is inspiring a growing body of academic research, management practices, and economic policies (Peters, Marginson, and Murphy 2009; Rooney, Hearn, and Kastelle 2012; Tsoukas and Shepherd 2009). We now have jobs whose purpose is the managing of online identities, where the product being sold is a business's reputation; interacting with customers and situating businesses in virtual communities has real world advantages, to the point where businesses without regularly updated websites or social media presences appear disingenuous. Writers in a range of areas hail the ability to work across borders as an opportunity for global growth and a possible solution to economic inequality.

In addition to this, there is an increased optimism about the ability of everyday, or "vernacular" creativity online to translate into meaningful civic engagement which may help to strengthen communities (Burgess, Foth, and Klaebe 2006). However, Burgess (2006, 206) cautions us that it is necessary to center questions around "access, self-representation, and literacy" in our discussions of vernacular creativity. With this in mind, it is important to examine the way in which racist and colonial discourses shape Internet communities, as well as to recognize community-built artifacts that challenge these structures. This not only allows us to build a better understanding of online culture as it already exists, but also to imagine possible alternatives which might be more welcoming of marginalized or colonized voices and forms of creativity.

It is also important to recognize media, including digital media, as being the outcome of labor that takes place under specific conditions. Important work, including early research by Tiziana Terranova (2000) and more recent interventions by the "Turkopticon" project (Irani and Silberman, 2013), has emphasized that digital content is often produced through exploitative labor conditions. However, more attention is necessary for understanding the ways in which race, and racism, shape the online content which we consume. Lack of visibility has been a problem for indigenous communities both on- and offline. A glut of available information has dual results: it theoretically provides opportunities for indigenous voices to be more available to non-indigenous consumers while simultaneously drowning legitimate productions in conflicting and unsorted information. As Nathan writes, "reporting of Indigenous matters has been as prolific as it has been negative. . . . Such negativity confirms a view that *Aboriginal* viewpoints do not have a place: only when Aboriginal issues appear in relation to an 'other,' and problematised, can they become media content" (2000, 39). This cannot be separated from the fact that minorities, and in particular indigenous Canadians, continue to be excluded from Canadian newsrooms due to a systematic bias in hiring processes (Ojo 2006, 349–351). The context of structural exclusion from mainstream media is therefore an important factor in the ongoing oppression which First Nations peoples in Canada face.

Visibility is the key to social change, and an important step in creating change is for those voices which have previously been excluded to be heard. Perley (2009) argues that gaining a voice for members of First Nations communities in the public sphere of the Internet can be a useful step in challenging racist mainstream representations. Perley's work also demonstrates the important role that online communications can play within First Nations communities, allowing people to create media that is relevant to their own needs and interests and which addresses issues from an indigenous perspective.

However, the use of digital technologies may also pose challenges for indigenous communities. Modern technological advances may, for example, contribute to a distancing from community and context; a user must, in many cases, be inside at her computer rather than interacting with in-person communities or landscapes, although this is changing with the growth of mobile Internet. The structure of computer-mediated communication is, arguably, based on Western ontologies; to participate completely in digital landscapes as they currently exist, users must often follow a pattern of thinking and interaction that is dominated by the colonizing culture, rather than one built by indigenous peoples (Iseke-Barnes and Danard 2007). As Eglash (2002) and Kendall (2011) note, the cultures which have dominated the computing revolution have been structured by whiteness, and while there have been attempts to challenge the gatekeeping function this plays, it continues to discourage minority participation in the programming industries. Disproportionately low employment rates for minorities in the computing industry also hint at a hiring bias similar to that seen in the newsroom (Kendall 2011, 520). Given the structural marginalization of minorities in the development of computing and computing culture, it is unsurprising to find that these spaces may not meet indigenous peoples' needs.

This is particularly clear when it comes to the frameworks for sharing content online. Efforts to use digital technologies to preserve, share, and develop indigenous cultural heritage highlight some of these challenges. For example, while online culture is increasingly characterized by a tension between existing intellectual property law and the new shift toward "open access," neither of these frameworks is well suited to the needs of indigenous communities. On the one hand, strict intellectual property laws are based on a system of property "rights" and individual ownership that many indigenous communities find inappropriate (Seadle 2002). On the other hand, the history of colonization of native cultures, which are often embedded within distinct cultural values and transmitted through endangered languages, means that entering indigenous knowledge into the digital commons is problematic, as cultural context and tools for cultural interpretation are lost (Schneiter 2011, 149). Cultural or technological shifts toward open access and sharing of cultural content do not often take into account the history of colonial appropriation and commodification of indigenous knowledge which many First Nations have experienced, and the ongoing commodification of indigenous culture (Brown and Nicholas 2012, 309; Iseke-Barnes and Danard 2007, 174). Inequalities between cultures and the ongoing impact of colonialism may temper many indigenous communities' enthusiasm about creative commons, unfettered sharing, and the public domain.

Open sharing of content may also clash with cultural prohibitions on the sharing of knowledge outside particular contexts. The broadcast of indigenous media engages with several issues that mainstream media do not recognize. Broadcasting in a public arena opens material up to scrutiny by a wide and uncontrolled audience, meaning that there could be legal ramifications that would never have arisen with a purely indigenous audience. Indigenous concepts of the sacred and private as opposed to the profane also differ greatly from mainstream media's conceptions; for example, it is common for Australian Aboriginal culture to find images and recordings of the recently deceased "too sorrowful" to be viewed (Schneiter 2011). In addition, some information is intended to be shared only with certain tribes, or only by particular members of a community. Communities are adapting their responses to these challenges. Māori tribal group Te Aitanga a Hauiti have chosen to provide a database of cultural knowledge in which some content is only available to appropriate tribal members, restricting accessing by sharing information on CDs rather than online (Ngata, Ngata-Gibson, and Salmond 2012, 242), demonstrating that these problems are not insurmountable when technologies are controlled by indigenous communities.

However, digital technologies are rarely developed with Indigenous needs in mind. Support for Indigenous languages also remains limited both online and for most computing devices (such as PCs, laptops, and mobile phones). Indigenous languages, some of which may be completely oral, are sometimes difficult to transmit effectively without being situated in cultural knowledge that outsiders do not have access to: therefore, translating information into English is always approximate. Use of the Internet may therefore threaten Indigenous languages, as people without access to convenient transcription fonts for their languages use English, or a romanized alphabet, further separating indigenous knowledge from its original context. Both cultural appropriation and the dilution of traditional cultures contribute to social uncertainty and have created new difficulties. For the Inuit, this has "created high levels of stress and dislocation in the key systems that sustained Inuit—the Elders, the family, kinship relationships, and the underpinning beliefs" (Tagalik 2010, 5).

The threats posed to Indigenous identity include the perpetuation of racist stereotypes in online spaces, and racist abuse which may exclude Indigenous people from participation. As Iseke-Barnes and Danard note, this is linked to the commodification of Indigenous cultures as dominant cultures often hold the power to "define, classify, and reduce cultural groups to stereotypes and to use these reductions to market and sell products" (2007, 31). Binary constructions are often used to maximize differentiation; when a group seems as different as possible from the dominant paradigm, that group can then be fetishized. Aboriginal women in Canada report a rate of victimization in violent crimes that is three times that of non-Aboriginal women, which the Aboriginal Justice Implementation Commission (1999) attributes in part to the demeaning "squaw" image of Aboriginal women as provided by mainstream media imagery. This hypersexualized imagery of Indigenous women (particularly those from North America) is repeated online, and attempts to address it are often met with outright hostility (Keene 2012). On December 23, 2012, Metis activist Âpihtawikosisân, in reference to repeated online racism in comments sections of newspaper articles about Idle No More, tweeted: "Wondering how we can talk about these things when almost all the spaces are unsafe?" (Âpihtawikosisân 2012). Given these issues (as well as others which are not addressed here) it is not surprising that many Indigenous communities are underrepresented online, as well as in mainstream media.

In the face of changing environmental and productive factors and a lack of safe spaces for discussion, digital media have become an important tool for providing information and community support to remote indigenous communities, such as the Mapuche in Chile and Yolgnu of northern Australia (Cárcamo-Huechante 2010, p. 156) . Indigenous communication systems have been radically fragmented and dispersed by colonization and appropriation; communities that were once next door may have been relocated thousands of miles apart. Indigenous people frequently prioritize media that allow for community building, particularly using oral contact as an important part of communicating. While there may be problems with the use of digital technologies, indigenous streaming radio is more similar to traditional communications methods than any mainstream printed material, which may also be in a language or use a syntax with which indigenous people are not familiar or do not wish to use because of its association with colonizers' culture. Burarra people in northern Arnhem Land have described the configuration of the Internet—a network of networks—as corresponding with their own system of kinship (Carew cited in Nathan 2000, 42). IsumaTV's streaming radio project, Nipivut Nunatinnii (Our Voice At Home) was created to encourage discussion of issues that directly impact Inuit, in their own language, and as such is an important focal point for social change. By providing resources for Inuit to produce their own media independently and broadcast globally, Nipivut Nunatinnii becomes a tool for organizing and communicating within the community to effect broader social change.

IsumaTV's Nipivut Nunattinni program provides a space for Indigenous voices which is based on Inuit values and largely run by Inuit people. A caller to Nipivut Nunatinni on May 15, 2012, stated: "People are asking

'What do people think?' and it's always someone else's voice, but this show means we can hear the real voices" (IsumaTVDID 2012a). Flexibility and adaptation to new situations has been a necessary trait of Inuit culture for thousands of years, even more so in the face of forced relocations, abrogation of treaty rights, global warming, and discovery of resource-rich land in the Canadian north. Inuit people are able to adapt online media, as they have adapted to other changes, and use these to not only provide opportunities for growth and the building of community, but allow real change to ripple outward and affect non-indigenous online communities.

Radio has always played a role in remote Inuit communities that few other media can play; radio is a commonly accessible medium in locations that may not have television, Internet, or effective cellular service. Inuit use the medium of radio as a community bulletin board, calling in to make requests about family members, discuss the price of meat at the local store, or share hunting tips (Cohn, pers. comm., 2012). For Inuit, radio has replaced the increasingly impossible community gathering—as jobs become scarcer, many Inuit must move south to feed their families, and the forced relocation and settlement of a previously nomadic people by Canada's government in the 1950s prevented communities from being able to meet as they had previously. Since, for Inuit, "cultural wellbeing relies on the individual becoming situated within a cultural worldview" (Tagalik 2010, 1), placement and identification within a larger community structure is necessary not just for individual health, but for the health of Inuit culture as a whole.

IsumaTV's decision to use Internet radio, rather than radio alone, as a platform is not surprising given the success other indigenous communities have had with this tool. For example, the Ashaninka Internet radio project in Peru, begun in 1999, has had many benefits:

> Through the use of high frequency Internet radio, over 60 Ashaninka communities, located in a relatively extensive area of the Peruvian Andes, have been able to establish a network of intra-communal information that ranges from cultural revival to protection of native rights to natural resources and traditional medicine. In addition, e-commerce is promoted, whereby the communities are able to sell products—such as coffee—in big urban centers such like Lima (Salazar 2003, 21).

Ashaninka Internet radio is responsible not only for encouraging the growth of community identity, but also in developing commerce opportunities and supporting political action.

Similarly, the radio station Wixage anai! was developed by Mapuche, the indigenous peoples of Chile and Argentina, in the early 1990s. Cárcamo-Huechante writes, "the members of Wixage anai! exercise their agency by creating a Mapuche sonorous space from this location on the AM frequency, thus producing sound and meaning 'along the margin'" (2010, 162). The

Mapuche derive collective as well as individual support not only by creating the radio programming, but by listening to it; the "very act of listening to the radio program resonates with the political desire to voice and bestow meaning upon Mapuche radio communication. Listening to voices and sounds associated with the Mapuche language, culture, and music is part of a process of collective identity formation" (Cárcamo-Huechante 2010, 163). As anyone who has traveled in another country can attest, hearing one's own language spoken in a sea of confusing sounds and ideas can be refreshing, revitalizing, and heartening. In traveling the uncharted countries of cyberspace, indigenous voices are distinct in their uniqueness and rarity.

By providing an alternative to traditionally produced and controlled media, such as television or newspapers, streaming Internet radio also allows Nunavummiut (Nunavut residents) to engage with a medium in their own language, built and promulgated by them. This means Inuit can build a sense of autonomy and independence from governmental bias and impact, as mainstream media are filtered through the lens of the dominant culture. Cárcamo-Huechante (2010, 164) states, "Indigenous radio is clearly a response to demands from a community seeking its own space in a media environment seen to be undemocratic." Nipivut Nunatinnii therefore has the opportunity to encourage social activism and change by demonstrating that one does not have to act, look, or produce art in a particular way (that is, so that it fits in with the dominantly accepted paradigm) to be heard.

Isuma Production Company's enormously popular films, all of which are available in their entirety on the isuma.tv website, were made using Inuit storytelling techniques, nonlinear and metaphorical language, and entirely in Inuktitut; as Tumblr user blackfeatherasylum says, " *Atanarjuat* is one of the most incredible films I've ever seen" (cited in Ayiman 2012). Qitsualik writes, "There is considerable stress in trying to be the ones to blend into foreigner's social structure and language. Things that we trust in must continue to exist" (cited in Tagalik 2010, 7). Indigenous artworks, following indigenous storytelling techniques, are valuable not just for the building of strong diasporic communities, but also for maintaining a continuity of native culture as media change.

Because Inuit communities are already familiar with and have developed uses for radio as a communication and creative medium (Cohn, pers. comm., 2012), streaming Internet radio, available in high- and low-speed options for possible streaming on mobile devices, is an obvious outcome of technological advances. The cultural background and context of Inuit consensus decision-making, community-building, and the necessity of communicating over long distances have molded the available technology into a form that is very specifically Inuit: southerners (as Inuit tend to refer to people living anywhere below Nunavut), with their vastly increased access to high-speed Internet and low latency, would not value a streaming radio program over other forms of online interaction. In this way, Nipivut Nunatinnii, by virtue of being available online and by traditional radio, provides access to information on a much broader scope than Inuit would have previously had access to: radio has traditionally been the main means of "social networking" in Inuit communities, so listening to the radio appeals to elders and those who are unfamiliar with the digital commons, while younger people or those with more access to digital media can participate in a broader way that integrates within the commonly accepted "netizen" digital identity. Listeners can tweet questions to radio guests using Twitter, or post on the station's Facebook page, as well as calling in, and can not only develop dialogue with each other, but also guide the focus of upcoming programs. There is simultaneous translation into Inuktitut for English guests, and in-studio translation of questions asked them in Inuktitut, placing English and Inuktitut on equal footing.

However, while translations are sometimes provided, Nipivut Nunatinnii is difficult if not impossible to consume as an outsider to Inuit culture. Aside from programming in Inuktitut, the pacing, topics, and subject matter are purely Inuit, and require cultural and social context to comprehend. The very nature of having an Inuit-produced radio program allowing participants to call in and discuss whatever they want in Inuktitut is an act of subversion of the existing paradigm; in some ways, encouraging Inuit cultural community growth is subversive, as "southern" western society valorizes individualistic interactions and assimilation to the dominant ideal (Buddle 2004). A history of several hundred years of concerted effort on the part of colonial Canadians to absorb indigenous culture into the "mainstream" shows that any resistance to the dominant ideal, no matter how small, is an enormous achievement in and of itself (King 2012).

Nipivut Nunatinnii, therefore, is both significant and unique in its attempts to situate Inuktitut and Inuit-friendly programming within a larger social and cultural context, by valuing a communications medium that is preferred by the indigenous group using the product. Aside from strengthening community ties by allowing Inuit in local communities to share ideas and information, it also allows diasporic Inuit and other indigenous people to develop a distinct identity. A caller to Nipivut Nunatinnii on May 15, 2012 asked "What about people who are away from home?" Human rights lawyer Lloyd Lipsett, a guest on the show, responded: "It's terrific that the radio can reach around the world now!" (IsumaTVDID, 2012b). Diasporic identity has become a fluid, constantly changing ideal as all participants contribute to a singular identity that may or may not be made up of people they know offline: Inuit from Nunavut can contribute to an Inuit identity with other Inuit living elsewhere in the world, those of partial Inuit descent, or other indigenous groups with similar backgrounds, such as the Inupiat of Alaska (Landzelius 2001). Due to the accessibility of Nipivut Nunatinnii as a streaming radio station, users can access programming by and for Inuit no matter where they are, and the website has listeners from South America, Europe, and Australia.

As tourism becomes a primary economically viable industry for Inuit, it is more important than ever to support products that allow Inuit to feel rooted in both traditional lifestyles and modern living. When cruise ship passengers arriving in Nunavut demand an "authentic Inuit experience" that involves packaging Inuit history as something that has already completed its lifecycle, thereby encouraging the depiction of Inuit as a defunct or static society, Inuit are forced into supporting this viewpoint if they wish to take advantage of the financial rewards that are available. Twitter user Clare Kines (2012) tweeted: "[I]n many cases we have nothing else to 'sell' that is remotely competitive." In this sense, the lifecycle of Inuit culture has been artificially constructed to either continue without ending (as in, demonstrating that Inuit supposedly continue on using traditional methodologies with no access to, or desire for, modern technological advances) or to have ended long ago (showing Inuit as a society that exists only in the past, such that no modern Inuit can be acknowledged). At the Smithsonian Institute's conference on Inuit Studies in October 2012, speaker Nelson Graburn stated: "Most of tourism is oriented towards nature, not the modern Inuit world, so tourists want to keep the dream of the pristine Arctic" (IsumaTV 2012b). In response, then-mayor of Iqaluit Madeleine Redfern (2012) tweeted: "Not surprising that some tourists don't want human arctic experiences when so much of arctic portrayal is w/o human context." It is immensely important to find a way to maintain individual native identities within the larger context of global access to information. This wrongheaded cultural depiction of the arctic as *terra nullius* then becomes a product to be marketed and sold by non-Inuit, further contributing to the isolation and marginalization of Inuit from their cultural context (Buddle 2004; Tagalik 2010). Nipivut Nunatinnii provides a vital space for negotiating Inuit identity that is not shaped by the priorities of non-Inuit culture.

While identity is an important component of Inuit life, Inuit communities are also deeply affected by development projects in Nunavut, and Nipivut Nunatinni has played a key role in discussion around these issues. In fact, Nipivut Nunatinni was originally developed to facilitate discussion among Nunavummiut on the topic of Baffinland Corporation's proposed mine and tanker superhighway in Mary River and Steensby Inlet, and the radio show quickly became a community focal point with participants calling in to ask questions and discuss issues as well as participating in conversations with radio staff on Facebook and IsumaTV. During the 2012 deliberations over the proposed iron mine placement at Mary River, Nunavut and the accompanying supertanker highway and port to be built at Steensby Inlet, the iron ore company Baffinland (a subsidiary of larger steel conglomerate ArcelorMittal) was required to provide data produced by the environmental impact review to the communities that would be impacted by the mine and port.

These data were provided as densely written English documents of several thousand pages. The majority of communities that are affected by the mine and port are remote and predominantly Inuit; most of the older community members speak only oral Inuktitut and can neither read nor understand English (Cohn, pers. comm., 2012). Even if the documents had been translated into Inuktitut, the syllabic alphabet developed for writing Inuktitut by Moravian missionaries in the mid-1800s is not universally known or taught in schools, which by Canadian law are only required to teach English and French. Inuktitut is not taught in schools after grade four, and the budget for developing bilingual programs focusing on Inuktitut as a primary language in Nunavut are one-fourth the budget for developing bilingual programs in Nunavut focusing on French as a first language (King 2012, 262). In northern Quebec and Labrador, Indigenous politicians protested new laws that stated all public officials were required to pass proficiency tests in French, although that was not their native language or the language of their constituency (Curtis 2012; King 2012). Therefore, Nipivut Nunatinnii provided a venue for community members to air concerns, ask questions, and participate in a political process that was previously unavailable to them.

To facilitate the spread of information, Nipivut Nunatinnii brought in employees of Baffinland; of the Nunavut Impact Review Board (NIRB), who would be deliberating on whether or not Baffinland's projects could proceed; of the Qikiqtani Inuit Association (QIA), which administers the land claims process for the Baffin region of Nunavut; and human rights lawyer Lloyd Lipsett, who was hired by IsumaTV to work on behalf of the Inuit. Although there were official hearings to discuss the impact of the proposed mine and port, these only took place in Iqaluit, Igloolik, and Pond Inlet during a small window of days. Travel across long distances in Nunavut is prohibitively expensive and difficult so many impacted community members were unable to attend the hearings. Nipivut Nunatinnii provided an opportunity for them to be involved. Furthermore, Inuit values and traditional ways do not support asking a lot of questions in a public forum (this is seen as rude to the person being questioned) or the expressing of negative opinion (Pauktuutit Inuit Women of Canada 2010). Nipivut Nunatinnii therefore acted as a safe space for participation in the process, allowing those who might not have been physically able to attend the hearings a chance to be heard, while those who were able to go could express their opinions in a more culturally appropriate way.

The radio show has also performed a key role in facilitating broader social change on other important issues: a topic of much discussion on Nipivut Nunatinnii is the Extractive Industries Transparency Initiative (EITI), which encourages mining companies to improve transparency over payments by companies from the oil and mining industries to governments and to government-linked entities, as well as transparency over revenues by those host country governments. Without discussion of the EITI in Inuktitut on community radio, many Inuit would have been unable to ask questions, request information, or encourage enforcement of transparency requirements for procedures occurring on their land.

The remoteness of Nunavut communities, which is partially responsible for Nipivut Nunatinnii's success, also contributes to logistical difficulties: for example, the power lines to the radio building were cut accidentally by construction and unable to be fixed for two weeks, which left the radio off the air (Rituit, pers. comm., 2012). In order to provide a wider range of participation and programming, radio station employees have also attempted to record from out "on the land" or other more remote communities, which requires a technical knowledge of microphones and simulcasting that must be learned with very little background. Furthermore, because the radio is a ground-breaking project in Nunavut, there are no frameworks in place for quality control: there are occasionally translation glitches and if the radio reporters decide not to go in one day, the resource is not there for the rest of the community. Finally, although developing media services in an Inuit cultural context is not just necessary but mandatory for effective participation and discussion, many facets of Inuit culture do not lend themselves well to consistent productions. Inuit traditionally follow a more nonlinear, relaxed temporal worldview, and value politeness over conflict resolution and listening over speaking (Pauktuutit Inuit Women of Canada 2010). Therefore, deadlines, invasive questioning, and some organizational techniques are not valued by the Inuit producers. This can lead to frustration, particularly on the part of non-Inuit listeners, who may not know that the scheduled guests were delayed hunting and therefore will not be appearing on the show until the next day.

The lack of funding and infrastructure for preserving indigenous broadcasts also restricts access to information that should be accessible by a particular group. That is, an online radio broadcast is only accessible to those with radios, computers, or mobile devices: this discounts community members who may be too poor or remote to have effective Internet or mobile service, may have had electrical problems due to storms or wind, may be out hunting or unable to access their electronic devices, and so on. While these broadcasts act as digital archives for information created by and for a particular indigenous group (in the case of Nipivut Nunatinnii, the Inuit), there may be many Inuit who are simply unable to access the program, either while it is broadcast or in the preserved online archives. It is therefore necessary to develop systems that allow indigenous groups to access information which is rightfully theirs, not just for the purpose of maintaining a free flow of data, but also for the purpose of developing an ongoing indigenous identity and heritage. As Schneiter (2011, 155) argues, "The most ethically and epistemologically robust way to preserve Indigenous heritage is through community collaboration, especially in the design of the infrastructure and contextualization of the content." The goal of IsumaTV and DID is to provide resources for communities to build upon in their own ways, thereby empowering and encouraging them to create new, vibrant content that can be shared effectively in the digital commons in ways that are appropriate and useful for First Nations.

Part of the challenge involved is that, aside from Nipivut Nunatinnii, there are few online spaces that specifically support or encourage an Inuit worldview. Facebook, Twitter, Tumblr, and other social networking tools have been developed using colonial paradigms; while other native groups have adapted them effectively, even to the point of developing the Aboriginal Peoples Television Network (APTN, Canada's only entirely indigenous broadcasting network), the remoteness and isolation of Inuit mean they are at a disadvantage in terms of participating in the creation of their own discourse. Inuit are often excluded from productions developed even by other indigenous groups. Green and Jenkins state, "When material is produced according to a one-size-fits-all model, it necessarily imperfectly fits the needs of any given audience" (2011, 116). It becomes crucial, therefore, that Inuit are given space and funding to continue specifically Inuit-developed projects. Unfortunately, lack of funding is often the decisive factor for the failure of innovative native-guided programs; resources are limited, which means several worthy projects are frequently competing with each other, occasionally creating divisions along gender or generational lines, and certainly between indigenous groups (Buddle 2004). This means that the future of Nipivut Nunatinnii, and of IsumaTV as a whole, is uncertain.

Limited access to resources also limits the ability of Nipivut Nunatinnii and other Indigenous media to impact mainstream society. In an age in which participation in media creation is relatively cheap and easy, we need to be asking questions about who is heard, as well as who has a chance to speak (Burgess 2006, 203). Idle No More is an ongoing indigenous protest movement that began in Canada in December 2012, and was initiated in response to Prime Mininister Stephen Harper's introduction of omnibus bill C-45, which weakens environmental protection laws on a national scale. Idle No More has since spread to include indigenous peoples on most continents; this means that indigenous groups are gaining public, mainstream attention in ways that were previously unheard of. Many indigenous groups have moved away from the need for basic rights or complaints to the desire for a decentralized, multifaceted, and autonomous cultural expression (Salazar 2003). For Inuit, who are a minority in Canada's indigenous landscape, there have been few opportunities to be included in the larger protest movements of Idle No More. While there was a significant amount of community action surrounding food security, where the Facebook Group "Feeding My Family" acted as an organizational tool in increasing protests against high prices in northern supermarkets, the voice of Inuit in mainstream and other indigenous media is sadly lacking. Even when Inuit concerns are addressed in more mainstream areas, they frequently lack a support base to effect real solutions. For example, a conversation in April on Twitter noted both the ways in which the idea of "giving" marginalized groups a voice can obscure the fact that they already have a voice, which goes unheard (IsumaTV 2013), and the need to link 'voice' to access to vital resources (Kovats 2013). Landzelius (2001, 40) states, "Internet performances and exchanges currently underway permit the articulation of subaltern voice, but do not show evidence of changing the structural and discursive appropriation of the other's self-narratives." Nipivut Nunatinnii provides an important space for Inuit voices, but this is not enough in itself to create change.

For Inuit, "cycles of life are based on belonging and in collective identity" (Tagalik 2010, 3); this is equally applicable to media and other cultural content, as Inuit culture sees anything "living" (that is, something that changes, develops, grows, or alters its form, whether tangible or intangible) as having a lifecycle, including weather, the seasons, and rocks (Tagalik 2010, 4). With this understanding, sentimental attachment and residual positive feelings for items may continue long after the goods have been produced, as with materials that were completed or formed in the past but are still active in the cultural process. An excellent example of this is the Isuma Productions film *Atanarjuat: The Fast Runner*, which was completed and released in 2001, but continues to shape and assist in the creation of Inuit identity. This is known as "residual value" (Green and Jenkins, 2011). Nipivut Nunatinni is at the beginning of its lifecycle as a tangible product—that is, a consumable radio program that broadcasts regularly through streaming Internet—and also at the beginning of a lifecycle that may stretch much further than the actual existence of the radio itself. Its existence has already impacted the way Inuit interact with non-Inuit and with political systems, and has laid the groundwork for community-directed communication specifically by and for Inuit.

As we look for ways to effect change, we need to think beyond interventions in production, consumption, and disposal of material objects. We also need to think about the ways in which our communications and media, and both shape and are shaped by broader social and political structures, and produced: Who is excluded, and who has a voice, and how does this affect the final product which we consume? As technology impacts accessibility to information and provides new platforms for people that were previously excluded from social activism in the public sphere, we need to look more closely at who participates, and how. Inuit in particular are both product and produced, marginalized even within indigenous groups and the media they are developing. Therefore, the production and support of specifically Inuit products is vitally important for the continuation and preservation of Inuit culture and worldview. To this end, Nipivut Nunatinnii is breaking new ground in demonstrating how new technology and traditional lifestyles can be combined, changing the technology and opening new avenues for change.

REFERENCES

Aboriginal Justice Implementation Commission. 1999. "The Justice System and Aboriginal People: The Aboriginal Justice Implementation Commission." Manitoba Government. http://www.ajic.mb.ca/volumel/chapter13.html.

Âpihtawikosisân. 2012. "Wondering How We Can Talk About These Things When Almost All the Spaces Are Unsafe? #racism #hatred #idlenomore." Microblog. *@apihtawikosisan*. https://twitter.com/apihtawikosisan/status/283052576721747969.

Ayiman. 2012. "Ayiman: Blackfeatherasylum: Atanarjuat Is One . . ." http://golden-zephyr.tumblr.com/post/33398243977/ayiman-blackfeatherasylum-atanarjuat-is-one.

Bradsher, Keith, and Charles Duhigg. 2012. "Signs of Changes Taking Hold in Electronics Factories in China." *The New York Times*, December 26, sec. Business Day. https://www.nytimes.com/2012/12/27/business/signs-of-changes-taking-hold-in-electronics-factories-in-china.html.

Brown, Deidre, and George Nicholas. 2012. "Protecting Indigenous Cultural Property in the Age of Digital Democracy: Institutional and Communal Responses to Canadian First Nations and Māori Heritage Concerns." *Journal of Material Culture* 17 (3) (September 1): 307–324. doi:10.1177/1359183512454065.

Buddle, Kathleen. 2004. "Media, Markets and Powwows Matrices of Aboriginal Cultural Mediation in Canada." *Cultural Dynamics* 16 (1) (January 7): 29–69. doi:10.1177/0921374004042750.

Burgess, Jean. 2006. "Hearing Ordinary Voices: Cultural Studies, Vernacular Creativity and Digital Storytelling." *Continuum* 20 (2): 201–214. doi:10.1080/10304310600641737.

Burgess, Jean, Marcus Foth, and Helen G. Klaebe. 2006. "Everyday Creativity as Civic Engagement: A Cultural Citizenship View of New Media." In *ARC Centre of Excellence for Creative Industries and Innovation, Creative Industries Faculty; School of Design*. Sydney. http://eprints.qut.edu.au/5056/.

Cárcamo-Huechante, Luis E. 2010. "Wixage Anai!: Mapuche Voices on the Air." *CR: The New Centennial Review* 10 (1): 155–168.

Chang, Leslie T. 2009. *Factory Girls: From Village to City in a Changing China*. Reprint. Spiegel & Grau.

Curtis, Christopher. 2012. "Marois Statement Angers Aboriginals." *Montreal Gazette*. August 23. http://buffalosfire.com/Marois-statement-angers-aboriginals-M/.

Eglash, Ron. 2002. "Race, Sex, and Nerds: From Black Geeks to Asian American Hipsters." *Social Text* 20 (2): 49–64.

Green, Joshua, and Henry Jenkins. 2011. "Spreadable Media: How Audiences Create Value and Meaning in a Networked Economy." In *The Handbook of Media Audiences*, edited by Virginia Nightingale, 109–127. Wiley-Blackwell. http://onlinelibrary.wiley.com.dbgw.lis.curtin.edu.au/doi/10.1002/9781444340525.ch5/summary.

Irani, Lilly, and M. Silberman. 2013. "Turkopticon: Interrupting Worker Invisibility in Amazon Mechanical Turk." In *Proceeding of the Annual ACM SIGCHI Conference on Human Factors in Computing Systems*.

Iseke-Barnes, Judy, and Deborah Danard. 2007. "Indigenous Knowledges and Wordview: Representations and the Internet." In *Information Technology and Indigenous People*, edited by Laurel Evelyn Dyson, Max A. N. Hendriks, and Stephen Grant. Idea Group Inc (IGI).

IsumaTV. 2012a. "DID Overview May 5, 2012." *IsumaTV*. May 5. http://www.isuma.tv/lo/en/DID/DIDoverview5May2012.

IsumaTV. 2012b. "Most of Tourism Is Oriented Towards Nature, Not the Modern Inuit World, so the Tourists Want to Keep the Dream of Pristine Arctic. #18thISC." Microblog. *@IsumaTV*. https://twitter.com/IsumaTV/status/261836972195196930.

IsumaTV. 2013. "Minnesotans Will Haul 200 Lb Sled Packs Towards the Arctic, to Bring Voice to the Inuit. None of Them Are Inuit. Hmm. http://bit.ly/ZOSWCC." Microblog. *@IsumaTV*. https://twitter.com/IsumaTV/status/322335070646067201.

IsumaTVDID. 2012a. "Marie-Helene: Ppl Asking "What Do People Think?" and It's Always Someone Else's Voice, but This Show Means We Can Hear the Real Voices." Microblog. *@IsumaTVDID*. https://twitter.com/IsumaTVDID/status/202614985225023488.

IsumaTVDID. 2012b. "Long-distance Call from Ottawa: What About People Who Are Away from Home? Lloyd: Terrific That Radio Can Reach Around the World Now!" Microblog. *@IsumaTVDID*. https://twitter.com/IsumaTVDID/status/202613127219646465.

Keene, Adrienne. 2012. "So You Wanna Be an Indian for Halloween?" *Native Appropriations*. October 13. http://nativeappropriations.com/2012/10/so-you-wanna-be-an-indian-for-halloween.html.

Kendall, Lori. 2011. ""White and Nerdy"": Computers, Race, and the Nerd Stereotype." *Journal of Popular Culture* 44 (3) (June). http://search.proquest.com.dbgw.lis.curtin.edu.au/docview/877020867?accountid=10382.

Kines, Clare. 2012. "Twitter / NunavutBirder: @RadicalOmnivore @kivalliqboy . . ." *Twitter*. October 26. https://twitter.com/NunavutBirder/status/261837940857114624.

King, Thomas. 2012. *The Inconvenient Indian: A Curious Account of Native People in North America*. Doubleday Canada.

Kovats, Stephen. 2013. "@IsumaTV It Seems Inuit Already Have Pretty Strong Voices, Esp. W/ Http://www.isuma.tv/ . . . Maybe They Can Bring Fresh Vegetables Instead?" Microblog. *@intertwilight*. https://twitter.com/intertwilight/status/322340818725773312.

Landzelius, Kyra. 2001. "Mapping the Unfathomable Frontiers of Indigenous Cyberspace: a Survey of the Expanding/contracting Boundaries of Going Native on the Net." In *IT-Users and Producers in an Evolving Sociocultural Context*, 41–50. Uppsala. http://atlas.dsv.su.se/~kjellman/Norberg%20report.pdf#page=41.

MacKinnon, Rebecca. 2012. "The Netizen." *Development* 55 (2) (June): 201–204. doi:10.1057/dev.2012.5.

Nathan, David. 2000. "Plugging in Indigenous Knowledge: Connections and Innovations." *Australian Aboriginal Studies* (1/2): 39.

Ngata, Wayne, Hera Ngata-Gibson, and Amiria Salmond. 2012. "Te Ataakura: Digital Taonga and Cultural Innovation." *Journal of Material Culture* 17 (3) (September 1): 229–244. doi:10.1177/1359183512453807.

Ojo, Tokunbo. 2006. "Ethnic Print Media in the Multicultural Nation of Canada A Case Study of the Black Newspaper in Montreal." *Journalism* 7 (3) (January 8): 343–361. doi:10.1177/1464884906065517.

Pauktuutit Inuit Women of Canada. 2010. *The Inuit Way: A Guide to Inuit Culture*. First Nations Child and Family Caring Society of Canada. http://www.fncaringsociety.com/publications/1271.

Perley, Sonja. 2009. "Representation and Participation of First Nations Women in Online Videos." *The Journal of Community Informatics* 5 (2) (December 9). http://www.ci-journal.net/index.php/ciej/article/view/559.

Peters, Michael A., Simon Marginson, and Peter Murphy. 2009. *Creativity and the Global Knowledge Economy*. Peter Lang.

Redfern, Madeleine. 2012. "@IsumaTV Not Surprising That Some Tourists Don't Want Human Arctic Experiences When so Much of Arctic Portrayal Is W/o Human Context." Microblog. *@madinuk*. https://twitter.com/madinuk/status/261840562125152256.

Rooney, David, Greg Hearn, and Tim Kastelle. 2012. *Handbook on the Knowledge Economy*. Edward Elgar Publishing.

Salazar, Juan Francisco. 2003. "Digitising Knowledge: Anthropology and New Practices of Digitextuality (IELLCC)." *Media International Australia, Incorporating Culture & Policy* (107).

Schneiter, Teague. 2011. "Ethical Presentation of Indigenous Media in the Age of Open Video: Cultivating Collaboration, Sovereignty and Sustainability." In *Video Vortex Reader II: Moving Images Beyond YouTube*, edited by Geert Lovink and Rachel Somers Miles, 147–161. Amsterdam: Institute of Network Cultures.

Seadle, Michael. 2002. "Whose Rules?" *D-Lib Magazine* 8 (3). doi:10.1045/march2002–seadle. http://www.dlib.org/dlib/march02/seadle/03seadle.html.

Tagalik, Shirley. 2010. "Inuit Qaujimajatuqangit: The Role of Indigenous Knowledge in Supporting Wellness in Inuit Communities in Nunavut." Child and Youth Health. National Collaborating Centre for Aboriginal Health.

Terranova, Tiziana. 2000. "Free Labor: Producing Culture for the Digital Economy." *Social Text* 18 (2): 33–58.

Tsoukas, Haridimos, and Jill Shepherd. 2009. *Managing the Future: Foresight in the Knowledge Economy*. John Wiley & Sons.

Chapter Nine

Reflections on Lessons for Social Change

Sky Croeser and Shae Garwood

This chapter aims to draw out some of the recurring themes from the book, as well as suggesting further directions for reading and research for those wanting to explore these themes further. The work in this volume demonstrates the complexity and difficulty involved in trying to achieve change. There are multiple potential sites for action, which are frequently separated from each other geographically and/or politically. A key part of the work is the need to reconnect these sites, building coalitions or other alliances which may cross national boundaries and incorporate groups with different interests and experiences. Ultimately, however, there are reasons for hope. These authors write from the perspective of strong connections to struggles which are ongoing, and which are seeing at least some successes, despite the challenges which they face.

The lessons that emerge from the chapters include connecting sites of production and consumption; translating awareness into action; identifying and targeting points of leverage; acknowledging the contradictory role of the state; understanding limitations of corporate social responsibility; recognizing the role of NGOs and unions in creating change; building coalitions and alliances; incorporating intersectionality in analysis and practice; employing short- and long-term strategies; creating and modeling viable alternatives; and holding on to hope that change is possible. Each of these are discussed in more detail below.

One of the challenges faced by those attempting to create change is reconnecting the disjunctures between sites of production and consumption. Workers' rights advocates with the Asia Monitor Resource Centre, Sanjiv Pandita and Fahmi Panimbang, put this in perspective in chapter 7, noting that global supply chains have been in existence at least since the use of cotton from Asia in the British textile industry in the nineteenth century. At the same time, they emphasize that the last three decades have seen a rapid expansion and increased complexity in global supply chains, involving the development of new links between different parts of the supply chain as well as a greater geographical spread in production processes. Gereffi and Lee (2012) provide a brief overview of some important shifts in global supply chains over recent years, including the role of regional supply chains and some of the effects of the global financial crisis on the relationship between developing economies and the Global North. The relatively small role given to social activists concerns in Gereffi and Lee (2012, 29) does, however, highlight the need for critiques such as those Pandita and Panimbang have provided in this volume, as well as for interventions into global supply chains. When discussing strategies for action, people are often encouraged to "think global, act local." Complex, geographically dispersed supply chains make it difficult both to understand the full impacts of production globally, and to act locally.

The distances, both literal and metaphorical, mean that conditions of production—and of disposal—are often invisible to consumers. Someone buying a laptop in North America is unlikely to know much about the factory in which it was assembled, the places where its components were created, the mines which provide key components, or what will happen after they throw it in the trash or give it to one of the increasingly common electronics recycling programs. Raising awareness about these issues is a vital first step to creating change. In chapter 2 Sarah Adler-Milstein, Jessica Champagne, and Theresa Haas write that the work around garment industry conditions which happened among US consumers throughout the mid-1990s helped to set the stage for the formation of student anti-sweatshop groups. Leisbeth Sluiter's (2009) *Clean Clothes* gives more detail on this, helping to understand the work that went into setting the stage for the anti-sweatshop movement. The process of awareness-raising which anti-sweatshop activists have engaged in for the garment industry is, it seems, still in its infancy for the electronics sector. In chapter 6 Sandoval and Bjurling make it clear that this is not an easy process. Getting details about actual working conditions requires that researchers find ways to contact and speak with workers outside of factories, as employment is often precarious and there are few protections for workers. This research then needs to be shared in such a way that it will engage consumers, as makeITfair is currently attempting to do through campaigns, online petitions, and other means. Awareness-raising therefore requires two important steps: gaining access to information about production conditions, which may be difficult, and then ensuring that this reaches consumers effectively, which may be even more challenging.

This awareness-raising is, of course, only one part of the story. Change also requires that awareness is translated into action. However, complex supply chains mean that it can be difficult to know where to locate activism. Even if those at the site of consumption want to act on their newly gained awareness, it may be difficult to locate sites of production: labels indicating a country of origin rarely give factory names. Adler-Milstein, Champagne, and Haas note that even once a national network of anti-sweatshop activism emerged in the United States, its power was limited by the convoluted and concealed nature of supply chains involved in collegiate apparel production. Apparel is produced across thousands of factories, many of which also produce other goods. This means that even universities which have been convinced to seek better working conditions for the production of their licensed goods have limited leverage in their negotiations, and little power to monitor any agreements. The situation in the electronics sector is, if anything, worse than this. While leaks of photos, stories, and news articles about conditions inside electronics plant Foxconn in China have led to improvements in workers' conditions at Foxconn itself and renewed commitments to labor standards from Apple (Bradsher and Duhigg 2012), preliminary evidence suggests that this has not created the positive ripples in working conditions in the electronics industry that some were predicting, and may not even lead to long-term change within Apple or the Foxconn plant (Nova and Shapiro, 2013). A recurring theme within this book is the challenge of translating awareness into action, even at sites where consumers occupy a relatively privileged place within the global economy.

At the other end of the supply chain, workers' attempts to challenge unjust working conditions are frequently limited by structural inequalities in the global system. Several authors in this volume discuss attempts among countries in the Global South to gain some competitive advantage in the global system through the creation of Special Economic Zones (SEZs), tax breaks for foreign investment, and limited labor protections. Sandoval and Bjurling point out that even in countries which have ratified key International Labour Organization (ILO) conventions, governments may be unwilling to implement labor protections. In the Philippines, for example, laws protecting freedom of association and collective bargaining have not protected union officials from ongoing and deadly attacks. SEZs can exacerbate these issues. Vaish (2011) argues that in India, SEZs have been developed within a regulatory environment which gives companies greater freedom to fire workers, makes it difficult to unionize workers, and diminishes workers' access to protections available to workers outside SEZs. Similarly, Ngai (2004) and Chan (2006) emphasize the ways in which women working in SEZs in China are particularly disadvantaged. These problems are not unique to the Global South. Litton-Cohn and Croeser's discussion of IsumaTV in chapter 8 hints at some of the ways in which structural racism limits workers' power even in countries like Canada, as do many of the issues which affect workers in the Global South, such as precarious employment and poor labor protections.

Recognizing these limits on workers' activism is not, however, to say that they are powerless. It should be clear from this collection that important organizing is happening at sites of production.

In addition to considering different sites for action, the chapters in this volume draw out the multiple points of leverage which may be involved in activism. Attempts to create change may focus on, or be organized through, governments, corporations, workers, consumers, or non-governmental organizations (NGOs). Each point of leverage is accompanied by its own constraints and opportunities, and may be easier to access from different points in the global supply chain of a product: those at the point of consumption, for example, will obviously find it easier to focus on their own buying habits than on supporting workers' unionization. The closest or most obvious point of leverage is, however, not necessarily the most effective one.

One of the most obvious targets for action is the state. The state plays a complex role in the struggles discussed here, as activists attempt to use regulatory mechanisms to secure environmental and labor protections at the same time as they critique the state's role in limiting workers' options and facilitating the expansion of neoliberal capitalism. Adler-Milstein, Champagne, and Haas for example, place binding commitments within the rule of law as the first principle which must shape any agreements for garment workers, arguing that this is crucial to enforcing any commitments made by corporations to improve conditions. Sandoval and Bjurling, like Adler-Milstein, Champagne, and Haas see legislation as playing a key role, arguing that even when it is not enforced it provides a valuable tool which workers might use to hold governments accountable. There are also other ways in which state support may be useful. An electronics dismantler quoted in Chaturvedi's chapter suggests that if the state provided space for dismantling work it would improve their working conditions; Litton-Cohn and Croeser refer to the need for funding for indigenous media projects; and Baillie and Feinblatt mention the importance of legal recognition for "recovered" factories in Argentina. However, even authors who argue for legislative protections or the provision of resources by the state are far from sanguine about the role played by the state in these struggles.

The growth of SEZs, discussed above, highlights the contradictory role played by the state, which often acts to diminish worker and environmental protections, as noted by Pandita and Panimbang. This is especially visible in cases where the state forcibly acquires land to set up SEZs, dispossessing farmers and other land-users, as has frequently been the case in India over recent years (Levien 2012; Ramachandraiah and Srinivasan 2011). Sandoval and Bjurling argue that states may also be complicit in human rights violations, such as restricting workers' rights to freedom of association and collective bargaining or outright attacks on trade unionists such as those happening in the Philippines. However, even cases of seemingly benign regulation can create problems. In chapter 3, Baillie and Feinblatt, for example, discuss the effects of the 2005 Zero Garbage (*Basura Cero*) law, which legislates a sharp reduction in the amount of garbage sent to landfill. Although this seems positive from an environmental perspective, it led to rifts in the relationship between *cartoneros* and environmental groups and created a market in recycling collection which may act to reduce *cartoneros* employment. Similarly, in chapter 4, Chaturvedi notes that attempts to regulate e-waste recycling in India have created problems for those working in the sector, diminishing their ability to carry out even non-polluting work. Some groups therefore attempt to limit their involvement with the state, or seek to limit state regulation in key areas.

One alternative to seeking increased state regulation is to effect change through consumer action, although these strategies are not necessarily mutually exclusive. While the chapters on anti-sweatshop work in the garment and electronics industries all mention initiatives which encourage consumers to seek more ethical products, these are usually intended to support other strategies, such as economic support for factories paying a living wage or punitive boycotts which encourage changes in corporate policies. Michael Heasman and Ralph Early's chapter argues that in order to create a socially just and fair food system the food industry requires change at a structural level rather than being left to one of individual consumer choice.

Attempts to change consumer behavior are often linked to strategies which put pressure directly on corporations. In response to the ongoing pressure from activists which corporations have faced over the last few decades, many companies have adopted Corporate Social Responsibility (CSR) programs. Carroll (2008) provides a useful overview of dominant perspectives on CSR, including the acceleration of the concept and practice from the 1970s on and its increased adoption within business literature and practice throughout the following decades. However, even mainstream business perspectives on CSR have raised questions about the extent to which it is effective in creating change (Vogel 2006), and the results of these programs are often far from what activists would desire. Although Adler-Milstein, Champagne, and Haas see some benefit in CSR initiatives which are legally binding, they argue that voluntary CSR programs which were developed in response to anti-sweatshop activism have done little to nothing to improve workers' conditions. Pandita and Panimbang take a more critical perspective, arguing that CSR programs are worse than ineffective in that they undermine calls for state regulation and lead to a problematic focus on corporate-led community development. This, they argue, has been particularly clear in the case of Hindustan Unilever's use of rural women's involvement in CSR initiatives to increase profits and open markets which might otherwise be inaccessible to Unilever. While CSR programs are not the only way in which corporations have attempted to answer critics, they do highlight some of the problems with seeking change through corporate partnerships.

This is linked to the broader critique of capitalism which many of these chapters raise, and an accompanying ambivalence about market-based strategies. Pandita and Panimbang are the most openly critical of the global capitalist system, arguing that effective change will only come about when people seek to dismantle neoliberal capitalism. Other authors, while remaining critical of global structures of capitalism, write about the difficulty of developing strategies within a framework which is critical of the market while still needing to engage with it. Baillie and Feinblatt discuss their discomfort at realizing that efforts to assist the cooperative to find a market for their products were leading them, unintentionally, to become a part of the market system. They go on to discuss their decision not to enter into partnerships with large companies who they saw as wanting to work with the *cartoneros* only as a green-washing exercise, to soothe consumers' guilty consciences about consumption. Despite misgivings such as these, finding a market for more ethical products plays an important role in sustaining alternative models for production. Chaturvedi, for example, writes that Chintan is currently helping to develop key infrastructure which will provide funding for grassroots collection operations. The Alta Gracia factory, which Adler-Milstein, Champagne, and Haas highlight as a success story, has been reliant on gaining a reliable market with US consumers. None of these chapters provide simple answers to the question of how to relate to the market, but they do raise interesting and important questions about the compromises and possibilities involved in different strategies.

Similarly, there are important questions to be asked about the role of NGOs, including those that are at the center of many of the efforts discussed here. Mitlin, Hickey, and Bebbington (2007) provide a useful overview of the debates surrounding the role of NGOs in development, particularly in the Global South. This work outlines key issues in the field, including around NGO effectiveness and accountability. Baillie and Feinblatt address these issues most directly, critically reflecting on the role of the Waste for Life organization and reviewing some of the problems associated with NGOs' historic role in development. In outlining their five guiding commitments, they provide a framework which could be used in evaluating the work of other NGOs. Chaturvedi's work also touches on some of the dilemmas faced by NGOs. In this case, Chintan does not have to face the consequences of vast inequalities in access to resources which NGOs from the Global North must often confront when working in the Global South. However, there are always challenges in how NGOs are positioned in relationship to those they seek to help and these relationships often change. For example, Chintan shifted from its original position as an external facilitator helping to organize dismantlers to becoming a member of the dismantlers' association, having recognized the legitimacy of dismantlers' desire for more active participation from the NGO. Chintan has also taken on the role of providing help navigating bureaucratic hurdles, another shift from its original plan. These experiences highlight some of the difficulties—and possibilities—involved in NGOs' work.

Any discussion of how to organize around creating change must also acknowledge the critical role of unions. Sandoval and Bjurling note that in many locations, unions play an important role in organizing and informing workers, but unionization is either illegal, or legal but difficult and potentially risky for workers in many countries. In other cases, the challenge is building unions around labor sectors which have not traditionally been unionized, particularly informal sectors. Chaturvedi, for example, writes that one of the most important tasks Chintan identified was helping to organize workers (through an association) in the e-waste sector in order to gain a sense of security and empowerment which they had previously not had access to. Baillie and Feinblatt, on the other hand, make no mention of unions in their work with informal workers apart from to cite hostility from a truckers' union. This is, perhaps, symptomatic of the tension that can exist between organized labor and many informal sectors. Despite an increasing recognition of the importance of informal sectors to economies around the world, and of the particular needs of workers in these sectors, in many cases unions and other organizing bodies have not fully committed to working with informal workers (Bonner and Spooner 2011). Adler-Milstein, Champagne, and Haas provide an example of some of the benefits for workers of effective union action, with unions having played a key role in the establishment and ongoing success of the Alta Gracia factory. Creating and sustaining independent structures for workers to advocate for themselves and collectively bargain for better working conditions is crucial to ensuring better conditions for workers now and into the future.

As well as outlining different points of leverage in the global system, the chapters in this volume suggest the need to reconnect different locations in the global supply chain in order to build effective alliances. All of the case studies examined here demonstrate the value of this strategy, whether through the transnational coalitions that helped to establish and maintain the Alta Gracia living-wage factory; the work currently underway to improve labor conditions in the electronics industry; the ability of local cooperatives to build strong connections with surrounding communities in Buenos Aires; or even the ways in which online radio enables connections between geographically dispersed communities around key issues. However, it is important that these alliances remain grounded and that there is attention to, and negotiation around, the inequalities and differences between different coalition partners, as discussed above in reference to NGOs' roles. Sen's (2003) *Stir It Up: Lessons in Community Organizing and Advocacy* offers further suggestions on how to manage these issues. Waste for Life's extensive on-the-ground research in Buenos Aires suggests one potentially fruitful approach, as does makeITFair's partnerships with local organizations. Chaturvedi also notes the importance of visits from the Silicon Valley Toxics Coalition in helping US activists to understand the situation of dismantlers in India, at the same time as it gave Chintan more information about trends in the US electronics industry. While each of these examples offers contributions to the thinking about how to build alliances, the methods of building and sustaining alliances will differ across industries, issues, and locations.

Part of the challenge of building alliances across different locales and with different groups is developing an intersectional analysis. Intersectionality refers to understanding the complex ways in which different structures of oppression—such as race, class, and gender—interact. Although the concept of intersectionality has only gained attention in the mainstream press relatively recently, it has played an important role in many struggles—especially those by people of color—for decades, and is vital for research which is strongly interlinked with practice (Cho, Crenshaw, and McCall 2013). While, for example, global inequalities clearly play a considerable role in shaping working conditions at electronics factories, Sandoval and Bjurling also point to the role of gender in determining how workers are treated, with women being more likely to be hired based on gender stereotypes and frequently subject to discrimination when seeking to advance beyond the lowest paid positions. Organizing for change in various industries may also need to take structures of race, sexuality, and caste, among others, into account.

Another lesson which emerges from this volume is the need to offer alternatives to the current system. Adler-Milstein, Champagne, and Haas's work demonstrates that initial campaigns around better working conditions in the garment industry were initially hampered by the lack of a viable alternative model: when activists succeeded in making changes in a factory, the companies buying from that factory were likely to cancel orders, reinforcing the idea that only factories which paid poorly could survive. The establishment—and ongoing success—of the Alta Gracia factory was necessary to show that alternatives are possible. Similarly, the waste-collecting, dismantling, and recycling (or "upcycling") work being carried out by informal workers in conjunction with Chintan and Waste for Life offers models for alternative ways of dealing with the mountains of waste generated by modern consumption; Heasman and Early suggest an alternative way of conceptualizing consumers' relationship to the goods they consume; and Litton-Cohn and Croeser demonstrate the value of alternative media models. It is important to highlight the ways in which these alternatives are built and developed, as they are a vital part of opposition to the status quo.

Most of the chapters in this volume discuss a particular campaign or project, but in each case there is an accompanying recognition that broader structural change is necessary. The relationship between short-to-medium term activism and advocacy and long-term change is not an easy one to negotiate. For example, Pandita and Panimbang argue that strategies which focus on achievable goals for the short-to-medium-term may at times be ultimately counter-productive, giving up hopes of more significant and deep-reaching change. Other authors position short-term changes as incremental steps toward long-term change: by gaining higher wages and access to unionization, workers are able to organize more effectively. Similarly, Heasman and Early's chapter suggests that individual and structural changes need to be underpinned by a broader framework of justice and fairness to ensure a lasting impact. Litton-Cohn and Croeser's chapter also addresses the need to build media which will incorporate marginalized voices as part of a longer-term strategy aiming to create political change. Linking short-term and long-term goals is not easy, especially given the complexity of the structures involved, but it is a vital component for all of the struggles discussed in this volume.

Finally and perhaps most importantly, these chapters offer the hope that change is possible. It may be difficult, and gradual, but we are seeing signs that new models are emerging. We should take heart from the development of living wage factories through transnational coalitions; the growth of informal economies which demonstrate new ways of dealing with recycling; challenges to the cycle of consumption and planned obsolescence posed by awareness-raising around e-waste; social justice and fairness movements that aim to transform peoples' relationships to the food they eat; and new spaces for marginalized groups to be heard and to communicate with each other. All of these point to ways forward to create social, political, and economic change in a globalized world.

REFERENCES

Bonner, Christine, and Dave Spooner. 2011. "Organizing in the Informal Economy: A Challenge for Trade Unions." *In ternational Politics and Society* 2: 87—105.

Bradsher, Keith, and Charles Duhigg. 2012. "Signs of Changes Taking Hold in Electronics Factories in China." *The New York Times*, December 26, sec. Business Day. https://www.nytimes.com/2012/12/27/business/signs-of-changes-taking-hold-in-electronics-factories-in-china.html.

Carroll, Archie B. 2008. "A History of Corporate Social Responsibility." In *The Oxford Handbook of Corporate Social Responsibility*, edited by Andrew Crane, Dirk Matten, Abagail McWilliams, Jeremy Moon, and Donald Siegel. Oxford University Press. http://www.oxfordhandbooks.com/view/10.1093/oxfordhb/9780199211593.001.0001/oxfordhb-9780199211593–e-002.

Chan, Jenny Wai-Ling. 2006. "Chinese Women Workers Organize in the Export Zone." *New Labor Forum* 15 (1) (April 1): 19–27. doi:10.2307/40342591.

Cho, Sumi, Crenshaw, Kimberlé Williams, and Leslie McCall. 2013. "Toward a Field of Intersectionality Studies: Theory, Applications, and Praxis." *Signs* 38 (4) (June 1): 785–810. doi:10.1086/669608.

Gereffi, Gary, and Joonkoo Lee. 2012. "Why the World Suddenly Cares About Global Supply Chains." *Journal of Supply Chain Management* 48 (3): 24–32. doi:10.1111/j.1745–493X.2012.03271.x.

Levien, Michael. 2012. "The Land Question: Special Economic Zones and the Political Economy of Dispossession in India." *Journal of Peasant Studies* 39 (3–4): 933–969. doi:10.1080/03066150.2012.656268.

Mitlin, Diana, Sam Hickey, and Anthony Bebbington. 2007. "Reclaiming Development? NGOs and the Challenge of Alternatives." *World Development* 35 (10) (October): 1699–1720. doi:10.1016/j.worlddev.2006.11.005.

Ngai, Pun. 2004. "Women Workers and Precarious Employment in Shenzhen Special Economic Zone, China." *Gender & Development* 12 (2): 29–36. doi:10.1080/13552070412331332170.

Nova, Scott, and Isaac Shapiro. 2013. "NYT Story Emphasizes Apple's Positive Statements, Obscures Ongoing Labor Abuses." *Economic Policy Institute*. http://www.epi.org/blog/new-york-times-apple-statements-labor-abuses/.

Ramachandraiah, Chigurupati, and Ramasamy Srinivasan. 2011. "Special Economic Zones as New Forms of Corporate Land Grab: Experiences from India." *Development* 54 (1) (March): 59–63. doi:10.1057/dev.2010.99.

Sen, Rinku. 2003. *Stir It Up: Lessons in Community Organizing and Advocacy*. John Wiley & Sons.

Sluiter, Ms. Liesbeth. 2009. *Clean Clothes: A Global Movement to End Sweatshops*. Pluto Press.

Vaish, Varun. 2011. "Special Economic Zones in India: Labor Issues and Key Considerations." *Indian Development Review* 9 (1): 143–154.

Vogel, David. 2006. *The Market for Virtue: The Potential and Limits of Corporate Social Responsibility*. Washington, D.C.: Brookings Institution Press.

Index

About the Contributors

Sarah Adler-Milstein is the Field Director for Latin America and the Caribbean for the Worker Rights Consortium (WRC). Previously, she served as the field representative for the Caribbean for the WRC, carrying out in-depth investigations of labor rights violations in apparel factories in the Dominican Republic, Puerto Rico, and Haiti. Her work has focused on the monitoring and development of the Alta Gracia factory, the first factory in the Global South to pay a genuine living wage (more than 300 percent of the minimum wage), and respect all workers' rights including freedom of association and exemplar health and safety standards.

Caroline Baillie is a materials scientist and, since mid-2009, the inaugural Chair in Engineering Education at the University of Western Australia. Prior to this appointment, Baillie worked as Chair in Engineering Education at the Faculty of Applied Science at Queen's University, Kingston, Ontario, Canada. Baillie is founder of the Engineering, Social Justice and Peace network (ESJP.org) and co-founder and co-director, along with Eric Feinblatt, of Waste for Life (wasteforlife.org), a network of scientists, engineers, academics, designers, and local communities working together to research, implement, and disseminate poverty-reducing solutions to specific environmental problems.

Mark Barenberg is the Sulzbacher Professor of Law at Columbia University in New York City, and the Director of the Columbia Program on Labor Law and Policy. He received his undergraduate and law degrees from Harvard University and his master's degree in economics from the London School of Economics. His research and teaching focus on labor rights in the global economy. He has been a consultant to the administration of President

Barack Obama on the methodology for assessing compliance with labor rights by countries around the world. Professor Barenberg is the Founding Chairperson of the Worker Rights Consortium and continues to serve on its Advisory Board. He has advised many labor unions and workers' centers in their domestic and global campaigns. He has also served as an independent expert for the International Labor Organization's global research on corporate codes of conduct. Professor Barenberg has been a visiting professor at Yale University, the European University Institute, Beijing University, Tokyo University, Cologne University, and other universities.

Kristina Areskog Bjurling is senior researcher with Swedwatch. She has over 15 years experience working on companies' responsibilities for environmental and human rights in developing countries. She is one of the co-founders of the Swedish NGO Fair Trade Center and initiator to Swedwatch and the Clean Clothes Campaign in Sweden. Her fields of specialty are the manufacturing industry in Asia and social public procurement. In 2010 she was project leader in Swedwatch for the European makeITfair campaign, which aims to improve conditions in the electronics industry.

Jessica Champagne is the Director of Research and Advocacy of the Worker Rights Consortium, an independent labor rights monitoring organization. Prior to joining the WRC, she served as Organizing Coordinator for Global Organizing at the Service Employees International Union (SEIU). She began her international work in Indonesia, initially as a Fulbright research scholar and subsequently coordinating trainings for the Indonesian Society for Social Transformation (INSIST).

Bharati Chaturvedi is the founder of an India based non-profit, Chintan, which advocates for the rights of the informal recycling sector and facilitates green jobs for them, to create a win-win for the poor and for India's dirty cities. Chaturvedi writes a column for a leading national daily, the *Hindustan Times* and occasionally blogs with the *Huffington Post*. She has Masters degrees, in History from Delhi University and in International Public Policy from the School of Advanced International Studies, Johns Hopkins University. She is the editor of *Finding Delhi : Loss and Renewal in the Megacity*, published by Penguin India (October 2010). Chaturvedi is the recipient of the prestigious 2009 Johns Hopkins Alumni "Knowledge for the World Award." She has previously received the LEAD fellowship and is a fellow at the Synergos Institute, New York.

Sky Croeser is currently a lecturer and adjunct fellow at Curtin University. Her research and activism focuses on the ways in which activists are working to shape, as well as use, the technologies of everyday life. Her PhD was undertaken at University of Western Australia in the Department of Political Science and International relations, and will be published by Routledge in 2014 as *Global Justice and the Politics of Information*. Her subsequent research has included work on digital liberties activism in India; the ways activists in the United States, Tunisia, and Greece are using social media to organize and communicate; and the struggle for Internet freedoms in post-revolution Tunisia. She has spoken about her research at academic and activist events around the world, is a co-founder of the Bluestocking Institute, and is a member of The Ada Initiative's advisory board.

Ralph Early is head of the Department of Food Science and Agri-Food Supply Chain Managment at Harper Adams University. A food scientist and food ethicist, he has taught in higher education for 20 years. The other half of his career was spent in the food industry. He has experience in food production, quality assurance, food safety managment, and New Product Development (NPD), and has held senior managment positions in NPD and food quality managment.

Eric Feinblatt is coordinator of Waste for Life as well as a filmmaker, photographer, and education consultant specializing in online cross-cultural collaborative learning for the State University of New York.

Shae Garwood is an Honorary Research Fellow at the University of Western Australia and a researcher for Shelter, an Australian-based NGO. She received her PhD from the University of Western Australia, MSc in Gender and Development from the London School of Economics and BSc in Commerce from the University of Virginia. Her research is on civil society and transnational politics, gender, labor, and social change. Her scholarship has appeared in *Gender and Development*, *Third Sector Review* and her book, *Advocacy Across Borders: NGOs, Anti-sweatshop Activism and the Global Garment Industry* was published by Kumarian Press in 2011. She is a co-founder of the Bluestocking Institute for Global Peace and Justice and a Management Committee member of the Village Library Project.

Theresa Haas is the Director of Communications at the Worker Rights Consortium (WRC). The WRC is an independent labor rights monitoring organization that conducts investigations of working conditions in factories around the globe. The WRC's purpose is to combat sweatshops and protect the rights of workers who sew apparel and make other products sold in the United States—in particular, garments bearing the logos of the WRC's 180 affiliate universities and colleges. Her recent work at the WRC has focused on developing and expanding efforts to address the ongoing fire and building safety crisis in Bangladesh. She is a graduate of the Schreyer Honors College at Penn State University.

Michael Heasman has worked on food policy for more than 25 years as a social science researcher, teacher, and writer. He is currently senior lecturer in Food Policy and Management at Harper Adams University, UK and visiting fellow at the Centre for Food Policy, City University, London. His active research and teaching interests are food and nutrition policy, food sustainability, and food security. He is co-author, with Tim Lang, of *Food Wars: The Global Battle for Mouths, Minds, and Markets* (2004, second edition due 2014). He completed his PhD in the Food Policy Research Unit, University of Bradford, where he investigated the impact of nutrition policy on sugar consumption and the response of food business to diet and health concerns.

Claire Litton-Cohn is IsumaTV's digital and social media coordinator. She has been an employee of IsumaTV since 2001, when she accompanied Isuma Igloolik Productions' blockbuster hit Atanarjuat to the Cannes Film Festival. Since then, she has moved through several roles within the company, ultimately working as social media and web coordinator for IsumaTV's Digital Indigenous Democracy project since 2010. Litton-Cohn holds a postgraduate diploma in public health from Curtin University.

Sanjiv Pandita is Executive Director of the Asia Monitor Resource Centre (AMRC) He has been on the front lines of labor activism in Asia for more than a decade. Having graduated in Microbiology from University of Pune in India, he went on to earn his Masters Degree in Environmental Sciences from the same university. His expertise in Occupational Health and Safety has won international awards, including from the Silicon Valley Toxics Coalition, and recognition as one of the 50 most influential Environmental, Health, and Safety leaders in 2008. Pandita's writings on grassroots movements and workers' health issues have been published widely. Pandita has also authored two chapters on China and India in the 2006 book, *Challenging the Chip* on labor rights and environmental justice in the global electronics industry.

Fahmi Panimbang is a program coordinator at Asia Monitor Resource Centre (AMRC), Hong Kong. Before joining AMRC, he was a labor activist with Sedane Labor Resource Center (Lembaga Informasi Perburuhan Sedane), an NGO specializing in labor issues in Indonesia. He graduated from Driyarkara School of Philosophy in Jakarta, Indonesia and earned his MA in sociology at Sungkonghoe University in Seoul, South Korea.

Marisol Sandoval is a Lecturer in Culture, Policy and Management at City University London. Her current research interests include alternative media, critical political economy of media and communication, the global division of labour in the culture industry, and Corporate Social (Ir)Responsibility. She has co-edited the collected volumes *Internet and Surveillance: The Challenges of Web 2.0 and Social Media* (Routledge 2012) and *Critique, Social Media and the Information Society* (Routledge 2013). Sandoval is managing editor of tripleC: Communication, Capitalism & Critique. Open Access Journal for a Global Sustainable Information Society (http://triplec.at/).

Christalla Yakinthou is a fellow in the Institute for Conflict, Cooperation, and Security at the University of Birmingham. She also works with the International Centre for Transitional Justice in the Middle East and North Africa. Her areas of research interest include transitional justice and conflict transformation, and the protection of human rights. She is the author of *Constitutional Design for Divided Societies: Consociationalism and Cyprus* published by Palgrave in 2009, and the editor of *Conflict Management in Divided Societies: Theories and Practice* (with Stefan Wolff), published by Routledge in 2011. She received her PhD in 2008.

CPSIA information can be obtained at www.ICGtesting.com
Printed in the USA
BVOW08*0343091213

338542BV00002B/5/P

9 780739 187753